MORE THAN 250 Illustrations

New Comp

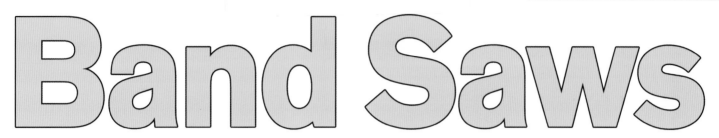

Band Saws

Everything You Need to Know About the
Most Important Saw in the Shop

Mark Duginske

New Complete Guide to

Band Saws

Everything You Need to Know About the
Most Important Saw in the Shop

Mark Duginske

Fox Chapel
PUBLISHING

Acknowledgments

I would like to thank Alan Giagnocavo and Peg Couch for giving me an opportunity to do this book and for being so easy to work with. Gretchen Bacon, Troy Thorne, and Lindsay Hess worked hard to make the book pleasing to look at and easy to use. John Kelsey did a superb job of editing and overseeing the project. I would especially like to thank my wife, Kate Morris, who spent hours and hours editing rough text.

I would also like to thank Larry Anderson, Jesse Barragon (Eagle Tools), Garry Chinn (Garrett Wade), Scott Clark (Kreg Tool), Erik Delaney (Felder), Jon Drew, Gene Duginske, Tom Gabriel, Brent Gantenbein (Kreg Tool), Aaron Gesicki, Torben Helshoj (Laguna), Carl Knapp (Laguna), Jeff Kurka, Jim Langlois, Brad Lillienthal (Kreg Tool), Tom Loeser, The Minnesota Woodworkers Guild, Jeff Miller, Chris Morris, Toshio Odate, Laure Olender, Chuck Olson (Olson Saw), John Otto (JET), Lee Perez (Carter Products), Barbara Reifsneider, Peter Segal (Garrett Wade), Alex Snodgrass (Carter Products), Craig Sommerfeld (Kreg Tool), Todd Sommerfeld (Kreg Tool), Jeff Trapp, Matt Williard (Delta), Brad Witt (Woodhaven), Roger Zimmerman, Kevin Harding, Chris Roland (Appleton Woodcraft), and Keither Rucker (OWWM).

To learn more about the other great books from Fox Chapel Publishing, or to find a retailer near you, call toll-free 800-457-9112 or visit us at *www.FoxChapelPublishing.com*.

Note to Authors: We are always looking for talented authors to write new books. Please send a brief letter describing your idea to Acquisition Editor, 1970 Broad Street, East Petersburg, PA 17520.

Printed in China
First printing

About the Author

Mark Duginske is a lifelong woodworker who lives in Merrill, Wisconsin. He is the inventor of many patented woodworking aids and devices, notably Cool Blocks replacement guides for the band saw and the Kreg band saw fence for resawing. Duginske has written extensively on woodworking techniques in general and on the band saw in particular—his favorite machine tool. His previous books include *Precision Machinery Techniques*, *Band Saw Bench Guide*, *Band Saw Handbook*, *Mastering Woodworking Machines*, *Band Saw Basics*, *Band Saw Pattern Book*, *Cutting Shapes and Profiles*, and *Shaker Band Saw Projects*.

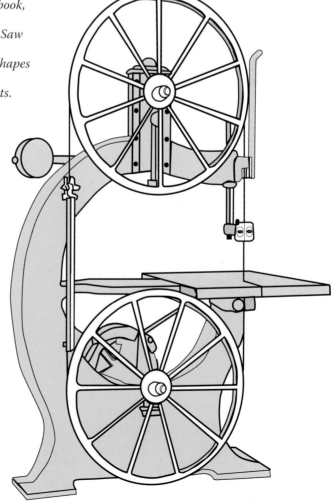

Contents

The Versatile Band Saw

Photo courtesy of the Minnesota Woodworker's Guild

A woodworker making curvaceous chairs like this would find a band saw essential—the only alternative would be to saw all the curved parts by hand.

No matter what woodworking project you choose to undertake, there is a good chance that you will need a band saw. Band saws can be used for a variety of tasks—from the clean, simple cuts of the popular Arts and Crafts furniture to more intricate designs—and it is this versatility that makes the band saw one of the most common power tools in the workshop. For example, you can make straight cuts in wood of almost any thickness. At the same time, because the band saw blade is narrow, you can also saw curves better than with any other machine, simply by moving the workpiece. This characteristic makes it essential for such projects as the graceful chair shown at left. Though it is used primarily for cutting wood, a band saw can cut many other materials, including most metals and plastics. Interestingly enough, it's also widely used in food processing to cut meat.

The band saw is named for its blade, a thin and narrow band of steel with teeth on one edge that is welded together to form a loop. The blade is stretched over either two or three large wheels, which are driven by an electric motor. As the wheels rotate, the blade orbits tightly around them, creating a continuous cutting action, as shown in the illustration on page ix.

The blade and the way it moves make the band saw unique among cutting machines, most of which use a circular blade or a bit that spins. Since the blade moves smoothly and continuously, it applies downward pressure on the workpiece. This makes the band saw safer than a circular saw, which applies a backward force that may kick the workpiece back toward the machine operator. Because the direction of the band saw blade is always downward, there is no danger of kickback. Safety is another reason why many woodworkers prefer the band saw for general cutting, and especially for cutting small pieces of wood.

The band saw's thin blade also cuts wood with a minimum amount of effort and waste. This is particularly important when cutting an expensive exotic wood or a highly figured domestic wood. The band saw is also the tool of choice when cutting through thick wood—nothing slices through a log like a band saw with a sharp hook-tooth blade. Throughout the pages of this book, you will see numerous examples of just how adaptable the band saw is to virtually any woodworking scenario and how—with practice and the right know-how—you can create both simple pieces and more complex, beautiful designs just like a pro.

I grew up as a woodworker in Wisconsin, and I have been using the band saw in my woodworking shop throughout my career. I am among the many woodworkers who prize the band saw for its versatility and its safety. Today, I have two band saws in my workshop: a 14-inch Delta that I use for general woodworking and cutting joints, and a 20-inch Agazzini, an Italian

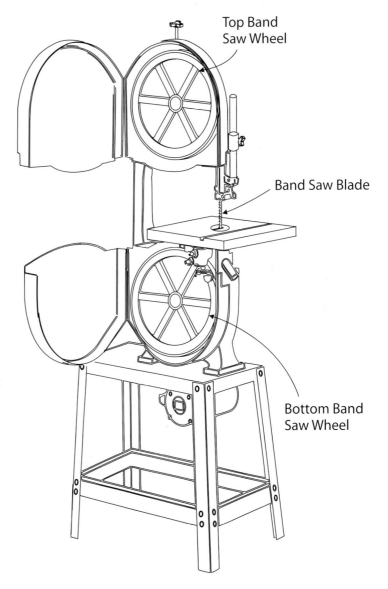

Top Band Saw Wheel

Band Saw Blade

Bottom Band Saw Wheel

The band saw is named for its blade, a thin band of steel with teeth on one side that is welded together to form a loop. As the saw's wheels rotate, the blade moves with them, creating a continuous cutting action.

Many projects, such as this graceful Arts and Crafts sideboard, require straight cuts and long, gentle curves. This piece is made of quarter-sawn oak, a material that is expensive to buy, but easy to cut from small logs using the band saw.

beauty I use for resawing, or cutting a board into thinner planks through its width, and making veneers. In this book, you will also see a shiny new 14-inch Jet that I borrowed for some of the photos. I've written several books on the band saw and have invented and patented a number of band saw accessories. My goal in writing this all-new handbook is to share with you the experience I have gained from a lifetime of using the band saw—something you won't find in any instruction manual—so that you begin to think like a woodworker and can feel confident with the band saw in your workshop.

Chapter 1 will provide you with a general overview of how band saws work so that you will become familiar with common terminology and the band saw's inherent safety

features. After you have a basic understanding of what a band saw can do in your workshop, Chapter 2 will help you to shop like an expert (even if you aren't one) to find the new or used band saw that's the right investment for you; I'll provide you with a checklist for evaluating a used band saw and will arm you with the information you need to compare models and test how they perform.

Naturally, once you've purchased your band saw, knowing how to use it properly and maintain it is crucial to extending the life of your machine and getting the quality results you want for your projects. Chapters 3 and 4 are devoted to maximizing your saw's performance. These chapters focus on the different types of band saw blades, how to choose the best blade for each application, and how to maintain them. You will also learn exactly how to make adjustments to your band saw—those you make when you acquire a saw, those you make every time you change the blade, and those you make while you are sawing—and how to know when you've done it right so that you can avoid the frustration that comes with an improperly adjusted machine.

The next several chapters spend time illustrating the mechanics of how to make the desired cuts in your wood. The band saw excels at making straight cuts (Chapter 5) and long, gentle curves in thick or thin wood (Chapter 6). You will learn all about guiding a straight cut using a fence as well as by eye and how to saw boards out of small logs. I'll prove that cutting curves with the band saw is not difficult and is a lot of fun. In fact, many first-time users get acceptable results right away. You will learn how to use the band saw in place of the scroll saw for cutting delicate curves, how to start and extract the blade in complicated layouts, and how to make

curved chair backs and graceful cabriole legs for fine furniture. I'll also teach you how to use patterns, templates (Chapter 7), and accessories, such as jigs and fixtures (Chapter 8), to help you work more accurately and efficiently and how to finish your projects to look polished and professional.

As your expertise and confidence grow, you can refer to Chapter 9 to learn how your band saw can be used for making interlocking mechanical joints, such as the mortise and tenon and the dovetail, traditionally crafted by hand and still the benchmark of high-quality workmanship when producing frames, stands, and cases. Once you've mastered these practical and efficient techniques, you'll be able to construct almost any type of furniture with relative ease. Finally, for those eager to put their newly found skills to use, there are four useful and attractive projects included throughout the book that utilize all you've learned in this book and showcase why the band saw may be the most indispensable tool in your workshop.

Traditional furniture pieces such as highboy chests often have a sweeping gooseneck molding, which can be cut on the band saw and then routed and sanded.

Photo courtesy of the Minnesota Woodworker's Guild

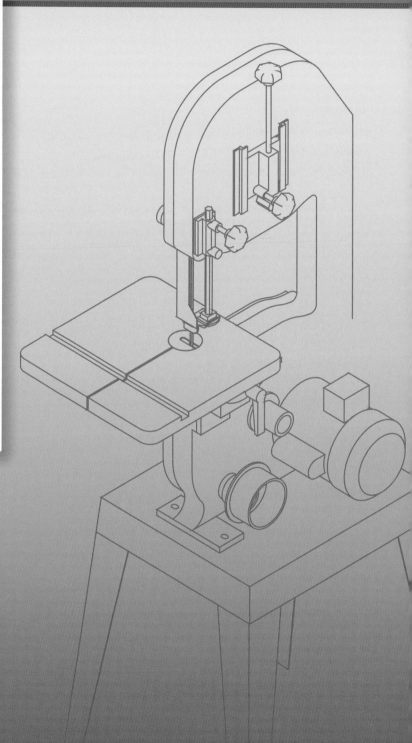

Figure 1.1. The most common band saw design is the stand-mounted two-wheel 14-inch Delta. The saw shown is fitted with three accessories: the 6-inch riser block, a roller stand, and an aftermarket rip fence.

Band Saw Basics

The band saw you will see in most woodworking shops is the stand-mounted two-wheel Delta 14-inch machine shown in **Figure 1.1** (and starring in the photos throughout this book), or one of its many imitators. Large shops with larger band saws most often will also have a little 14-inch machine like this one ready to work. First made in Milwaukee, Wisconsin, in the early 1930s, this saw has been the standard of the industry for 75 years. Today, there are many Asian-made imported saws that mimic this basic design and that even use the same standard 93.5-inch blade. It's probably the first band saw you encountered, and it's likely that—if you own a band saw already—you own one like this. So let's begin with a basic introduction of standard band saws.

Band saws for woodworking are manufactured in a variety of vertical and horizontal configurations that range from small portable units to large industrial heavyweights. There are three basic styles of band saws: floor models, stand-mounted models, and bench-top models. Most have two wheels, though three-wheel saws do exist. The most common horizontal configuration is what you see on portable saw mills, where the rail-mounted saw moves through the log, the heart of which is a wide-blade gas-powered band saw.

Band saws are generally classified according to either the wheel diameter or the throat width, which describes the distance between the column and the blade, as shown in **Figure 1.2**. Because the moving blade must be guarded at the column, a two-wheel band

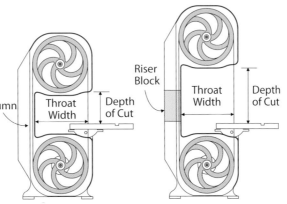

Two-Wheel Saw   Two-Wheel Saw with Riser Block   Three-Wheel Saw

saw with 14-inch wheels has a throat width of slightly less than 14 inches. A three-wheel saw may have a very large throat width, also shown in **Figure 1.2**, and is likely to be less expensive than a two-wheel machine with a similar throat width. However, the three-wheel design has a number of drawbacks: it is more difficult to track and more difficult to align the wheels, and some users report premature blade wear, perhaps due to the fact that the blade must flex more tightly over smaller wheels.

Band saws are also classified by depth of cut, which means the thickest material that the saw can fit between the saw table and the upper blade guide. A typical 14-inch band saw can saw a 6-inch-thick piece of wood. An optional 6-inch height riser can be bolted between the top and bottom castings of some 14-inch band saws, allowing for the cutting of material up to 12 inches thick (see **Figure 1.2**). Few 14-inch saws have the power to handle such a deep cut in solid hardwood, but they may be able to manage 8 inches or thereabouts. This increased capacity is nevertheless useful in many other situations, for example, when trimming furniture subassemblies or for clearance when using some jigs and fixtures.

Figure 1.2. Band saws are classified according to the wheel size or the throat width, the distance between the column and the blade. Most popular 14-inch saws have a throat width of 13 inches and a wheel diameter of 14 inches. Three-wheel saws have wide throats. A typical 14-inch saw can cut a 6-inch-thick piece of wood, but with an optional 6-inch height attachment, some can cut 12-inch-thick material.

Parts of the band saw

The major parts of the band saw include the blade, the machine frame, the wheels, the table, and the blade guides. The various parts of the band saw may be called different names by various manufacturers, books, and magazines. Each of the major parts is discussed under the following titles and is shown in **Figure 1.3** and the following illustrations. If you are not already familiar with the band saw, please take the time to study the drawings and identify the part names as they relate to your particular machine. While features are pretty much standard among various brands of 14-inch band saws, you will find much more variation on both smaller and larger machines. Sometimes one variation is better than another, sometimes not. Even though each manufacturer makes a slightly different machine, the same general principles apply.

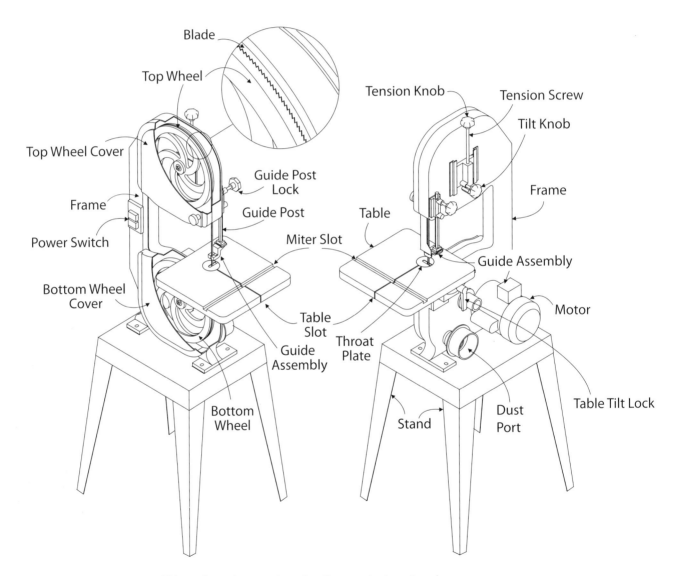

Figure 1.3. This small stand-mounted saw has the same basic parts as larger machines, though they may be named differently by various manufacturers and in other books and magazines. Take the time to study the part names as they relate to your particular machine.

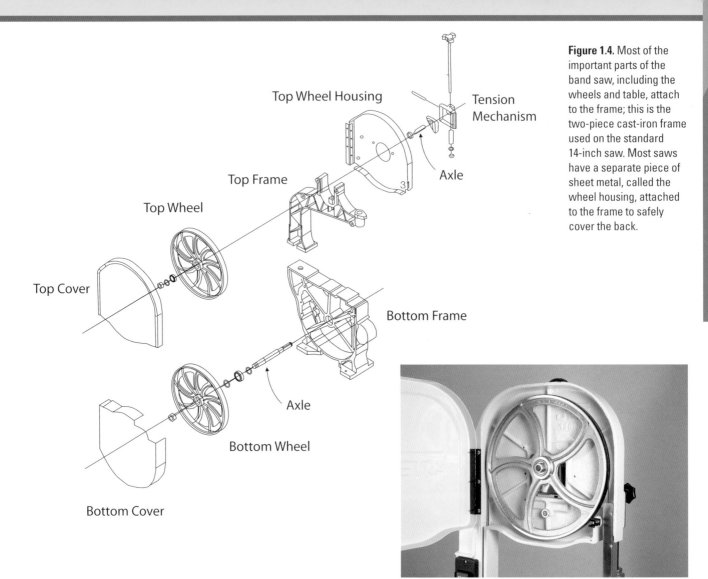

Top Wheel Housing

Tension Mechanism

Top Frame

Axle

Top Wheel

Top Cover

Bottom Frame

Axle

Bottom Wheel

Bottom Cover

Figure 1.4. Most of the important parts of the band saw, including the wheels and table, attach to the frame; this is the two-piece cast-iron frame used on the standard 14-inch saw. Most saws have a separate piece of sheet metal, called the wheel housing, attached to the frame to safely cover the back.

Figure 1.5. Some saws have a one-piece casting that provides both the main framework and the cover for the back of the wheels, such as this 12-inch Jet. The cast iron adds weight, which dampens vibration. The wheels on most small band saws are made of cast aluminum, with a rubber tire to cushion the blade.

Blade

The band saw blade is a thin band of steel with teeth either punched or ground on one edge with its two ends welded together to form a smooth loop. The blade is mounted on either two or three wheels. As the wheels rotate, they move the blade along with them, creating a continuous cutting action. More expensive blades have hardened teeth including high-speed steel and carbide tipped. Band saw blades are covered in detail in Chapter 3, "Band Saw Blades," page 37.

Frame

Most of the important parts of the band saw—including the motor, wheels, and table—attach to the frame, as shown in **Figure 1.4**. The frame is the saw's backbone. There are various styles of frames, and each manufacturer makes its frames differently. The most common types of frame are the one-piece casting and the skeletal frame, an assembly of sheet steel with cast and welded pieces of metal. A separate piece of sheet metal, called the wheel housing, is attached to the frame to safely cover the back of the saw. Some saws have a large, one-piece cast-iron frame that incorporates the wheel covers, such as the 12-inch Jet saw shown in **Figure 1.5**. The cast iron adds to the weight of the saw, which helps dampen vibration. In the past, both INCA and Sears have used lightweight aluminum one-piece castings, but both of those designs have been discontinued, though you may still see an aluminum frame on a used machine.

Power Switch

The band saw motor is turned on and off with a switch. On some models, the switch is attached to the saw frame, as in **Figure 1.6**. On other models, it is on the stand. Some switches have built-in safety interlocks, which prevent use of the saw unless a plastic key has been inserted. If there is any risk that children may be tempted to turn on your band saw, make sure that you use some kind of protection. A locked electrical panel box protects the entire shop.

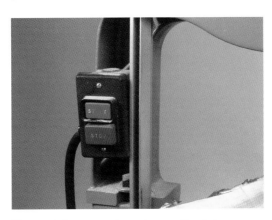

Figure 1.6. Some saws have the on-off switch mounted on the machine frame, while others have it on the stand.

Motor

The typical consumer-grade band saw is equipped with a ¾ hp or 1 hp motor as standard equipment. This size motor is adequate unless you plan to resaw a lot of thick material, in which case a 1½ hp motor is the minimum requirement. Many band saw motors can be converted from standard 110-volt electrical current to 220-volt, which also increases the motor's efficiency. The conversion is a simple matter of swapping wires guided by instructions usually found inside the electrical box on the motor; it does require a new 220-volt plug on the power cord and 220-volt breaker-protected service to a nearby outlet.

Wheels

The size of the band saw wheels determines many of its characteristics and abilities. The band saw wheels usually are made of cast aluminum with a hub (see **Figure 1.5**), thick spokes, and a flat or crowned rim; some older saws have a solid disk for a wheel. The rim usually is covered with a strip of rubber called a tire. The tire cushions the blade and protects the teeth from damage due to contact with the metal wheel. The bottom wheel is the drive wheel. It is attached to the motor either directly or through a V-belt running on pulleys. The top wheel is not powered but rotates by contact with the blade, which is being driven from below. The top wheel has adjustments for the tension on the band saw blade and also for how the blade centers, or tracks, on the wheels, as shown in **Figure 1.7**.

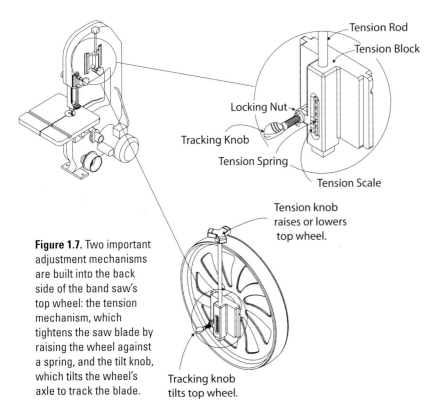

Tension Rod

Tension Block

Locking Nut

Tracking Knob

Tension Spring

Tension Scale

Tension knob raises or lowers top wheel.

Tracking knob tilts top wheel.

Figure 1.7. Two important adjustment mechanisms are built into the back side of the band saw's top wheel: the tension mechanism, which tightens the saw blade by raising the wheel against a spring, and the tilt knob, which tilts the wheel's axle to track the blade.

Tension Screw

Band saw blades operate best under some tension, with the amount of tension primarily determined by the blade's width. The tension on the blade is adjusted with a threaded screw, which moves the top wheel up and down, as shown in **Figure 1.7**. When you rotate the knob atop the tension screw to increase the tension, it compresses the tension spring inside the tension block. These functions are described more fully in Chapter 4, "Adjusting the Band Saw," page 69.

Tilt Knob

Though it is not powered, the top wheel has the job of balancing or centering the blade on the wheels, which is called tracking the blade. This is done using an adjustable tilt mechanism. Turning the knob counterclockwise tilts the top wheel forward, and rotating the knob clockwise tilts the wheel backward (see **Figure 1.7**). Very small changes in wheel tilt can have a large effect on exactly how the blade travels over the wheels; more on this can be found in Chapter 4, "Adjusting the Band Saw," page 69.

Wheel Covers

Wheel covers protect the operator from the spinning wheels and the blade. If the blade breaks, the covers contain the pieces. Some saws have hinged covers, while others have covers that attach with knobs or clips. The two most common materials used for covers are plastic and metal. Plastic is quieter and less susceptible to vibration. Metal covers should be secured tightly to avoid vibration and noise.

Table

The band saw table is attached to the saw frame by means of two semicircular metal parts called trunnions, as shown in **Figure 1.8**. The workpiece rests on the table as it is fed into the blade. The table surrounds the blade, which passes through a large hole in the middle. The

hole also helps the operator gain access to the blade-guide adjustments below the table. The table includes a throat plate with a blade slot that fills the center opening, a slot from the edge to the center that allows the blade to enter, a miter gauge slot milled in the table surface parallel to the direction of cut, a tilt mechanism mounted under the table (see **Figure 1.9**), and a fence rail mounted on the front edge of the table.

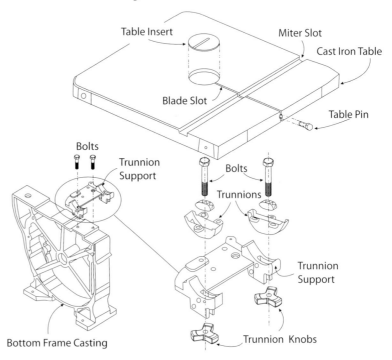

Figure 1.8. Two semicircular metal trunnions attach the table to the frame. Bolts located in the trunnions secure them to the trunnion support casting. This system allows the table to tilt. The cast-iron table has a center opening for the blade, an insert that fits the opening around the blade, and a milled slot for the miter gauge.

Figure 1.9. This under-the-table view shows the trunnions, which allow the table to tilt, and blade guide mechanism on a 14-inch Jet saw. The bottom guide assembly is situated between the two semicircular arcs machined in the trunnion support casting. The pointer is secured to the trunnion support and should be adjusted to an accurate 90-degree setting.

Table Slot

A narrow slot in the table, running from the outside edge to the center hole, allows the blade to enter. There is usually some device to keep the table surfaces aligned on either side of the slot. It may be a bolt, a pin, or a screw; some manufacturers use the front rail to align the table across the slot. Make sure that you do keep this device in place; without it, you risk the two halves warping in opposite directions, causing an uneven table.

Table Throat Plate

A throat plate with a blade slot fits into the hole in the table. The throat plate is made of either plastic or metal. A plastic plate is quieter and won't cause any damage if the blade accidentally touches it. On some saws, the setscrew adjustments for the guide holder and thrust bearing are made through the hole in the table, after removing the throat plate. On other saws, all of the adjustments are made from underneath the table.

Table Miter Gauge Slot

Most saws have a miter gauge slot milled across the surface. This slot runs parallel to the blade and accepts the miter gauge bar, which is usually used for crosscutting (cutting across the grain of the wood). The miter gauge slot also is very useful for guiding owner-built jigs, which are discussed in Chapter 8, "Jigs and Fixtures," page 145.

Table Tilt Mechanism

The saw table on most band saws is designed to tilt, which means that it can make beveled or angled cuts, as shown in **Figure 1.10**. The table tilts away from the column up to 45 degrees. On some models, it also tilts toward the column up to 10 degrees (see **Figure 1.10**), a handy feature for cutting dovetail pins, but not a necessity. Underneath the table on some saws, there is an adjustable bolt or screw to help level the table back to 90 degrees after it has been tilted.

Figure 1.10. The trunnion mechanism allows the band saw table to tilt 45 degrees away from the column, and about 10 degrees toward it.

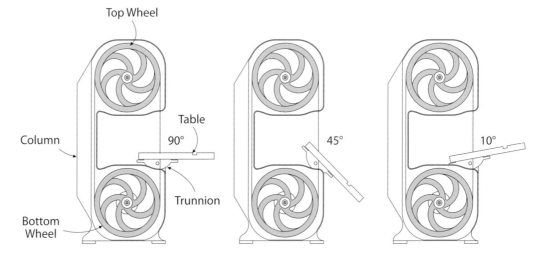

Top Wheel

Column

Table

90°

45°

10°

Trunnion

Bottom Wheel

Guide Assembly

Two guide assemblies support the blade. One is located below the table and one is above the table. Each guide assembly consists of two guide blocks, one on each side of the blade, which keep it from deflecting sideways and twisting. Each assembly also houses a thrust bearing, which supports the back edge of the blade and keeps the blade from being pushed backward under the load of cutting, as shown in **Figure 1.11**. The guides and bearing are held in place by a metal casting called the guide assembly. Each guide assembly contains a mechanism for the independent forward and backward movement of the guides and thrust bearing. The guide-assembly design shown accommodates different blade widths.

Blade Guides

There is a pair of blade guides above the saw table and another pair below, with each pair flanking the blade on either side, as shown in **Figure 1.12**. The guides are also called blocks, pins, or guide blocks. These guides can be bearings, or they can be made of solid material such as steel, or of high-tech materials such as phenolic plastic, which may contain a patented dry lubricant.

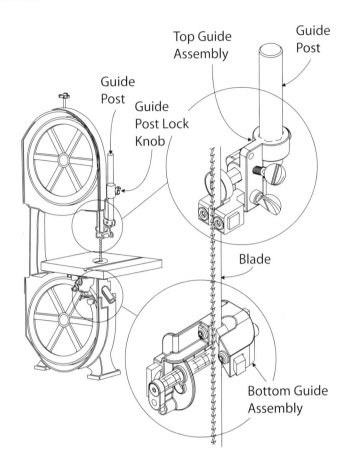

Figure 1.11. The guide assemblies keep the blade from deflecting sideways and from twisting. Each one consists of two guide blocks located on each side of the blade, plus a thrust bearing, which keeps the blade from being pushed backward. Both guide assemblies allow the independent forward and backward movement of the guides and thrust bearing to accommodate different blade widths.

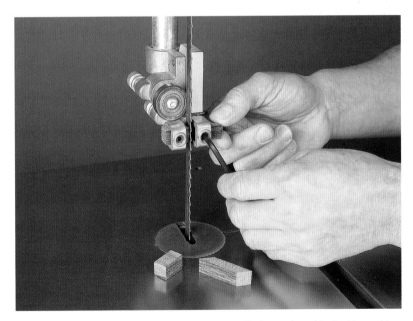

Figure 1.12. Blade guides typically can be removed, changed, and locked in position with an Allen wrench.

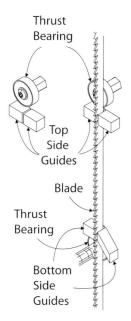

Figure 1.13. Thrust bearings limit the backward movement of the blade.

Thrust Bearing

On most saws, a round wheel bearing called the thrust bearing is used to limit the backward movement of the blade (see **Figure 1.13**). A bearing is used because it decreases friction at the back of the blade. There are usually two thrust bearings, one above and one below the table. The thrust bearing is called by a number of other names, including blade support and roller guide, but in this book it will be called a thrust bearing.

Guide Post

The top assembly is attached to a metal rod called the guide post. The whole upper guide assembly is adjustable up and down so it can be set just above the workpiece, as shown in **Figure 1.14**. The guide post lock screw locks the post at the desired height. The blade guard is attached to the front of the guide post. In most situations, you want about ¼ inch of clearance between the top guide assembly and the workpiece. This prevents the operator's finger from coming into contact with the blade. This also reduces the unsupported blade span between thrust bearings, decreasing the likelihood of blade deflection.

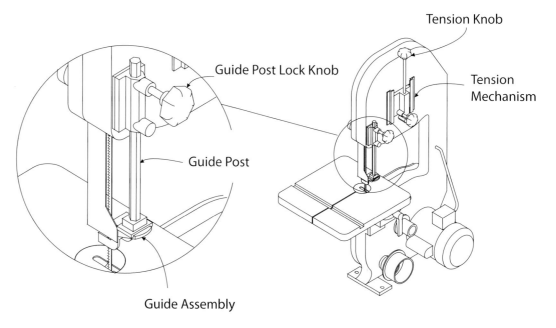

Figure 1.14. The top guide assembly is secured to the end of the guide post and is adjustable up and down to accommodate various board thicknesses. The post is normally locked with about ¼-inch clearance above the workpiece to keep the operator's fingers safely away from the blade.

BAND SAW SAFETY PROCEDURES

The band saw is so popular because it is versatile and relatively safe and easy to use. Many schools, especially junior high schools that offer shop classes, have the students do all of their ripping, or sawing along the grain of the wood, on the band saw, as shown in **Figure 1.15**, because it is so much safer than the table saw. Even though the machine is fairly safe, you must never take safety for granted. Read the following safety rules carefully, and practice each and every one.

1. Before operating the saw, read and understand the instruction manual that comes with it.

2. If you are still not thoroughly familiar with the operation of the band saw, get advice from a qualified person.

3. Make sure that the machine is electrically grounded and that the wiring codes are followed.

4. Do not operate the band saw while you are tired or while under the influence of drugs, alcohol, or medication.

5. Always wear eye protection (safety glasses or a face shield) and hearing protection.

6. Wear a dust mask. Long-term exposure to the fine dust created by the band saw is not healthy.

7. Remove your tie, rings, watch, and all jewelry. Roll up your sleeves and pull back your hair. You do not want anything to get caught in the saw.

8. Make sure that the guards are in place, and use them at all times. The guards protect you from coming into contact with the blade.

9. Make sure that the teeth of the saw blade point downward, toward the saw table.

10. Adjust the upper blade guard so that it is about ¼ inch above the material being cut.

11. Make sure that the blade has been properly tensioned and tracked.

12. Stop the machine before removing the scrap pieces from the table.

Figure 1.15. Many schools that offer shop classes have the students rip lumber on the band saw because it is so much safer than a table saw. Here an eighth grader, wearing her safety glasses, is using the band saw with a fence to make a straight cut.

13. Always keep your hands and fingers away from the blade.

14. Make sure that you use the proper size and type of blade.

15. Hold the workpiece firmly against the table. Do not attempt to saw stock that does not have a flat surface that can rest on the table, unless a suitable support is used.

16. Use a push stick at the end of a cut. This is the most dangerous time because the cut is complete and the blade is exposed. Push sticks are commercially available, or they are easy to make in the workshop.

17. Hold the wood firmly and feed it into the blade at a moderate speed.

18. Turn off the machine if you have to back the material out of an incomplete or jammed cut.

19. When you are working inside the saw, whether for adjustments or repairs, always disconnect the power.

CHAPTER TWO

Figure 2.1. Retail woodworking machinery dealers often have a good selection of band saws.

Shopping for a Saw

The old adage "you get what you pay for" is especially true of the band saw. More than any other tool, quality makes a big difference in band saw performance. When shopping for a band saw, you must look beyond the sales hype to choose a saw that fits your needs. Like the lathe, the band saw is a skill-intensive machine. Since you are cutting freehand, you can feel how the machine is performing. The band saw should run smoothly and cut thick material without resistance or vibration. If the saw vibrates, either there is something wrong with the setup, or else it is not a good piece of equipment.

Which saw you buy naturally depends on your plans for it and your budget. But because the band saw requires skill to cut well, you will also want to compare features carefully to find the machine that suits you best. In this chapter, I'll run down all the systems and parts of the machine and explain what your choices are, and what you might be trading off. My remarks apply equally to new machines and to used ones, which you may discover at auctions or in newspaper or online classified ads. At the end of this chapter, there will be a section on buying used equipment with a checklist to help you evaluate the machines you may be offered.

Band saws for woodworking are available in a variety of sizes and prices, and retail dealers often have a good selection, as shown in

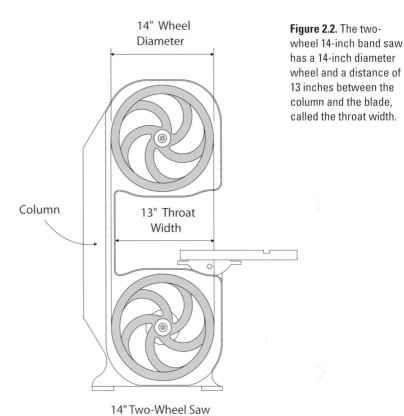

14" Wheel Diameter

Column

13" Throat Width

14" Two-Wheel Saw

Figure 2.2. The two-wheel 14-inch band saw has a 14-inch diameter wheel and a distance of 13 inches between the column and the blade, called the throat width.

Figure 2.1. Band saws range in size from small portable bench-top units to large industrial heavyweights. There are three basic styles of band saws: bench top, stand mounted, and floor model, further differentiated by wheel size, throat size, and number of wheels. As I mentioned previously, the most common design is the 14-inch two-wheel saw. Its 14-inch diameter wheels yield a throat width of 13 inches between the column and the blade, as shown in **Figure 2.2**.

Bench-top saws

Bench-top saws are the smallest and can be mounted directly on a worktable or on a purchased or shop-made stand or cabinet, as shown in **Figure 2.3**. Bench-top saws are typically lightweight and typically have wheel diameters in the range of 8 inches to 12 inches. They are ideal for small projects and small workshops. One characteristic of these saws is that the motor is mounted directly to the unit, so there is no belt system below the table. Although typically small and lightweight, there are exceptions, such as the 12-inch Jet, shown in **Figure 2.4**, and the 14-inch Shop Fox, **Figure 2.5**.

For a number of years, bench-top saws were manufactured with the three-wheel design, but those models have been discontinued. Remember that a three-wheel saw offers the widest throat in the least amount of space, but the design has drawbacks: It is more difficult to align the wheels and track the blades, and some users report premature blade wear.

Figure 2.3. Bench-top saws are the smallest size and can be mounted directly on a workbench or on a purchased or shop-made stand or cabinet. The motor on these saws is mounted directly to the unit so there is no motor or belt system below the table.

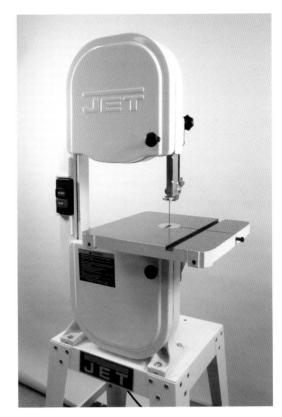

Figure 2.4. Although bench-top models are often quite small and lightweight, there are exceptions. The 12-inch Jet is a small but heavy-duty machine. The frame and back wheel guard are cast iron.

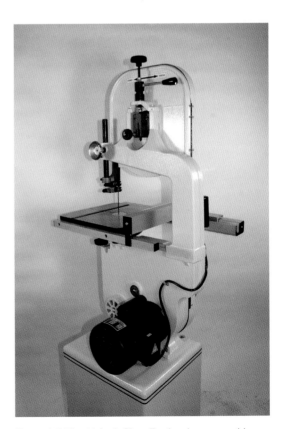

Figure 2.5. The 14-inch Shop Fox is a heavy machine that is technically a bench-top saw. It features a quick-release tension lever and a rack-and-pinion guide post, unusual on a 14-inch saw.

Stand-mounted saws

The stand-mounted model is characterized by the familiar 14-inch band saw with the cast-iron frame and stamped steel stand that is either an open frame or an enclosed cabinet. The motor is usually mounted in the stand under the saw and is connected by a drive belt to the lower wheel. The 14-inch size, shown in **Figure 2.6**, is adequate for most woodworking tasks and is the most popular size sold. These band saws are so popular because they're very versatile, small, and relatively inexpensive. Although these saws all look very much alike, their quality varies widely, with price being a reasonable indicator of quality.

The 14-inch saw market is very competitive, and the imported saws have pressed prices downward. Prices vary widely, so it is worth researching a purchase. While you might find the lowest price through a distant dealer, a locally purchased saw would not require additional charges for shipping, though you might have to evaluate that against having to pay sales tax.

Since the 1930s, with the advent of the 14-inch Delta saw, this category of saws has been made with a frame consisting of two iron castings supporting the top and bottom wheels, as shown in **Figure 2.7**. Sheet-metal blade guards are secured to the frame members. The two frame members mate together at the base of the column. A height extension, which is also called a riser block, can be installed between the frame castings, as discussed in Installing the Riser on page 14.

The typical consumer-grade band saw comes with a ¾ hp motor as standard equipment. This size motor is adequate unless you plan to resaw thick wood, in which case a 1 hp motor is the minimum requirement. More expensive models use a 1½ hp motor. Some manufacturers offer the same saw with your choice among these three motor sizes.

These 14-inch saws can handle blades up to ⅝ inch wide and .025 inch thick for heavy work and resawing. They can accept either block-style guides or ball bearing guides. With block-style guides and phenolic replacement blocks, blades as narrow as ³⁄₃₂ inch can be used.

Although the 14-inch band saw with a larger motor will handle a variety of tasks, there are limitations. These saws typically have a pronounced crown on their wheels, which helps track narrow blades. Although most owners' manuals state that a ¾-inch blade can be used, these blades are usually .035-inch thick and are prone to break prematurely from metal fatigue caused by bending the thick band over the relatively small wheels.

Catalogs can be full of numerous expensive accessories meant to soup up the 14-inch saw, and you could easily spend $500. However, I think the money would be better spent on a bigger saw in the first place. You would be making fewer compromises, with less risk of pushing the machine past its limits.

If you are doing a lot of cutting in thick stock, you will max out the capabilities of a 14-inch saw rather quickly. In automobile terms, the 14-inch saw is a small four-cylinder pickup truck. It will do a lot, but don't expect to turn it into a dump truck.

Figure 2.6. The 14-inch band saw is the most popular size because these saws are versatile, small, cost effective, and adequate for most woodworking tasks.

Figure 2.7. Since the 1930s, these saws have been made with two iron castings supporting the top and bottom wheels, and sheet metal blade guards. The two cast-iron frame members mate together at the base of the column. This very early 14-inch saw has a height extension and a shop-made pulley guard.

Photo courtesy of Laure Olender

Buying a new band saw

Buying a new saw has several advantages, just like buying a new car. You can get exactly what you want, or at least what you think you want. You get service and a warranty, and a current model that has parts readily available. You also get the peace of mind of knowing the history of the saw so you know it wasn't abused or broken and welded.

Research and compare tools before you buy. Here are some questions to consider:

- Can you buy it locally?
- How long is the warranty?
- Is labor covered as well as parts?
- Upon unpacking, if the band saw is defective, what is the procedure, and who pays to transport the machine to a service center?
- How many miles to a service center?
- How many years into the future will parts be available?

Because a band saw is older or industrial doesn't guarantee that it's a better choice than a new one. Recent models often have advantages, such as ease of adjustment, safety features, better guides, and better choice of accessories.

Perhaps the biggest consideration in deciding whether to buy new versus used is your time. Acquiring and fixing older equipment is a hobby for some. But if your real interest is woodworking and you want to get on with it, spending the summer attending machinery auctions may be a waste of your time, not to mention the hours you will spend moving a large used machine, installing it, getting it running, and adjusting it so it can do the work you have in mind.

Buying a used band saw

The alternative to buying new is to buy a used piece of equipment. Theoretically, one can save a lot of money. Occasionally, equipment in good working order can be acquired at a fraction of the cost of a brand-new machine. The downside is that you have to have a good knowledge of band saws to be able to evaluate a used one. Buyer beware! There are a lot of "great deals" in the back corner of shops gathering dust because the machine needs work or parts. If you buy one of these, you may never get the "bargain" to be a working machine. If a machine is not making sawdust in a month, it was a mistake, not a bargain.

Of all the woodworking machines, band saws are probably the most frequently abused. Band saws do wear out, and a machine from a shop or a factory may be for sale because it would be too expensive to fix. In a commercial setting, a machine often can be replaced for less than the cost and hassle of repairs, especially if it is simply worn out. One or two custom-made repair parts may exceed the price of a new machine.

A missing part or parts is often the deal breaker. The essential part may no longer be available, or it may require very expensive custom fabrication.

It is easy to romanticize about old big equipment, but the reality is that newer equipment, and band saws in particular, have better designs, better bearings, better dust collection, better guides, and better guards. This is especially true since the advent of the steel-frame saws. I'll go into more detail on how to buy a used saw later in this chapter, on page 30.

Important band saw features

In this section, I'll discuss the features you'll find offered on various band saws. This discussion continues and expands the basic introduction to the parts of the saw in Chapter 1, "Band Saw Basics," page 1. While features are pretty much standard among various brands of 14-inch band saws, you will find much more variation on both smaller and larger machines. Sometimes one variation is better than another, sometimes not. In any case, when you are shopping for a saw, you want to go in with as much information as you can muster. That's the only way you will be able to evaluate what you see and what you are told by sales personnel.

Frame Type and Weight

Bench-top saws weigh between 75 and 200 pounds. Although they should be bolted to the bench top for stability, they are relatively portable. Most 14-inch stand-mounted saws weigh between 200 and 300 pounds. They can be disassembled to be transported up or down stairs. A big European floor model saw or imitation European unit, with a welded steel frame, can weigh anywhere from 400 to 600 pounds, which is the weight of an eight-cylinder car engine, and they cannot be disassembled for transport. Cast-iron floor models can weigh 800 to 3000 pounds; they can be disassembled only up to a point, and they probably will have to be bolted to a concrete floor.

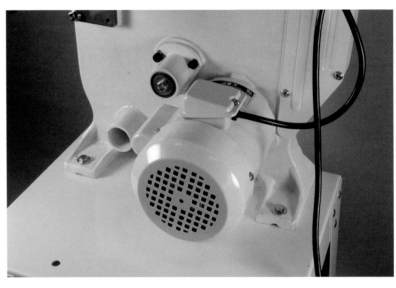

Figure 2.19. The 110-volt motor on the 12-inch Jet bolts directly to the cast-iron frame and back wheel guard, making it a very compact unit.

Electrical Requirements

Most bench-top and stand-mounted saws are 110-volt and draw 15 amps of current (see **Figure 2.19**), though many can be reconfigured for 220 volts by following the instructions inside the electrical cover on the motor. Normal household current, whether 110 volt or 220 volt, is single phase. It's a good idea to have a separate circuit breaker for each shop machine. You'll need a 220-volt outlet for most big saws, and 24-inch European band saws can require a 40-amp breaker.

Many older cast-iron floor model saws have three-phase motors, which require industrial-grade three-phase electrical power. This can make an attractive older industrial band saw turn out to be problematic if you do not have a three-phase electrical supply. Many of these saws have direct-drive motors that cannot be replaced, so a phase converter is required along with some extra wiring, which could cost $500 or more. If the saw's three-phase motor is a freestanding unit, it can be replaced with a single-phase motor, but that too can be quite expensive.

Motor Power

Wheel diameter and weight are related to power. Bench-top saws generally have motors in the ⅓ hp to ½ hp range. Most consumer-grade 14-inch band saws are equipped with a ¾ hp or a 1 hp motor as standard equipment. More expensive commercial grade models use a 1½ hp motor. Manufacturers sometimes offer the same saw with your choice of motor size.

Figure 2.20. Resawing thick material with a wide blade requires power. A saw with 16-inch diameter wheels, such as this one, should have at least a 2 hp motor.

Figure 2.21. The drive belt on this Jet 12-inch motor is short, and the saw pulley is behind the bottom wheel, which means you will need to remove the wheel to replace a worn belt.

Resawing thick material with a wide blade requires a lot of power. This is perhaps the most important characteristic of a heavy-duty saw, as shown in **Figure 2.20**. It is hard to have too much power in a band saw. If the saw has 16-inch-diameter wheels, it should have at least a 2 hp motor.

While some older saws and some small bench-top saws have the motor directly connected to the saw's lower wheel, most modern saws use pulleys connected by a V-belt, as shown in **Figure 2.21**. V-belts are readily available, and you can always replace a worn one. You might want to replace the pulleys on a used saw since out-of-balance pulleys can be a source of vibration.

Throat Depth

Bench-top saws typically have a throat depth between 4 and 5 inches, while an unmodified 14-inch stand-mounted saw will have 6 inches. You may not use it often, but having a resaw capacity of 11 or 12 inches is ideal. You can get 12-inch cutting capacity with a 14-inch saw, a riser block, and the largest available motor. On larger floor models, an 11- or 12-inch resaw capacity is essential, as you can see in **Figure 2.20**.

Wheels

More than any other part of a saw, the wheels determine how the saw will perform and what tasks it will do best, what the throat width and depth are, and therefore what the saw's limits on workpiece size are. The key factors are the diameter of the wheels, what they are made of, and whether or not they are crowned. These in turn determine the kind of tires that will be on the wheels, the range of blades the saw can accept, the motor horsepower it will need, and the overall weight of the machine.

Wheel diameter

One crucial factor is the size of the saw's wheels. The smallest bench-top saws have 9-inch wheels with a throat depth around 8½ inches. Each additional inch of wheel diameter also adds an inch to throat width. Large wheels have a lot of advantages. The larger the wheel, the longer the blade, and the cooler the blade runs. The larger the wheel, the longer blades last because there is less blade metal fatigue from bending around the wheel. Some deluxe blades are not recommended for saws with wheel diameter less than 20 inches, as shown in **Figure 2.22**. An 18-inch or 20-inch wheel is ideal for the serious woodworker as well as for the average small professional shop. Larger wheels, especially ones with a minimum crown, can also easily handle thick ¾-inch-wide to 1-inch-wide blades for ripping and especially resawing.

Bigger is not necessarily better. Although I had a 24-inch Italian saw at one time, when I moved my shop, I replaced it with a 20-inch Italian model and have no regrets. The 20-inch saw handles all of my needs. Band saw size soon reaches the point of diminishing return in terms of floor space in the shop, power requirements, and more expensive blades. Theoretically a huge saw can manage very large work, but do you actually need it? Do you think you can even lift a 15-inch log for resawing, let alone steer it through the blade?

Wheel materials

There are a number of band saw wheel designs, including solid cast iron as used on the Italian saws, as shown in **Figure 2.22**, and spoked aluminum as usually used on 14-inch saws, shown in **Figure 2.23**. The Italian saws use a very heavy solid cast-iron wheel, which increases the momentum and adds to the flywheel effect, helping the saw run smoothly and consistently in such variable material as thick wood. Spoked aluminum wheels are light and relatively easy to balance.

Figure 2.22. The European saws like this 20-inch Agazzani have a heavy cast-iron wheel with an almost flat rim. Some deluxe blades, like this carbide-tipped one, should not be used on saws with wheels smaller than 20 inches.

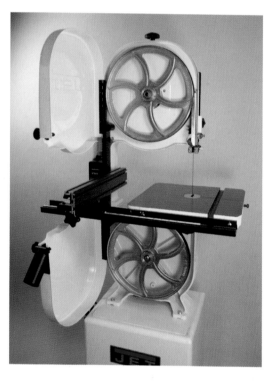

Figure 2.23. Spoked aluminum wheels are usually used on 14-inch saws.

More important than what the wheel is made of is how round and how well balanced the wheel is. Vibration is usually caused by eccentricity or imbalance. To run smoothly, the band saw wheels must be round and balanced, just as they must be on a car. Balancing equalizes the forces on the blade and dampens vibration so that the blade and the machine run smoothly. Wheels can be balanced by either removing material or adding material near the periphery. If you notice holes drilled in your wheels, it shows that material was removed for balance.

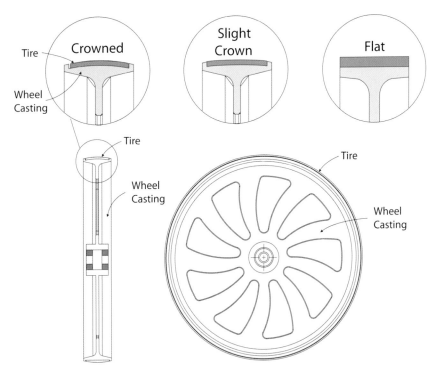

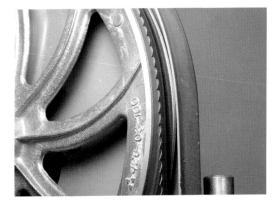

Figure 2.24. A crowned wheel helps to track a blade in the middle of the wheel, which is desirable for blades 3/8 inch wide or narrower. Flat wheels are best for wider blades because they give the blades more support. A compromise design has a very small crown.

Figure 2.25. Most 14-inch band saw wheels have a pronounced crown designed for tracking narrow blades toward the center of the tire.

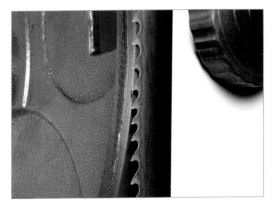

Figure 2.26. Flat wheels will support wide blades. Blades can be tracked in various positions on the wheel, and large blades can be tracked with the teeth off the front of the wheel, as shown here.

Wheel crown

Band saw wheel rims have evolved with two different design philosophies. On some saws, the rim of the wheel is almost flat, while on others it has a curve, or crown, as shown in **Figure 2.24**. A crowned wheel helps to track a blade in the middle of the wheel, which is desirable for narrow blades, or those ⅜ inch or smaller. However, if the wheels are not perfectly aligned, the crowns on each wheel compete for control of the blade, and this misalignment causes vibration and shortens blade life. Most bench-top and 14-inch band saws have a very pronounced crown because these smaller saws were designed for running narrow blades, as shown in **Figure 2.25**. Crowned wheels are not the best for wide blades because the front and back edges of the blade don't touch the tire and aren't well supported. Flat wheels are best for wide blades because they give the blade more support, as shown in **Figure 2.26**. Although they take more care to track, flat wheels allow you to track blades in various positions on the wheel, either in the middle of the wheel or toward its front edge. Wide blades track best toward the front of the tire on a flat wheel. Narrow blades are best tracked toward the middle.

Having said all that, unless you are considering a large floor model saw, you probably do not have a choice between crowned or flat wheels.

Tires

Band saw wheels have a rubber or plastic tire to cushion the blade from contact with the metal wheel. The tire also provides traction for the blade. Some tires, as on the typical 14-inch saw, are stretched to fit tightly on the metal wheel. Other tire materials are glued to the metal wheel. All of the tire materials work well, so there is no reason to seek out some specific type. The orange part of the wheel on the 14-inch saw in **Figure 2.25** is the tire.

Footbrake

One of the characteristics of the bigger saws, especially those with heavy wheels and good bearings and guides, is that they run for a long time after the motor is turned off. Some saws have motor brakes, which stop the blade shortly after the saw is turned off. If the saw does not have a motor brake, a handy feature is a footbrake, which stops a band saw blade almost instantly, as shown in **Figure 2.27**. As a safety feature, some footbrakes are connected to a switch that turns the motor off as soon as the brake is touched.

Blade guides

Two sets of guides are located above and below the saw table, as shown in **Figure 2.28**. Each set of guides is a two-part system of support for the blade. One part, the thrust bearing, supports the back of the blade during the cut and prevents the blade from being shoved off the back of the wheels under the load of feeding the wood. The other part, the guide blocks or guide bearings, prevent sideways deflection and twisting of the blade. Guide blocks are located on either side of the blade and are fitted to the guide holder, as shown in **Figure 2.29**. Pairs of bearing guides are held in line with each other

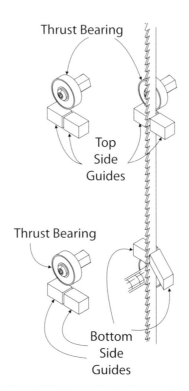

Thrust Bearing

Top Side Guides

Thrust Bearing

Bottom Side Guides

Figure 2.28. Each set of guides, located above and below the saw table, has a thrust bearing that supports the back of the blade and prevents it from being shoved off the wheels. The guide blocks or guide bearings prevent side deflection and rotation of the blade.

Figure 2.29. These inexpensive phenolic replacement guide blocks contain a graphite dry lubricant. Because these blocks can be used in contact with the blade, they provide more support for narrow blades as well as for tasks such as resawing.

Figure 2.27. Some big saws have motor brakes that stop the blade shortly after the saw is turned off. This saw has a footbrake connected to a motor safety off switch.

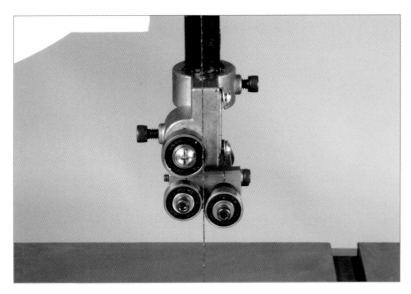

Figure 2.30. Bearing guides are held in line with each other in the guide holder so that both move forward and backward in unison. These Shop Fox side bearings are adjustable on an eccentric cam.

in the guide holder so that both move forward and backward in unison. Each guide bearing is locked in place with a setscrew. Both the guide bearings and the thrust bearings are held in place by a cast piece of metal called a guide assembly, as shown in **Figure 2.30**, which also shows bearing-style guides.

The 14-inch saws are available with either bearing or block guides. Wide blades can be used with either kind of guide, but narrow blades require block guides. Standard steel block guides can destroy the teeth on a narrow blade, so they should be replaced with phenolic blocks or with shop-made wooden blocks. Some European saws have disc-style bearing guides instead of ball bearing guides, but the effect is the same.

I prefer block guides for ease of setup with narrow blades. Disc or ball bearing guides are the standard with floor model saws. The bearing systems require very little maintenance while the blocks do need to be resurfaced occasionally. Blocks, European disc bearing, and ball bearing guides all perform well if adjusted properly. No one is better than the other; they're just different. While blade guides might seem to be as crucial as the wheels,

they are not because usually you can replace inferior guides with high-quality aftermarket ones. Adjusting and replacing the guides are discussed in Chapter 4, "Adjusting the Band Saw," page 69.

Guide Post

The top guide assembly is attached to a metal rod called the guide post, which is adjustable up and down so it can be set just above the workpiece. Some guide posts have a crank that moves a rack-and-pinion mechanism to raise or lower the heavy part, as shown in **Figure 2.31**. **Figure 2.32** shows the rack-and-pinion from inside the saw. Although it is not a necessity, the crank makes it easier to set the height of a heavy guide post and makes it much more likely that the guide post will remain square to the saw table.

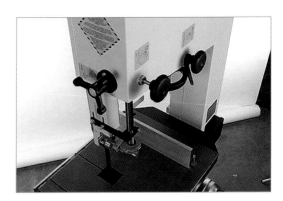

Figure 2.31. The top guide assembly is attached to the guide post, which is adjustable up and down.

Figure 2.32. Some saws have a rack-and-pinion guide post mechanism.

Tensioning Mechanism

The blade tensioning mechanism is located on the back of the top wheel on the 14-inch saws, as shown in **Figure 2.33**. A hinge holder houses the tension spring and the tension rod, which can be seen from the back of the saw in **Figure 2.34**. A thin tongue on each side of the hinge holder fits into a mating groove in the top frame casting and slides up or down to increase or decrease the tension on the blade. On the inside of the hinge holder box is the hinge and threaded rod that support the top wheel, as shown in **Figure 2.35**.

The tension spring adjusts the amount of tension applied to the blade. It also acts as a shock-absorbing or buffer system to mitigate any eccentricity of the wheels. Occasionally, increasing the tension on a blade can improve its performance, especially when the blade starts to become dull.

If too much tension is applied to the blade, the top wheel hinge will either break or bend, as shown in **Figure 2.36**. Remember that the 14-inch Delta saw was designed to run a ¼-inch blade. When using wider blades, it is important not to over-tension the saw or the hinge will bend like the one shown on the right in the photo. A new Delta hinge is shown in the middle of the photo. The broken hinge on the left of the photo is from a Taiwanese saw.

The tensioning system is skimpy on many bench-top saws. It is so important to the proper functioning of the saw that I would

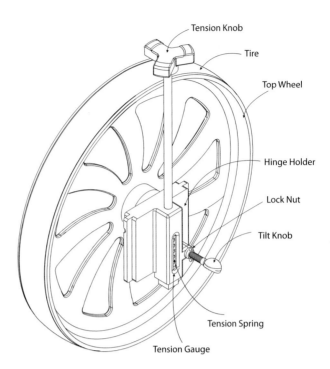

Figure 2.34. The hinge holder slides up or down to increase or decrease the tension on the blade.

Figure 2.35. On the inside of the hinge holder box is the hinge and threaded axle that support the top wheel.

Figure 2.36. If too much tension is applied, the top wheel hinge will either break (left) or bend (right). A new hinge is shown in the middle of the photo.

Figure 2.33. On the 14-inch saws, the blade tensioning mechanism is located on the back of the top wheel.

Figure 2.37. On European saws, the tensioning mechanism and the spring are massive.

evaluate it very carefully. If it feels like a kid's toy, it probably is.

On European saws, the tension adjustment wheel is often conveniently located under the saw's top frame member, making it easy to adjust from either the front or back of the saw. The tensioning mechanism and the spring on the European saws are massive, as shown in **Figure 2.37**. You can apply as much tension as is needed without fear of damaging the mechanism. Some of the clones have minuscule springs compared to the Italian saws. Resawing requires adequate blade tension, but be careful not to over-tension because that can damage the machine and shorten blade life.

Tension gauge

The tension spring regulates the amount of tension applied to the blade, and a gauge usually registers the amount of tension. The gauge on the 14-inch saws is on the back of the saw near the tension spring, as you can see in **Figure 2.33**. With most steel-frame saws, the tension gauge is inside the top cover. On many floor model saws, a tension gauge window allows viewing the gauge from outside the saw without the need to open the wheel cover. Although the window is not essential, it is convenient.

Quick-Release Tension Lever

A recent innovation is the quick-release tension lever, which allows the tension on the saw to be released by moving a lever, as shown in **Figure 2.38**. The quick-release tension lever eliminates the tedious task of cranking the tensioning knob. Although this mechanism is handy, it is by no means essential. This mechanism is more often found on 14-inch saws than on smaller bench-top units or larger floor models. Releasing the tension is good for extending blade and tire life, though, contrary to popular misconception, it has no effect on

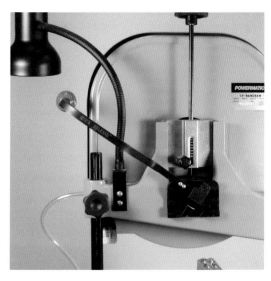

Figure 2.38. The quick-release tension lever eliminates the tedious task of cranking the tensioning knob. Releasing the tension extends blade and tire life, though it has no effect on the life of the spring.

the spring, which does not deteriorate if left under tension. To re-establish tension, the wheels should be rotated as the tension is gradually increased. This allows the blade to be tracking correctly by the time proper tension is achieved.

Blade Changing System

Changing the blade on most bench-top and stand-mounted saws is simply a matter of opening or removing the guard. The European saws have a hinged top guard, and the blades can be changed without tools, as shown in **Figure 2.39**. However, one of the European imitation saws requires four different tools to change blades, which is not much fun.

Blade Observation Window

Some saws have a small window in the upper wheel cover that allows you to observe the blade on the tire while the saw is running. This is a handy feature, but it is not necessary.

Dust Collection

Band saws generate a lot of fine dust, especially when cutting thick material. Dust collection is inadequate on most band saws, especially on the bench-top and 14-inch models, which

Figure 2.39. The European saws have a hinged top guard, and the blades can be changed without tools.

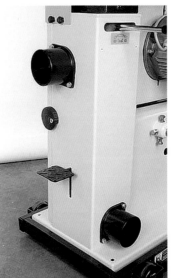

Figure 2.40. The European saws feature a large 4-inch dust port, and some have two. By moving a lot of air through the saw, much of the fine dust is transported to the collector.

Figure 2.41. Some saws have a sealed chamber under the table allowing a volume of air to transport sawdust directly from the blade. A replaceable block surrounds the blade. This saw also has a wheel brush (left).

have small dust ports designed to be connected directly to a shop vacuum. By comparison, most of the European saws feature a large 4-inch dust port, and some have two, as shown in **Figure 2.40**. Many European models have a sealed chamber under the table allowing a flow of air to transport sawdust directly from the blade, as shown in **Figure 2.41**.

Wheel Brush

A wheel brush for cleaning the bottom tire is a standard feature on some band saws, as shown in **Figure 2.41**. The brush helps to keep the wheel clean, which helps the blade track without vibration. This is important if you cut a lot of wood with pitch in it, such as pine.

Table

While most band saws have a cast-iron table whose working surface has been ground flat and smooth, some have a sheet-metal table,

and a few small bench-top units have a molded plastic table. I very much prefer a heavy cast-iron table. You want something solid under the workpiece with enough beef to support itself, the front fence rail, and the lower blade guide system without any flexing. The table trunnions and trunnion supports enable the table to tilt so you can saw beveled work.

Table height

Band saw table heights are a real consideration if you spend a lot of time at your saw. Of course this depends on the operator's height, and of course there isn't much you can do about it unless you want to stand on a platform or put the saw itself on one. The table on a 14-inch band saw is usually close to a height of 44 inches (3 feet, 8 inches). Most floor models have table heights in the 36-inch (3-foot) range. A small bench-top saw can be mounted on a bench of any height.

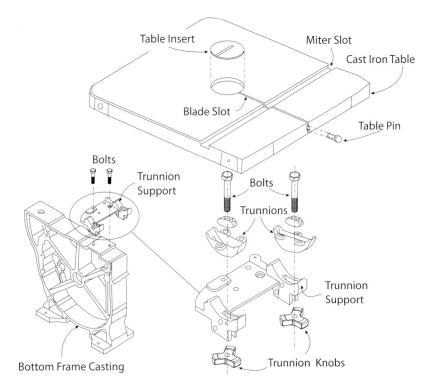

Table Insert

Miter Slot

Cast Iron Table

Blade Slot

Table Pin

Bolts

Trunnion Support

Bolts

Trunnions

Trunnion Support

Bottom Frame Casting

Trunnion Knobs

Figure 2.42. Two semicircular metal trunnions are secured to the bottom of the table. Bolts located in the trunnions secure them to the trunnion support casting. This system allows the table to tilt.

Table trunnions

Remember that the saw table is mounted on two semicircular metal pieces called trunnions, which mate with a semicircular piece attached to the saw frame called the trunnion support, as shown in **Figure 2.42**. This mechanism is what allows the table to tilt, as shown in **Figure 2.43**. After the table is adjusted to the desired angle, it is locked in place with the trunnion lock. A scale and a pointer register the angle of tilt, as shown in **Figure 2.44**, which is a view of the underside of the saw table.

Trunnion support

The trunnion supports are securely bolted to the saw frame, and the table is bolted to the trunnion system with adjustable bolts that are easy to loosen and tighten, as shown in **Figure 2.42**. Two semicircular arcs are

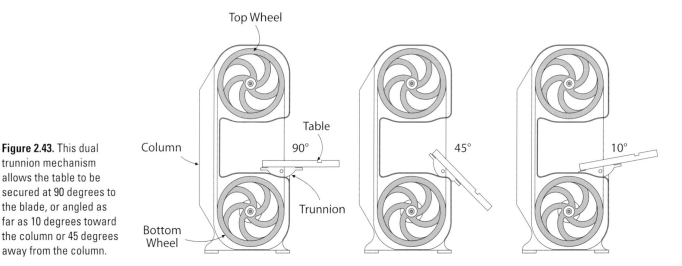

Top Wheel

Table

90°

Column

Trunnion

Bottom Wheel

45°

10°

Figure 2.43. This dual trunnion mechanism allows the table to be secured at 90 degrees to the blade, or angled as far as 10 degrees toward the column or 45 degrees away from the column.

Figure 2.44. A scale to register the tilt angle of the table is secured to the front of the trunnion in this view of the underside of the saw table. The bolts, which hold the trunnion to the cast table, can be adjusted to position the blade in the middle of the table slot.

cast and then machined to accept the curved trunnion on the bottom of the saw table, as shown in **Figure 2.45** and **2.46**. The guide assembly below the table is secured to the trunnion mount.

The table and trunnions on bench-top saws may be rather light, though most 14-inch stand-mounted saws are adequately built. In general, the floor model saw table and trunnion system is solid and very stable. Most of the European saws have heavy-duty cast-iron tables and trunnion systems with single lever locks, as shown in **Figure 2.47**. Some of the imitations of the European saws have large cast-iron tables but flimsy trunnion systems; you can actually wiggle the table when it is supposed to be locked tight.

Check that the trunnion locks are tight and easy to work. On some saws, they are like faucet knobs and mounted so close to the underside of the table that you will skin your knuckles every time you saw a bevel. Also look for an adjustable stop that will help you return the table to its square position without having to fuss.

Figure 2.46. This photo shows a 14-inch Delta saw with the table removed. The bottom guide assembly is situated between the two semicircular arcs machined in the trunnion support casting.

Figure 2.47. Most of the European saws have a heavy-duty cast-iron table and trunnion system. This Agazzani also features a handy single lever lock.

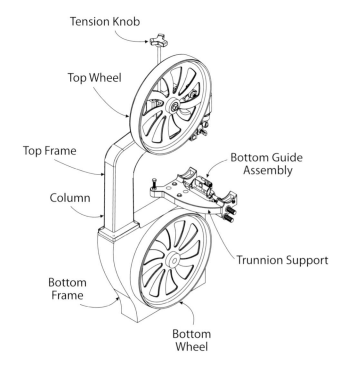

Tension Knob

Top Wheel

Top Frame

Column

Bottom Guide Assembly

Trunnion Support

Bottom Frame

Bottom Wheel

Figure 2.45. The table is attached to the saw frame by resting on a cast-iron piece called the trunnion support. Two semicircular arcs are cast and then machined to accept the curved trunnion on the bottom of the saw table.

Front Rail and Rip Fence

Most saws have a rail mounted on the front edge of the table on which to mount and move the rip fence. Some saws have a smooth rail that is essentially a flat or round iron bar. Other saws have a gear rack cast or cut into the metal to engage with a toothed wheel on the rip fence.

The rip fence extends across the saw table parallel to the side of the blade, as shown in **Figure 2.48**. Most rip fences have a mechanism for adjusting the distance from the saw blade and for locking this setting. Some fences also have a latch that grips the back edge of the table. The rip fence can be used to guide the workpiece when ripping. Since sharpening variations can cause the saw cut to drift or lead one way or another, most rip fences have adjustment bolts that can compensate for blade lead.

A number of aftermarket rail and fence systems are available, and you can always make a fence that clamps to the saw table, so the presence or absence of one is not a sufficient reason to reject a used saw.

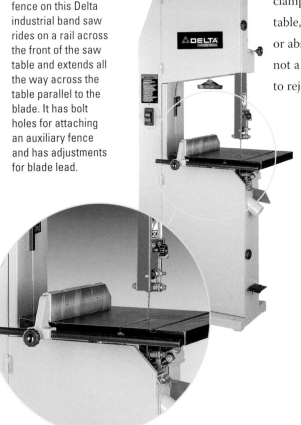
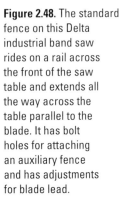

Figure 2.48. The standard fence on this Delta industrial band saw rides on a rail across the front of the saw table and extends all the way across the table parallel to the blade. It has bolt holes for attaching an auxiliary fence and has adjustments for blade lead.

Miter Gauge

The miter gauge on most band saws is the same as you would find on a table saw: a metal bar that rides in the table slot, with a semicircular head that can be adjusted from square to 90 degrees left or right. The miter gauge can be used to crosscut wood at 90 degrees or at any other angle. If the miter gauge is missing from a saw, it is easy to find a replacement.

Finding used equipment

Finding used equipment is a waiting game. Word of mouth, classified ads, used machinery dealers, estate sales, and auctions are some of the places to look. A bankruptcy auction can be a very good source because the machinery likely was being used until the sale. However, the demand for good used equipment is high, and the bidding at the auction may escalate rapidly to the point where it is no longer a good deal. Doing an online search for machinery auctions may be a good way to locate machines locally. Online sources, such as eBay, are popular, though I would never buy a used machine that I did not personally inspect. There are just too many potential problems that are hard to evaluate in photos.

As soon as you find an advertised tool, ask the seller a few simple questions. Ask for the manufacturer's name, model, and serial number if possible. There is usually a nameplate on the saw, as shown in **Figure 2.49**. Prepare yourself with a working knowledge of new band saw prices and repair parts' costs.

Evaluating a Used Saw

Used machines can be divided into two camps: "ready-to-go" and "needs-help."

Ready-to-go machines are ready to plug in and start sawing. They may need some adjustment and fine-tuning, but they have no missing parts, no unusual customizing, and no broken, abused, or worn-out parts. A ready-to-go band saw purchase is simply a matter of agreeing on a price.

Popular brands like Delta, General, Powermatic, and Jet are in demand. A huge advantage of these well-known brands is that these companies are still in business and repair parts are available. The price of lesser-known brands drops precipitously.

Used equipment prices depend on the condition and the desirability of a particular machine. The rule of thumb is that a brand-name band saw in running condition will often sell for 50% to 65% of a new unit. The fair price is adjusted up or down from 50%, depending on age and condition. On the high end, an almost new saw is probably worth about 75% of the new price. On the low end, a working older saw with a lot of use might be worth only 25% to 35%. Remember that you are not paying sales tax or shipping so that will save some money compared to the price of the new machine.

A needs-help saw is an entirely different situation. Needs-help saws, as the term implies, are machines that are worn out, are abused, or have missing or broken parts. Of course there are gradations of this category: For instance, a missing throat plate is less severe than a missing bottom guide assembly. A needs-help saw is worth no more than 50% of the new price, and its value goes down precipitously as the requirements for new parts and work increase. Replacement parts are expensive, and a pile of key parts can very quickly add up to the cost of a new saw. The needs-help

Figure 2.49. There is usually a nameplate on the saw identifying the manufacturer and giving the machine's serial number. This is the nameplate on the back side of an older 14-inch Delta Rockwell.

group can be further divided according to the condition of the machine. I usually drop a machine into a lower category of desirability for every $100-worth of parts or every three hours of work it needs. A saw that needs two new tires ($40), a new throat plate ($8), guide blocks ($15), a new top guard ($12), and a half-hour of work ($17.50) adds up to $92.50.

Just about anyone can handle a ready-to-go machine, but a needs-help machine is a different matter, and what the saw needs should be matched with your skill, time, and money. Each buyer has his/her own repair tolerance. A machinist who can make any part of a saw has a greater tolerance for repairs than someone with limited experience and tools. Be realistic about your limits and your tolerance for used machines.

Smaller machines from industrial brands like Northfield, Newman-Whitney, Oliver, and Tannewitz are especially desirable. A friend of mine recently picked up a beautiful 20-inch Northfield band saw at a retirement auction for the price of a new 14-inch machine. Northfield and Tannewitz are still in business, so parts are probably available, making their machines even more desirable.

USED BAND SAW CHECKLIST

Here is a three-part checklist you can use when you are hot on the trail of a used band saw.

Before you visit the machine, try to get the name of the manufacturer, the model number, and the serial number. Do your research and compare the cost with that of a new machine. Learn all you can about the manufacturer, and, if you have a model number, you may be able to get a parts drawing and obtain a copy of the original manual online. Many manufacturers and importers also publish their parts lists and replacement prices online. Online support groups, such as the Wood Online Old Tools and Machinery forum (*www.woodmagazine.com/oldmachinery*) and Old Wood-Working Machines (*www.owwm.com*), often can be a big help. Acquire a current catalog if one is available. Record the information on Part 1 of the checklist.

When you visit the seller to inspect the saw, wear old clothes (now is not the time to look well-to-do) because old machines usually are dirty. Bring such basic supplies as screwdrivers, Crescent wrenches, Allen wrenches, rags, oil, a flashlight, a magnifier, a small inspection mirror, hand cleaner, a tape measure, a good light with an extension cord, Band-Aids, and cash. If the purchase is for your business, bring a receipt the seller can sign.

Look for bent, broken, or customized parts, as shown in **Figure 2.50**. Saw parts will last a lifetime if they are not abused. The weakest link of the 14-inch saw is the top wheel hinge, which is the first part to be damaged by abuse such as over-tensioning. Record the results of your general inspection and your inspection of particular subassemblies on Parts 2 and 3 of the checklist.

Figure 2.50. The top blade cover on this 14-inch saw was cut away to make room for a bent wheel hinge after the owner over-tensioned the blade. When you are evaluating a used machine, modifications like this can be a danger signal.

Part 1: General Info

Date of call _____ Phone _____

Owner's first name _____

Address _____

_____

Date and time of appointment _____

Asking price _____ Band saw manufacturer _____

Is it a common brand? ❑ Yes ❑ No   Size _____

Model _____ Serial number _____

Accessories, blades, etc _____

_____

Part 2: General Inspection

General condition _____ How old is it? _____

Is it intact or has it been disassembled? _____

Has it been abused? ❑ Yes ❑ No

Are parts missing? ❑ Yes ❑ No

Are parts available? ❑ Yes ❑ No

Bent or broken parts _____

_____

Does the part need to be custom made? ❑ Yes ❑ No

Can you make the missing part
(i.e., throat plate)? ❑ Yes ❑ No

Block guides (best for narrow blades) ❑ Yes ❑ No

Bearing guides ❑ Yes ❑ No

Flat wheels (better for tracking wide blades) ❑ Yes ❑ No

Crowned wheels
(better for tracking narrow blades) ❑ Yes ❑ No

Metric threads ❑ Yes ❑ No

SAE threads ❑ Yes ❑ No

Is the motor direct drive? ❑ Yes ❑ No

Is the motor three-phase electrical? ❑ Yes ❑ No

240 volt or 120 volt? ❑ 240V ❑ 120V

Throat depth _____ Height _____

Width _____

Part 3: Individual Parts and Mechanism Inspection

Tension knob _____ Tension spring _____

Casting _____ Covers _____

Wheels _____

Shafts (replacing a worn shaft can be expensive)

_____

Pulley _____ Top wheel bearing _____

Bottom shaft bearings _____ Guide post _____

Tires _____ Top guides _____

Bottom guides _____ Top thrust bearing _____

Bottom thrust bearing _____ Motor _____

Belt _____ Table _____

Table insert _____ Table trunnions _____

Damaged knobs, bolts, or screws _____

_____

Pulley wobble or damage _____

Does it run? ❏ Yes ❏ No

Noise or vibration _____

_____

Does it need work? ❏ Yes ❏ No

How much work will it take? _____

Can you do the work? ❏ Yes ❏ No

What is the cost of parts? _____

What is the final price? _____

Can you move the saw? ❏ Yes ❏ No

Is it worth it? ❏ Yes ❏ No

DEAL KILLERS

"Deal killers" are problems with used machines that you should avoid trying to fix unless you have a lot of experience and you are going to get the saw at a very good price. These problems include:

- Cracks in castings, unless you are a very knowledgeable welder;
- Older direct-drive motors;
- Three-phase motors;
- Worn shafts and bearings;
- Key parts missing;
- A burned-out motor;
- A machine that has been disassembled;
- Babbitt bearings, unless you have the skill and inclination to maintain them;
- Broken parts, unless you know the replacement part is readily available.

Restoring old cars, tractors, and woodworking machines is a popular hobby. At the end of this chapter is a story about the restoration of an older Crescent band saw that had cracked castings, was missing parts, and required new babbitt bearings. A member of the Old Wood-Working Machines Group did this restoration. This group was founded as a public service to amateur and professional woodworkers who enjoy using and/or restoring vintage machinery. Their very informative website is *www.owwm.com*.

Making the deal

This is a short story about how to make a deal. At one time, Maxwell Street in Chicago was the largest flea market in the country. Every Sunday morning at dawn there were hundreds of people selling anything that you can imagine, including tools. My older brother got his PhD from the University of Chicago and lived in Chicago before Maxwell Street closed down. Unlike most academics, he loved tools and went to Maxwell Street just about every Sunday. Without going into great detail (because a whole book could be written about buying tools), he would ask a number of leading questions when he looked at a tool he was interested in. Sellers usually imagine that they have a great object for sale, so the buyer's task is to create doubt as to its real value.

My brother would ask these kinds of questions:

- Do you have the parts that are missing?
- Do you have the owner's manual?
- Do you have the rip fence?
- Do you have the height attachment?
- Do you have the circle cutting jig?
- Do you have the resaw attachment?
- Do you have the blades?
- Do you have the dust collection attachment?
- Are you aware that this _____ (fill in the blank) is a problem with this machine?

And only after all of that, he would casually ask, "What are you asking for this?" He never quite said it, but you could read in his expression and almost hear, "What are you asking for this . . . piece of junk?"

Just like a good auction buyer he had in mind the price he would pay. If the answer was less than that, he would buy the tool. And if not, he would walk away.

Band saw restoration

Although it not advisable to buy a pre-owned saw that needs too much work, there are exceptions. If the machine has been in your family and has sentimental value, it is worth keeping and repairing. If you have the skill and you know that you would enjoy tackling the project, the machine might also be worth buying and restoring.

To give you an example of what can be done, I've included these photos, which illustrate the story of the restoration of an older Crescent 36-inch band saw that had cracked castings, was missing parts, and required new babbitt bearings. The band saw was found in rough shape, as you can see in **Figure 2.51**. The broken castings were welded together and then used as patterns for sand-casting new parts, as

Figure 2.51. This Crescent band saw was found in rough shape with broken castings.

shown in **Figure 2.52**. The cost for the four new castings was $114 plus shipping from a supplier listed in the Resources section on page 184. For a local firm that can do this work, look under "Foundries" in the phone book. New babbitt bearings were poured around the new shaft, as shown in **Figure 2.53**. **Figure 2.54** shows the completed functioning band saw in very close to original condition.

Most cities have a working foundry that can cast new metal from patterns or old parts, and the cost is usually surprisingly modest. The castings for this project were done by Cattail Foundry.

Keith Rucker, who is a member of the Old Wood-Working Machines Group, did this restoration.

Figure 2.53. New babbitt bearings were poured around the new shaft.

Figure 2.52. The broken castings were welded together and then used as patterns for sand-casting new parts.

Figure 2.54. This restoration was done by Keith Rucker, a member of the Old Wood-Working Machines Group.

CHAPTER THREE

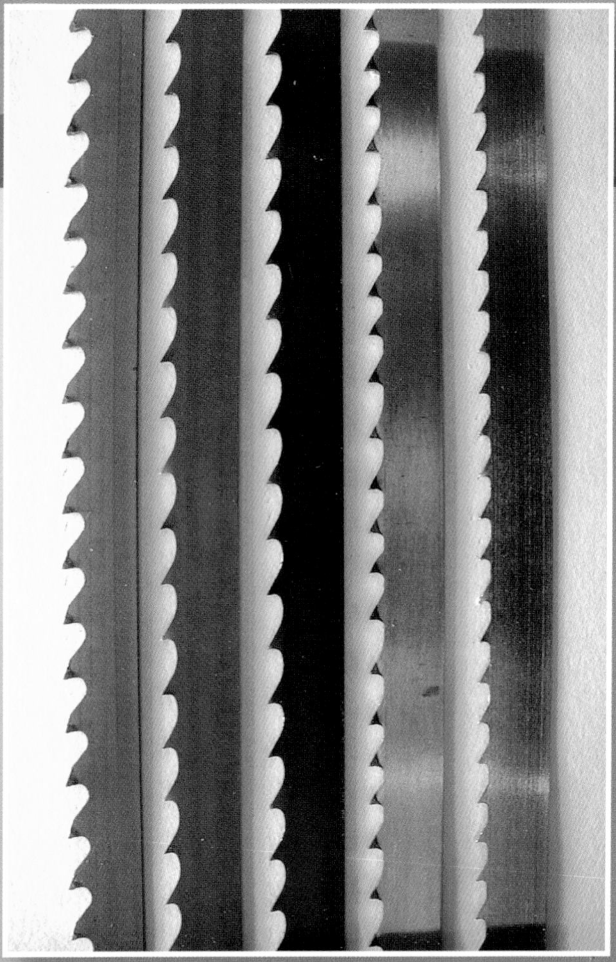

Figure 3.1. From most durable on the left to least durable on the right, the most popular blades are carbide tipped, bimetal, carbon steel, spring steel with hardened teeth, and spring steel. The carbide-tipped blade costs roughly 10 times as much as the least expensive spring steel blade, but will outlast it by close to 100 times.

Band Saw Blades

Though band saw blades all have the same basic design—an endless loop of steel with teeth cut into one edge—they each have their own particular cutting characteristics. To get the most out of your band saw, you have to use the blade that has the characteristics best suited for the given task. This can only be accomplished if you understand the different types of blades and their cutting characteristics (see **Figure 3.1**).

Of all woodworking machines, the band saw offers more creative potential than any other. Many projects, such as the chairs shown in **Figure 3.2**, require the unique ability of the band saw to make straight or curved cuts in wood of all thicknesses. With this single tool, you can exploit the beauty of a single board or log by resawing it into flitches, cut accurate dovetails, or quickly make a cabriole leg or an ingenious puzzle. But to do all of those neat things requires picking and adjusting the best blade for a given

task. The blade is really half of the saw. Most woodworkers have settled on one all-purpose blade for the miter saw or table saw, but the band saw is different. To use the band saw to its fullest potential, you will have to use a variety of blades.

In this chapter, I will discuss the various types and sizes of band saw blades so that you can decipher the catalog copy and have a knowledgeable conversation at your local saw shop or retail woodworking store. I'll also elaborate on which blades I've found to be best for particular woods and woodworking tasks.

Before exploring the general types of band saw blades available, you should familiarize yourself with the terms used to describe them, as shown in **Figure 3.3**. There's also a complete glossary of band saw and blade terminology at the back of this book (see page 180).

Figure 3.2. Complicated pieces of furniture, such as these elegant contemporary chairs by Jeff Miller of Chicago, require the unique ability of the band saw to make both straight and curved cuts in wood of all thicknesses. Photo courtesy of Jeff Miller.

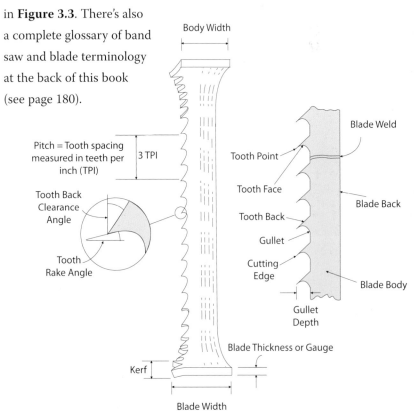

Body Width

Pitch = Tooth spacing measured in teeth per inch (TPI)

3 TPI

Tooth Back Clearance Angle

Tooth Rake Angle

Blade Weld

Tooth Point

Tooth Face

Blade Back

Tooth Back

Gullet

Cutting Edge

Blade Body

Gullet Depth

Blade Thickness or Gauge

Kerf

Blade Width

Figure 3.3. Blade terminology includes a number of specialty words, and some terms are used interchangeably. Manufacturers and catalogs often use different terms. The following standard terminology will be used in this book.

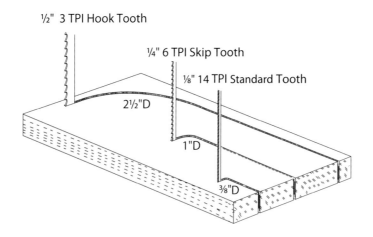

Figure 3.4. The blade width determines the smallest diameter that can be sawn.

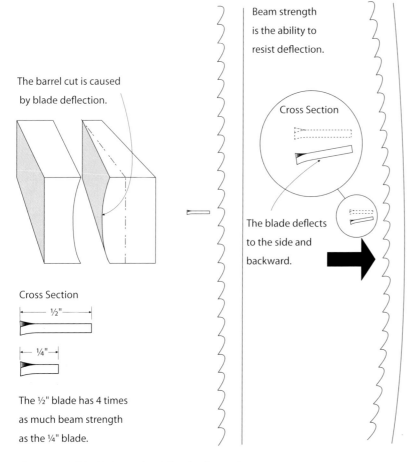

Figure 3.5. Wide blades resist deflection better than narrow ones, so they are preferable for sawing straight cuts and gentle curves. As a blade deflects under a load, it rotates and turns sideways, creating a barrel cut.

Blade specifications

Choosing the correct blade is the first step in attaining good band saw performance. The blade that you choose determines the type of work that you can do and how efficiently you can do it. If you choose a very coarse blade, it will cut like a chain saw. In contrast, a very fine blade will allow you to do very intricate scrollwork. You'll also prolong blade life and tooth sharpness by choosing the proper blade for each particular application. Using a blade for the wrong application is the best way to cause it to break or wear out prematurely. In this section, I'll discuss the differences among blades.

Blade Width

Blades are usually classified according to their width, which is the measurement from the back of the blade to the front of the teeth. The width of the blade determines how tight a turn the blade can make (see **Figure 3.4**). The narrower the blade, the tighter the turn. The wider the blade, the more likely it is to resist deflection. For this reason, wide blades are preferable to narrow ones for making straight cuts.

A ½-inch-wide blade that is .025-inch thick is the widest blade that is practical to use on a 14-inch consumer-grade band saw. Some owners' manuals say that you can use a ¾-inch blade on a 14-inch wheel, but those blades are usually .032-inch or .035-inch thick, and that's too thick. These thick blades are liable to break due to metal fatigue as a result of bending around a too small wheel radius. Do not use a .032-inch or .035-inch blade on a saw with wheels less than 18 inches in diameter. Thick blades also require more tension, which puts stress on the saw frame, bearings, tensioning mechanism, and shafts.

The wider the blade, the less likely it is to deflect because a wider blade has more beam strength. Think of a floor joist as an example of beam strength. A 2 x 8 has roughly four times as much beam strength as a 2 x 4. As the blade deflects, it rotates sideways and creates a barrel cut, as shown in **Figure 3.5**. The ½-inch blade has roughly four times as much beam strength as a ¼-inch blade. **Figure 3.6** shows that a ½-inch bimetal blade with 3 teeth per inch (TPI) is stiff enough to resaw a wide board from a cherry log.

A ¼-inch blade is the one most frequently used for general-purpose work. It is usually a good compromise, offering some beam strength along with the ability to make tight curves. **Figure 3.7** shows a ¼-inch blade with 6 TPI being used to cut a cabriole leg.

For years, the smallest available blade was ⅛ inch wide. This blade can saw a turn about the size of a pencil eraser. A ¹⁄₁₆-inch blade had been developed but was discontinued. A new ³⁄₃₂-inch blade is now available. **Figure 3.8** shows the work of a ¹⁄₁₆-inch blade in the oak piece on the right and the work of the new ³⁄₃₂-inch blade on the left. This very small blade requires replacing the saw's metal side guides with special nonmetal guide blocks, which can be set tight to the narrow blade. Regular bearing guides would interfere with the teeth on the blade, quickly dulling it. These blades are not usable with regular bearing guides.

Figure 3.6. These boards were cut from a small cherry log and then resawn using a ½-inch-wide bimetal blade, which is more than stiff enough for this demanding task. The wood figure on each board is a mirror image, called a bookmatch.

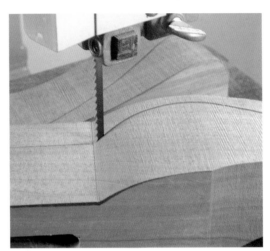

Figure 3.7. A ¼-inch blade is the most frequently used blade for general-purpose work. It is a good compromise, offering moderate beam strength and the ability to make tight curves. Here the ¼-inch blade with 6 teeth per inch (TPI) is cutting a cabriole leg.

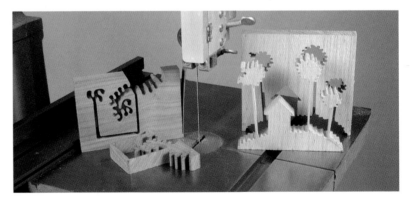

Figure 3.8. The cutout on the left was made with a ³⁄₃₂-inch blade. The oak piece on the right is the work of an older, now discontinued ¹⁄₁₆-inch blade. These very small blades require replacing metal guide blocks with phenolic guides.

UNDERSTANDING BEAM STRENGTH

Tensioned band saw blades obey the laws of structural engineering and function like a loaded beam spanning between two points. The band saw blade spans between the top and bottom thrust bearings and carries the load imposed by the material being sawn.

Beam strength is the ability to resist deflection and is a function of blade width and tension. The blade deflects to the side and backward, as shown in **Figure 3.5**. As a load is applied to the blade of the saw, the side receiving the load (the cutting teeth) goes into compression. The back of the blade is stretched and is under tension.

An architect friend once explained to me how his engineering professor used a huge ink eraser to demonstrate compression and tension stress. He had drawn closely spaced vertical lines on the sides of the eraser. When he bent the eraser, you could clearly see that the lines were now spaced further apart at the bottom, where there was tension, and closer together at the top, where there was compression. The only place the spacing of the lines remained unchanged was right down the center of the eraser. This is called the neutral axis, which, even in the most heavily laden beam or blade, remains unstressed.

Referring to the structural beam analogy, it is intuitively obvious that if you make the beam twice as wide, it will carry twice the load with the same sag. What is not so obvious is that if a beam is twice as deep, it will carry eight times the load with the same amount of deflection.

Because a beam will carry a great deal more load if it is deeper rather than wider, floor joists are 2 x 10s even though they contain the same amount of lumber as 4 x 5s. The lesson learned from the structural beam analogy is to use the widest possible band saw blade when cutting thick material.

USING A RADIUS CHART

The amount of detail and the size of the detail in your pattern determine the blade width you should use. It's best to choose the widest blade that will make the tightest curves with ease. You will have to identify the tightest curve in the pattern and match the blade to that radius.

Until you become well acquainted with your saw and the different blade sizes, use the contour (radius) chart in **Figure 3.9**. Radius charts can be found in many woodworking books, magazine articles, and on blade boxes. They differ slightly from one another, but are good indicators of how tight a curve can be cut with a particular blade.

A ¼-inch blade will cut a circle with a ½-inch radius or a 1-inch diameter. Everyday items such as coins or a pencil also can help determine which blade to use. A quarter is almost an inch wide, the tightest curve you can make with a ¼-inch blade. A dime is the size of the tightest curve that can be cut with a ³/₁₆-inch blade, and a pencil eraser is the size of the tightest turn that you can make with a ⅛-inch blade. Therefore, to test whether a ³/₁₆-inch blade would work for a particular curve, just drop a dime on the pattern. The ³/₁₆-inch blade can cut a curve bigger than the dime, but not smaller.

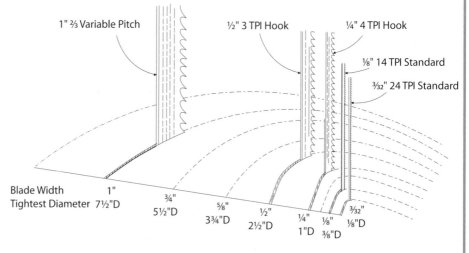

Figure 3.9. Until you become well acquainted with your saw and how the different blade sizes behave, it is best to use the radius chart. It shows, for example, that a ¼-inch blade will cut a circle with a ½-inch radius or a 1-inch diameter.

Tooth Size and Spacing

When you are talking about band saw blades, the word "pitch" does not refer to the sticky thick liquid found in pine boards. It is a term for tooth size. The pitch is usually given as a number that refers to how many teeth are in one inch of blade (called teeth per inch or TPI), as shown **Figure 3.10**. The words "coarse" and "fine" also are used to describe the number of teeth in a blade. A coarse blade has few teeth. A fine blade has many teeth. The coarser the blade, the faster and rougher the cut; the finer the blade, the slower and smoother the cut.

It is important that you match the pitch of the blade to the thickness of the material being cut, as shown **Figure 3.11**. There should always be at least three teeth in the material. A blade with more teeth will give a smoother cut, but one with too many teeth will create other problems, such as too much heat and too slow cutting. Excessive heat shortens the life of the blade because it draws the hardness from the teeth, allowing them to dull quickly. It also shortens the life of the band. With a little experience, you will learn how to tell whether a blade has the proper pitch, too fine a pitch, or too coarse a pitch.

Pay close attention to the feel of the saw and the resulting cut. Heat or burned wood indicates a dull blade or too fine a pitch. Vibration may indicate that the pitch is too coarse or that you are feeding too quickly.

When choosing a blade with the proper pitch, you also should consider the hardness of the workpiece. Harder materials require finer blade pitch. Exotic hardwoods such as ebony and rosewood require blades around 4 TPI or 5 TPI, while American hardwoods such as oak or maple will cut well at 3 TPI. Softwoods such as pine are best cut with a coarse blade because the resins in the pine will quickly clog a blade that is too fine, decreasing its ability to cut. Owning blades with a variety of tooth configurations in the same width will give you an acceptable choice for most jobs.

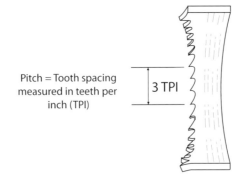

Pitch = Tooth spacing measured in teeth per inch (TPI)

3 TPI

Figure 3.10. The term "pitch" describes tooth size and usually is stated as the number of teeth in one inch of blade (called teeth per inch or TPI). This example has three teeth in one inch of blade so it is a 3 TPI blade.

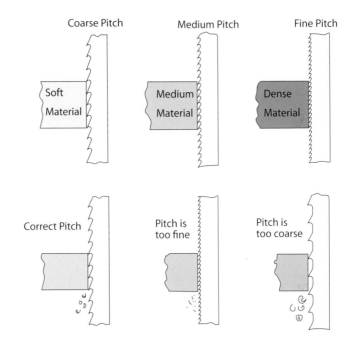

Figure 3.11. There should always be at least three teeth in the material being cut. A blade with more teeth makes a smoother cut, but too many teeth create other problems, such as excessive heat and slow cutting.

CHOOSING THE BEST PITCH

Proper Pitch
1. Minimum heat generated.
2. Cuts quickly.
3. Quality cuts.
4. Long blade life.
5. Minimum feeding pressure is required.

Pitch That Is Too Fine
1. Excessive heat.
2. Cuts slowly.
3. More feeding pressure is required.
4. Premature breakage or rapid dulling of blade.

Pitch That Is Too Coarse
1. Vibration.
2. Rough cut.

Tooth Characteristics

Two factors that indicate how a band saw blade will cut are the shape, or form, of the teeth and the set of the teeth. These factors are examined below.

Tooth shape

Band saw teeth are available in one of two shapes: The face of the tooth is either 90 degrees to the body of the blade, which is called a zero-degree rake or it has a slight positive angle, in which case it is called a hook tooth, as shown in **Figure 3.12**. A blade with a zero-degree rake cuts with a scraping action. This makes a smooth cut, but increases the heat caused by the cutting. A blade with hook teeth cuts more aggressively. It makes a rougher cut, but less heat is generated, which means that the blade can be used for a longer period of time. Thick wood is best cut with hook teeth not only because they are more aggressive but also because they are more efficient at removing the waste.

Blades can be broken down into four general groups according to the shape of their teeth.

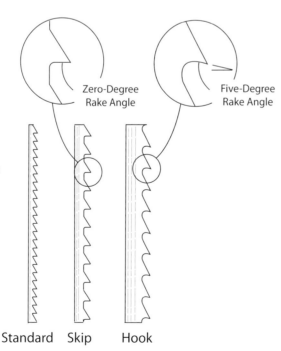

Figure 3.12. Band saw teeth are available in one of two shapes: zero-degree rake angle and five-degree rake angle. The standard tooth and skip tooth have a tooth face that is 90 degrees to the body of the blade, called zero-degree rake angle. The hook tooth has a slight positive angle, called five-degree rake angle.

Zero-Degree Rake Angle

Five-Degree Rake Angle

Standard   Skip   Hook

Standard

A blade with standard teeth has teeth spaced closely together. It has a zero-degree rake. This blade makes a smooth cut. It is especially useful for cutting small details and for cutting across (against) the grain of the wood because it doesn't tear the wood as it cuts. It is the best blade to use when smoothness is a consideration. When cutting thick stock with a standard tooth blade, make sure that you feed the stock slowly. This is the usual tooth form for small blades under $\frac{3}{16}$ inch.

Skip Tooth

The teeth on skip tooth blades have a zero-degree rake, like those on standard tooth blades, but every other tooth has been removed. Thus, this blade has only half as many teeth per inch. Because a skip tooth blade is coarse, it cuts very quickly, especially with the grain. A skip tooth blade is best suited for cutting long, gentle curves such as a cabriole leg. Although it doesn't cut against the grain as well as the standard tooth blade or rip with the grain as well as the hook tooth blade, it does offer the best compromise. This is the usual tooth form for medium-size blades between $\frac{3}{16}$ inch and $\frac{5}{16}$ inch wide.

Hook Tooth

The hook tooth blade is the most aggressive blade. This is because it has a positive rake angle and the fewest number of teeth per inch. It is particularly efficient at cutting thick stock with the grain. The large round gullet, the area at the base of the tooth designed to carry the chip from the kerf, can transport large amounts of sawdust. This makes it the best choice for ripping, or sawing along the grain of the wood, and resawing, or cutting a board through its width. This is the usual tooth form for blades wider than $\frac{5}{16}$ inch.

Variable Pitch

The variable pitch blade is the most recently developed blade for the metal cutting industry and is designed to decrease vibration on interrupted cuts such as those made on tubing, U channels, and I beams where excessive vibration is a problem, as shown in **Figure 3.13**. These blades have a positive rake angle like hook teeth, but the teeth progressively change in size from large to small and back to large again. The variable pitch blade also features varying set angles. The manufacturing process is complicated and expensive because the size of the tooth and the depth of the gullet both change from one tooth to the next, as shown in **Figure 3.14**. The design dampens vibration and produces a smooth finish. It is now being used in the meat cutting industry, as well as on woodworking blades designed for cutting thick stock and for resawing. **Figure 3.15** shows a variable pitch blade cutting oak.

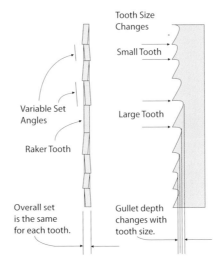

Figure 3.13. The variable pitch blade, recently developed for the metal cutting industry, decreases vibration on interrupted cuts such as those made on tubing, U channels, and I beams. The teeth progressively change in size from large to small and back to large again.

Figure 3.14. The variable pitch blade is complicated and expensive to manufacture because the size of the tooth and the depth of the gullet both change from one tooth to the next. The design dampens vibration and produces a smooth finish.

Figure 3.15. This 1-inch-wide carbide-tipped variable pitch blade, running on a 20-inch band saw, makes a superb cut in an oak log. It is called a 2/3, referring to the range of variation in the tooth pitch and gullet depth. This blade retails for more than $200.

Blade Set

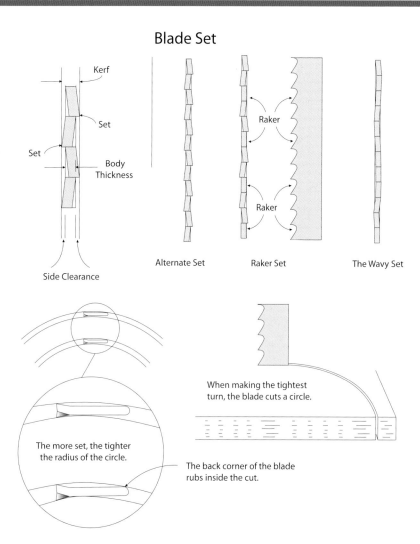

Figure 3.16. The teeth on the band saw are bent sideways, or set, so the saw kerf is wider than the body of the blade. Set makes it easier for the band saw operator to rotate the workpiece around the blade when sawing a curve. The side clearance also decreases friction between the blade and the workpiece on straight cuts.

WHICH TEETH ARE BEST FOR WHAT

Crosscutting wood and tight curves—Alternate set, standard pitch teeth with zero-degree rake.

Long, gentle curves—Raker set, skip tooth with positive rake.

Ripping and resawing wood—Raker set, hook tooth with positive rake.

Smoothest possible cut—Alternate set, standard pitch or fine pitch teeth with zero-degree rake.

Cutting metal—Wavy set, variable pitch with zero-degree rake.

Tooth set

The teeth on the band saw are alternately bent or set sideways, as shown in **Figure 3.16**. Thus, the saw cut (kerf) is wider than the body of the blade. Set makes it easier for the band saw operator to pivot the workpiece around the blade when sawing a curve. On straight cuts, the side clearance created by the set also decreases friction between the blade and the workpiece.

There are three basic set styles, as follows:

Alternate Set

Alternate set teeth have every other tooth bent in the same direction. A blade with alternate set teeth gives the most teeth per inch and thus the smoothest cut. Standard tooth blades usually have teeth with alternate set. This type of blade is well suited to crosscutting (sawing across the grain of wood).

Raker Set

Raker set teeth are similar to alternate set teeth except that some of the teeth, called rakers, are not set. Rakers clean the middle of the cut and are used most often on skip tooth and hook tooth blades. The design increases the efficiency of the cutting action but decreases the smoothness of the cut. This type of blade is best suited to ripping and resawing with the grain of the wood.

Wavy Set

Wavy set means that groups of teeth are alternately set in opposite directions. You can see wavy set teeth on an ordinary hand-held hacksaw designed for cutting metal. The variable pitch blade also has a variable or wavy set, which helps to decrease vibration. This type of blade is best suited to cutting metal.

Blade classifications

Band saw blades are usually classified in three different groups: small, medium, and large (see **Figure 3.17**). This takes into account the blade width, tooth shape, and pitch. Small blades usually have standard (regular) teeth and a fine pitch. Medium blades usually have skip teeth with a raker set and a medium to coarse pitch. Large blades often have hook teeth with a raker set and a coarse pitch. You can best prepare yourself by owning at least one blade from each group.

The Best All-Around Blade

A ¼-inch-wide hook tooth blade with 4 to 6 teeth per inch is usually considered the most useful all-around blade for small band saws.

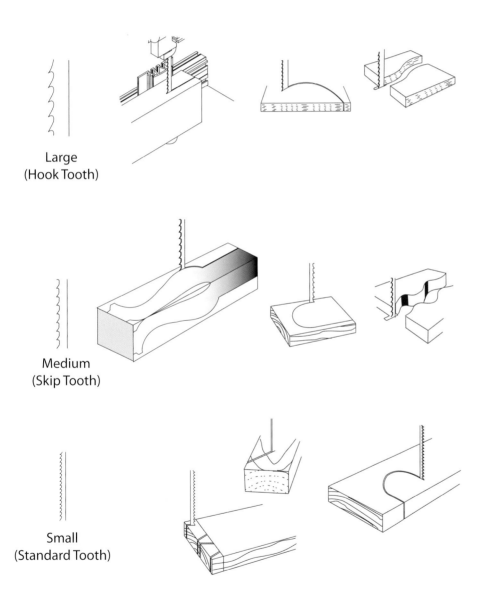

Large
(Hook Tooth)

Medium
(Skip Tooth)

Small
(Standard Tooth)

Figure 3.17. Band saw blades are usually classified as large, medium, and small. Large blades often have hook teeth with a raker set and a coarse pitch. Medium blades usually have skip teeth with a raker set and a medium to coarse pitch. Small blades usually have standard (regular) teeth and a fine pitch.

Choosing a blade

There are primary factors to consider when choosing a blade. The first is the tightness of the curves that you are cutting, as shown in **Figure 3.18** and in the radius chart on page 40. This will determine the width of the blade. Another important factor is the orientation of the wood grain that you are cutting.

The best blade to use to crosscut, to cut diagonally, and to cut curves that swing back and forth across the wood grain is a standard tooth blade. A skip tooth blade also works well on long, gentle curves with the grain and is often acceptable when making cuts that criss-cross the wood grain. A 1/4-inch-wide hook tooth blade with 4 TPI to 6 TPI is usually considered the best all-around blade. A hook tooth blade is good at long curves cut with the grain and is especially good at cutting with the grain when you are making straight cuts, such as ripping or resawing.

You should select a blade according to the following priorities:

Width

First, decide on blade width. If all of the cuts in your work are straight, use the widest blade your saw can accept, for maximum beam strength and resistance to deflection. If there are curves, you will determine blade width by how many and how large they are.

Form and Shape

The second most important choice is the tooth form. This is determined by the orientation of the grain, with standard teeth best for crosscutting, skip teeth best for gentle curves, and hook teeth best for ripping and resawing. Choosing the tooth form also affects the pitch. The standard tooth form has twice as many teeth as the other forms.

Pitch

The tooth spacing (pitch) is the final consideration, but after choosing the width and the form, you may not have much say about the blade pitch unless you have a very large selection of blades on hand.

Blade Length

All band saw blades are manufactured from straight lengths of blade stock that are cut to length and welded end-to-end to form a continuous loop. Band saw blades are readily available in lengths that will fit the most common saws—9-inch bench-top saws use a 59½-inch blade and the standard 14-inch saw uses a 93½-inch blade, or, with the riser block installed, a 105-inch blade. Unless your saw

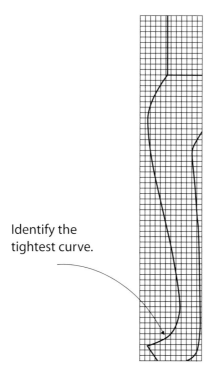

Identify the tightest curve.

Figure 3.18. When choosing a blade, consider the tightness of the curves to be sawn. Choose a blade width that can cut the tightest curves in the pattern.

blade requires an unusual length, buy blades that are already welded. If you need a custom size, you can order them (usually you can find a local supplier), and you also can learn to weld them yourself, as discussed on pages 61 to 65. However, making your own blades requires gas or electric welding equipment and a long learning curve. Just like owning a very small drill bit doesn't qualify you to be a dentist, owning a blade welder doesn't mean you can weld a blade. Commercially available blades are welded with expensive machines, and the quality is not easily replicated.

If you do need a custom blade, you will need to know how long it is. Band length varies among the different manufacturers. The correct blade length may be found on the machine, on the box a previous blade came in, or, if you have it, in the owner's manual.

You can also measure the length, but first park the upper (tension) wheel in between the fully up and fully down positions. This midpoint will allow adjustment if the blade comes out slightly long or short. Then, wrap a tape measure around the two wheels, the same as if it was an installed blade, and read the length.

If you can't find the length anywhere, or if you've measured it and you want to double-check, calculate it from the following formula:

L = (3.14D) + (2 x Y).

In this formula, *L* is the length (in inches) of the band saw blade, *D* is the diameter (in inches) of either the upper or lower wheel, and *Y* is the vertical distance (in inches) between the wheel centers. **Figure 3.19** shows how to determine the blade length.

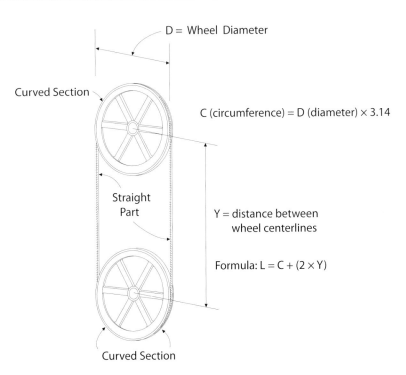

D = Wheel Diameter

Curved Section

C (circumference) = D (diameter) × 3.14

Straight Part

Y = distance between wheel centerlines

Formula: L = C + (2 × Y)

Curved Section

Figure 3.19. To determine the blade length, measure the curved part of the blade and add it to the straight part of the blade. Either measure around the wheel or measure its diameter (D) and multiply it by 3.14 to get the circumference (C). The two straight sections of the blade, on each side of the wheels, are represented by the letter Y. Length equals the circumference of the wheel plus the two straight sections, as in the formula L=C + (2 x Y).

STANDARD SAW, STANDARD BLADE

The common 14-inch band saw, whether American made or imported, uses a 93 1/2-inch blade. With the 6-inch riser block installed, the same saw takes a 105-inch blade. These lengths are standard and are readily available.

Spring Steel Blades

The original band saw blades were made of spring steel, which is usually silver in color. These are the blades that you find at local hardware stores and home centers. The teeth and body have the same hardness, Rc 36–42, which is not particularly hard. However, the body is soft enough to be flexible, thus avoiding band breakage. The teeth are hard enough to be used on softwoods, but they will dull quickly on hardwoods.

Spring steel is usually available in alloys specified as C1074, C1086, and C1095, where the last two digits indicate approximate carbon content. For example, C1074 has a carbon (C) content range of approximately 0.74% to 0.78%. C1086 is approximately 0.84% to 0.89%, and C1095 is approximately 0.94% to 0.96%. All are considered high-carbon steel.

In an effort to make an inexpensive blade, some manufacturers notch the blank, which is essentially punching the shape of the teeth with a die. Other spring steel blades are milled. Although most blades are .025-inch thick (the thickness of six pieces of paper), spring steel blades are available in thinner dimensions, down to a .014-inch blade for small tabletop saws.

Spring Steel Blades with Hardened Teeth

Another type of spring steel blade has a soft body with hardened teeth, which extend their life. Harder teeth stay sharp longer. The teeth are first cut in the soft body; then, they are ground and set.

The last stage is the hardening process. The tip can be induction hardened with an electrical current or flame hardened with torches. If the tooth tips of a spring steel blade are dark in color, this indicates that they have been hardened.

Spring Steel Hybrid

The spring steel blade is also manufactured with variably spaced teeth for the meat cutting industry. This blade has sharp impulse-hardened teeth that produce a smooth cut on moderately hard wood. The impulse hardening process darkens the tips of the teeth. The body is a thinner .022-inch with minimal set, so the kerf is narrower than other blades. The blade is initially very sharp and produces a smooth surface, but it is not very durable when cutting wood.

Plain Carbon Steel Blades (Flex-Back)

The plain carbon steel blade was designed during the 1930s to improve durability by increasing the carbon content. These blades are usually black in color and are used for both wood and metal cutting. The teeth of carbon steel blades are very hard, measuring 64–66 on the Rockwell C Scale. This is about the hardness of a good chisel.

The higher carbon content of approximately 1.30% makes the steel stay sharp longer because the metal has increased wear resistance. The teeth of a carbon blade can withstand heat up to 400 degrees F, which is important when cutting metal because of the high temperatures generated. This is less important when cutting wood, unless the blade is used in constant daylong production or is used to cut exotic woods like teak, which not only are rather hard but also contain abrasive minerals.

The back of a flexible or flex-back carbon steel blade, at Rc 28–32, is softer than the back of a spring steel blade. The teeth are hard and durable, and the blade's body is soft enough to not be brittle. These blades are the most reasonably priced for the serious woodworker.

There is also a hard-back version of the blade with a body hardness of Rc 43–47 that is used to cut metal in industrial settings. The increased hardness increases the tensile strength of the blade, while the hard back increases the beam strength, which helps the blade resist deflection under heavy sawing pressure in a production metal-cutting situation. The hard-back blade isn't especially important for woodworking and isn't worth the extra expense. A flex-back blade is sufficient.

Silicon Steel Blades

One variation of the carbon steel blade is blade stock with a high silicon content, from Sweden. Silicon steel blades have a carbon (C) content similar to C1074 spring steel, from 0.74% to 0.79%. Its silicon (Si) content is around 1.5%, whereas regular carbon steel has a silicon content of 0.16% to 0.19%. High silicon steel can tolerate heat. It is appropriately named "friction band" and is used primarily for friction-sawing metal, that is, cutting at speeds between 6,000 and 14,000 surface feet per minute (SFM). The metal being cut is heated to a very high temperature by the cutting action of the blade, and softens in front of the cut. Even though the blade is not designed for woodworking, it is aggressively marketed at a premium price. These blades have teeth in the Rc 60 range, with an Rc 30 blade body. They are initially sharp and cut well in the beginning, but I don't think they are as durable as a high-quality carbon steel blade. These blades are advertised as requiring less tension, but there is not a good technical explanation for using less tension than usual.

Bimetal Blades

The bimetal blade was developed during the 1960s for cutting metal. The blade looks like a carbon

steel blade but is a uniform medium gray in color. Like the carbon steel blade, it has hard teeth and a softer body, but it is made in quite a different way.

A small strip of flat high-speed steel (cobalt/molybdenum) wire is electron-beam welded onto a wider strip of alloy steel. The combined strip is then milled just like all the other bands, creating a blade with tooth tips of high-speed steel on an alloy steel body. Only the tooth tip cuts, so it's an ideal combination. The high-speed steel teeth have a hardness of approximately Rc 65, and the blade can withstand heat up to 1000 degrees F. The blade rarely reaches 300 degrees F when wood is being cut. The bimetal blade also can withstand much higher tension than the carbon blades, which increases its beam strength. This is useful in metal cutting because so much feed pressure is used. Bimetal blades are now available in the .025-inch thickness for use on 14-inch saws, with tooth configurations specifically designed for cutting wood.

Although bimetal blades are more expensive than standard carbon steel, they will outlast the steel blade by 10 to 25 times. They are not as sharp as some of the other blades, and they do tend to experience harmonic vibration, like a guitar string. The bimetal blade may be best in situations that require abrasion resistance, such as when cutting plywood, particleboard, fiberglass, and exotic woods with a high mineral content. My experience is that when resawing dense woods such as hard maple, this blade will greatly outlast everything except carbide by quite a margin—up to 20 times longer than a standard carbon steel blade. If you do a lot of sawing and the finish doesn't have to be the smoothest, this is the most economical choice. The blade I use is a 3 TPI hook tooth manufactured by Olson Saw and sold under the brand name MVP (see Resources, page 184).

Carbide-Tipped Blades

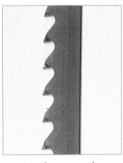

Like circular saw blades, the carbide teeth on band saw blades are individually brazed onto the blade back; then, they are precisely ground on the exposed surfaces. It is an expensive manufacturing process. This blade will outlast any other type of band saw blade and may be a good choice for woods like teak that have a high silica content, which dulls a regular blade very quickly. For the consumer grade 14-inch saws, this blade is available in the ½-inch by .025-inch thickness for about $100. The carbide blade requires some getting used to because it tends to vibrate unless the wood is fed at a smooth rate. It requires more tension to dampen vibration and should have the back rounded with a stone fairly often to prevent a crack from starting, which is the first step in blade breakage (see page 59). It would be hard to find a local shop that could weld this blade if it should break.

For large saws, carbide-tipped blades are available in wide widths with a variable tooth spacing pattern. I have had one of these blades for years on my 20-inch Italian saw, which I use like a table saw for ripping. It produces a high-quality cut similar to that of a circular saw blade. Resawing with a wide carbide-tipped blade is a dream.

Comparing the blades

To test the cut surface, I used four different blades with the ½-inch x 3 TPI hook tooth configuration to resaw a hard maple board. I used the same setup for cutting each board, as shown in **Figure 3.27**. So that a smooth surface was always presented to the resaw guide, I thickness-planed the board after each cut.

Each blade felt different during the cut. Surprisingly, the results were very similar. The photo in **Figure 3.28** shows four different pieces cut from the same board. The spring steel hybrid left the smoothest surface.

Although they will outlast the other blades, the carbide blade and the bimetal blade didn't cut quickly, and each tended to flutter, an indicator of harmonic vibration. Flutter leaves small diagonal waves on the surface of the cut, as shown in **Figure 3.29**. Increasing or decreasing the tension slightly, and/or changing the feed rate, can minimize harmonic vibration.

Practice using blades

The only real way to be sure that the blade and the saw will run correctly is to test it. Check the quality of the cut on a practice piece of scrap that is the same wood and the same thickness as your project. Don't be afraid to experiment, particularly if you are not confident.

Don't be too goal-oriented at first because that only leads to frustration. Figure out what the saw can do before you start planning what you can do with it. To use the band saw efficiently, you must be able to tension it correctly. As with developing most types of skill, this takes time, patience, and concentration. Tensioning and tracking the blade are discussed in detail in Chapter 4, "Adjusting the Band Saw," page 69.

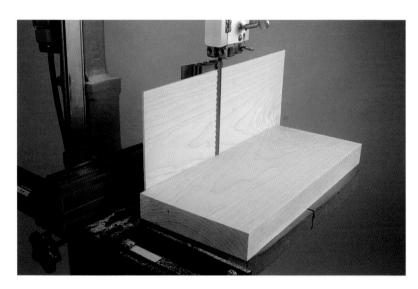

Figure 3.27. This is the setup for testing how the different types of blade took a slice off a piece of hard maple. This is the 1/2-inch x 3 TPI hook tooth blade.

Always pay attention to the performance of the blade. A well-adjusted blade will often change while you work. As it heats up from hard use, it will expand in length and decrease in tension. When sawing thick and dense wood such as hard maple, you may have to re-tension the blade to compensate for this expansion. And if you do increase the tension to maintain performance, it is important that after you have finished sawing, you release the tension and allow the blade to cool and shrink back to its original length. If you don't release the tension, you will have an over-tensioned blade by the time the blade cools down.

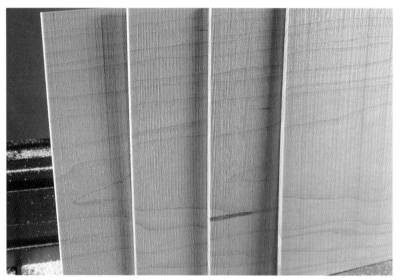

Figure 3.28. The test results are very similar. From left to right are the surfaces left by the carbide-tipped blade, the bimetal, the carbon steel, and the spring steel hybrid, which left the smoothest surface. For most straight cuts, the smoothness is not important because the surface will be finished by planing. It's usually more important on curved cuts.

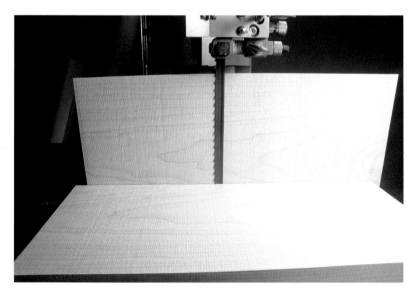

Figure 3.29. The carbide-tipped blade and the bimetal blade tend to flutter, leaving small diagonal waves on the surface. Increasing or decreasing the tension slightly, and/or changing the feed rate, can minimize flutter.

The blade's life

The life of a band saw blade is not an easy one. It must do two contradictory tasks: flex around the band saw wheel while at the same time remain straight in the cut. Moreover, it must do all of this at 30 miles an hour. The surface speed (surface feet per minute, or SFM) of the blade on a consumer saw is between 2,800 SFM and 3,000 SFM. On a large commercial saw, the speed may be up to 5,000 SFM or 6,000 SFM, or about 60 miles per hour.

When discussing blade life, there are two distinct factors that must be considered, the blade body and the tip of the tooth. These are the two blade parts that suffer the most from wear and tear. When the tip becomes too dull, the usable life of the blade is over. The same is true if the blade breaks, which it ultimately will, from metal fatigue due to flexing over the wheels. Welding the broken blade and sharpening the tooth tip will extend the usable life. However, this may not be cost effective.

Ideally, band saw teeth should be close to the end of their usable life when the blade body breaks. The body shouldn't break when the teeth are still sharp, but it can happen. The body of the blade has to withstand the constant flexing and straightening cycle. If the blade body is too hard, it will be brittle and break too easily. Blade teeth have to be hard to resist wear and heat. Cutting produces heat. The harder and thicker the material being cut, the more heat. When sawing metal, coolant fluid is often used to help dissipate the heat. Extreme heat decreases the tooth's ability to stay sharp and resist wear.

The Blade Becomes Dull

All cutting edges have similar and predictable dulling characteristics. The initial edge depends on the type of metal and the grinding process. Steels can be inexpensively sharpened to a higher degree than carbide. A tip that is too sharp or too pointed can dull quickly. Although the initial sharpness is often used in testing blades for magazine articles, I put more emphasis on durability. Although initial sharpness and durability are not mutually exclusive, my experience is that the band saw blades with the highest initial sharpness are not the most durable.

As tools dull, there is a predictable dulling curve, as shown in **Figure 3.30**. A blade begins sharp. It then starts to dull, but it is still cutting well. Then, the edge dulls at a geometric rate. The tool dulls quickly and eventually becomes so dull its usable life is over.

Figure 3.31 is a chart showing the dulling curve for the blades listed in this chapter. This chart is not to scale and is designed for representation only. It shows the dulling curves for the various blade metallurgies. Because the bimetal and the carbide blades have a much longer usable life, their dulling curves are much longer.

If you are doing a lot of resawing and are finding that your blades are not lasting as long as you would like, try a bimetal blade. The $30 bimetal blade will outlast a number of carbon steel blades.

Every blade has good points and not so good points. Despite the advertising hype, there is no perfect blade. As with life in general, band saw blades are always a compromise.

SHARPNESS CHART

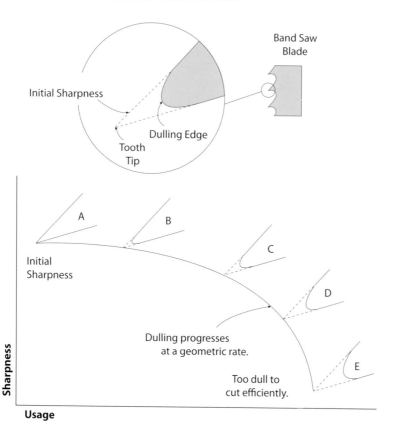

Figure 3.30. As tools dull, there is a predictable dulling curve. A shows the initial sharpness. B shows the tool dulling, but it is still cutting well. C shows the tool at the apex of the curve—so far the dulling has been gradual and slight—but C is the tipping point. After C, the curve drops dramatically as the edge dulls at a geometric rate. D represents the tool dulling quickly, and at E it is so dull that its usable life is over.

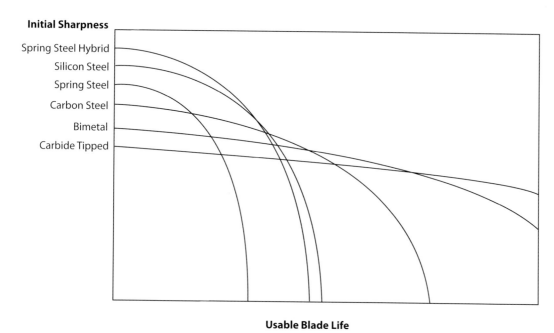

Figure 3.31. This chart (not to scale) shows the dulling curve for various blades. Because the bimetal and the carbide blades have a much longer usable life, their dulling curves are much longer.

Troubleshooting the blade

Although the band saw was invented in 1808, it was not a usable tool until the 1850s when a reliable technique for welding the blade was developed. Before that, blades had to be hammer-welded by a blacksmith, a somewhat imprecise method that requires a lot of skill. For the blade to track properly and cut well, the weld must be straight and aligned. Many band saw problems can be traced to a problem with the weld. Following is a list of some of the problems that can be encountered.

Premature Breakage

Experts feel that, when a blade breaks, approximately half the time the break should be attributed to the weld and half the time to the blade body. If your blade breaks consistently at the weld, you should return the blade for a refund or find another supplier. If the blade was cutting well and then breaks, it can be rewelded. A local machine shop usually can reweld a blade for a minimal price.

Breaking a blade should be a rare thing. I cannot remember the last time I broke a blade. I use quality blades, take care to round the back of the blade (see page 59), and spend time adjusting the guides and bearings. If you break blades often, something is wrong either with your blade supplier or with your technique.

The Blade Does Not Flex Properly

The blade should be flexible. If the metal adjacent to the weld was damaged during the welding process, it may be brittle and not flex well. If the blade breaks within an inch of the weld, it suggests the metal is damaged and it probably is not worth welding again. People sometimes break a blade when they fold it for storage because they put undue pressure on the weld. The weld should withstand gentle flexing, but it shouldn't be expected to make a sharp bend.

The Blade Is Not Welded Straight

When you get a new blade, the first thing to do is to check the weld. The back of the blade should be straight. Getting the weld straight is not as easy as it sounds. During the hardening of the teeth, the front of the blade shrinks in relationship to the back. If a blade is resting on its back, it will often rock because the back is convex and the front (tooth) side is concave. Some blades rock more than others. Because of this, it may be impossible to weld the blade perfectly straight. However, the blade should be welded as straight as possible. If the blade is not straight, it will pulsate back and forth on the saw. This can make tracking the blade difficult. It may be hard to keep the blade on the saw because it will pulse forward on the wheels. It may also damage the guides or thrust bearing.

Sawing puts stress on the back of the blade and the thrust bearing, especially if you are cutting thick material with a wide blade. The blade weld should move past the guides and thrust bearing without any noise. If there is pulsing contact between the weld and either the guides or the thrust bearing, you will hear a ticking sound with each revolution of the blade. If you do hear such a noise, stop the saw and investigate. The blade should be welded straight from front to back, as shown in **Figure 3.32** (A). If the back of the blade is concave, as shown in **Figure 3.32** (B), the blade will pulsate back and forth, which may be annoying but will not hurt anything. However, if the back of the blade is convex, as shown in **Figure 3.32** (C), the weld may pound against the thrust bearing and damage it.

When your blade makes the ticking sound that indicates a convex weld, run a stone against the back of the blade for a while. If it still makes the ticking sound, remove the blade and dress the back of the weld with a disk or belt sander. The back of the blade should be

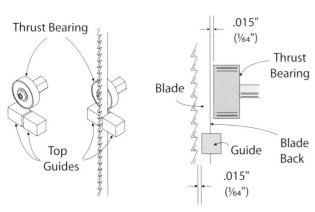

Thrust Bearing

Top Guides

.015"
(¹⁄₆₄")

Thrust Bearing

Blade

Guide

Blade Back

.015"
(¹⁄₆₄")

Figure 3.32. The blade should be welded straight from front to back, as shown at A. If the back of the blade is concave, as at B, the blade will pulsate annoyingly back and forth. If the back of the blade is convex, as at C, the weld sticks out and may damage the thrust bearing. If the blade is offset, as at D, send it back to the supplier. Don't put a blade like the one at E on the saw because it will destroy the thrust bearing. Send it back to the supplier.

A   B   C   D   E

straight. If it is offset, as in **Figure 3.32** (D), send it back to the supplier. Don't put a blade like the one in **Figure 3.32** (E) on the saw because it will destroy the thrust bearing very quickly. Send it back to the supplier.

Rounding the back of the blade

Years ago I was working on a job over the weekend and discovered that the weld on the new blade that I had just purchased had a problem. Since the local store was closed, I couldn't exchange the blade, so I tried to clean up the weld. As an experiment, I backed off the guides and stoned the back of the blade while the saw was running. To my surprise, it fixed the problem and improved the performance of the saw. I now stone the back of every blade, as shown in **Figure 3.33**. Stoning the back of the

blade smoothes the weld and removes the sharp corner where cracks start. The rounder the back, the less likely the blade is to crack.

The stoning process takes about five minutes. Begin by lightly touching the back corners with a dry (unoiled) sharpening stone (see Chapter 4, "Adjusting the Band Saw," on page 69 for more information on how stoning the back of the blade fits into the setup, alignment, and adjustment processes). I've had the best results using a silicon-carbide stone fitted on a wood handle designed for this purpose. Because this is a grinding process, be sure to wear safety glasses, and, since sparks are created, clean out the sawdust from the inside of the band saw, and turn off your dust collection system before you start.

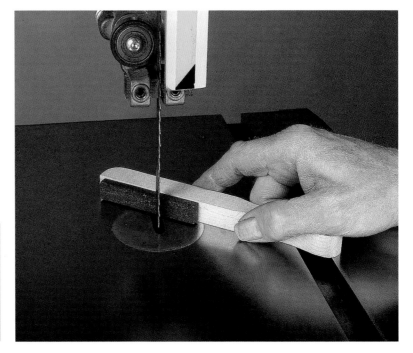

Figure 3.33. Stoning the back of the blade smoothes the weld and removes the sharp corner where cracks start. Rounding the blade decreases the chances that the blade will crack.

Figure 3.34. With small ⅛-inch and ³/₁₆-inch blades, the pressure of stoning the back of the blade may push the blade forward off the wheels. To prevent this, feed wood into the blade during the rounding process. Pass the wood underneath the stone.

Begin by holding the stone against the back corner of the running blade, and then move it back and forth for a minute or so. Do the same for the other corner. After rounding the corner, sweep the stone around the back of the blade in a continuous, smooth motion. Since rounding the back of a narrow blade can push it off the wheel, lightly feed a scrap of wood into the blade during rounding, as shown in **Figure 3.34**. It might also help to angle the top wheel back to prevent the band from being shoved forward off the wheel.

Resawing with a wide blade is especially hard on the back of the blade and the thrust bearing. The back corners can become quite sharp and even develop a burr like a cabinet scraper, as shown in **Figure 3.35**. Rounding the back removes the corner and is especially helpful if the blade twists during a turn because there is no sharp corner to dig into the thrust bearing, as shown in **Figure 3.36**. Another advantage is that the blade will cut a smoother and tighter radius, as shown in **Figure 3.37**.

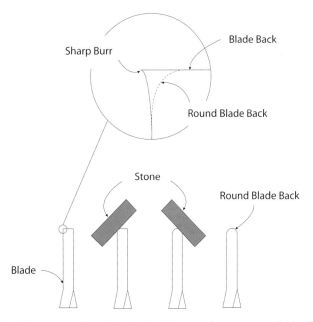

Figure 3.35. Resawing with a wide blade puts so much pressure on the back of the blade against the thrust bearing that the blade may develop a sharp burr like a cabinet scraper. Rounding the back of the blade removes the sharp corner.

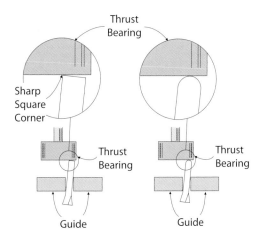

Figure 3.36. Rounding the back to remove the corner protects the thrust bearing in the event that the blade twists during a turn.

Figure 3.37. The rounded back enables the blade to cut a tighter radius and produce a smoother surface.

When to weld the blade

You can buy band stock in 100-, 250-, and 500-foot rolls, weld the blade yourself, and save money. That assumes that you can do a good job of welding. However, companies that manufacture blades invest at least $50,000 in equipment for cutting, tooth matching, welding, and annealing so that the teeth match and the blade is straight. Welding blades narrower than ¼ inch is especially difficult.

There are three situations that require a blade to be welded. One is when the blade is welded to form the continuous band after being cut to the desired length from coil stock. Another is when the blade is rewelded after it breaks to make it usable again. It makes sense to reweld a blade if it is in good shape. If, however, the blade is work-hardened, it will quickly break in another place. The third time a blade is welded is when it is used to make interior cuts. This often happens in metalworking. The blade is purposely sheared, threaded through a hole, and rewelded using a resistance-type welder that is mounted on the column of the saw, as shown in **Figures 3.38** and **3.39**.

Figure 3.38. Many professional metal cutting band saws have a welder mounted on the column to assist in making inside cuts by severing the blade, threading it through a hole, and rewelding it.

Figure 3.39. This welder has dials and levers for adjusting the weld. There's also a grinding wheel inside the round orange cap at the bottom of the machine for cleaning up the weld.

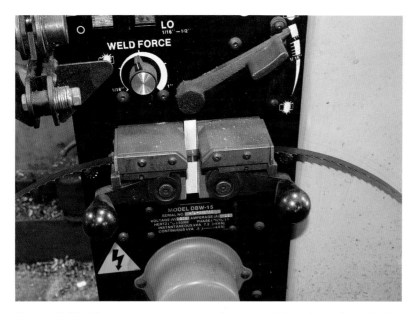

Figure 3.40. The blade ends are cut or ground square and then clamped together in the welder. An electrical current heats the ends until they fuse together.

Figure 3.41. The excess material left over from the weld is called flash and is removed by grinding.

Resistance Welding

To use a resistance welder, the blade ends are cut or ground square, and then the ends are clamped together in the welder, as shown in **Figure 3.40**. An electrical charge heats the ends until they fuse together to form the weld. Making a good weld takes skill, care, and practice.

When the band is heated during the welding process and then cools, it is very brittle. Before it can be used, you must anneal it to restore the weld joint to the same metallurgical hardness and strength as the rest of the band. Properly annealing the weld is as important as properly making the weld. It is done by reheating the weld to annealing temperatures and then cooling it slowly. The annealing temperature is detected by the color of the metal. For both carbon steel and high-speed steel bands, the proper color is dull cherry red. After the welding and annealing have been completed, file or grind the flash off the weld so that it is smooth (see **Figure 3.41**).

Silver Brazing

A low-tech and inexpensive alternative to resistance welding is brazing the blade ends together using a silver solder alloy. Properly done, this joint is very strong and flexible. It also has the advantage of not requiring expensive or complicated machinery, as shown in **Figure 3.42**. You probably already have most of the tools you would need: a grinder, a propane torch, a file, shears for cutting the blade stock, and a medium-grit diamond plate or stone. You'll also need a fixture to hold the blade ends together for brazing. The fixture is available from most catalogs, or you can make your own.

Silver brazing is a two-step process, as shown in **Figure 3.43**. First, grind the two blade ends at an angle of about 20 degrees in order to increase the surface area of the joint. You want a bevel that is slightly smaller than the adjacent

Figure 3.42. Silver brazing does not require expensive or complicated machinery. You probably already have most of the tools you need: a grinder, a propane torch, a file, shears for cutting the blade stock, and a medium diamond honing plate or stone.

gullet, as shown in **Figure 3.44**. Then, hold the two ends in a vise or fixture while you heat the metal with a torch. When the metal is hot enough, it melts the silver solder alloy so that it flows into the joint, usually with the aid of a chemical paste called flux. This technique takes some practice, but it is a good way of salvaging blades that break but still have usable teeth. The technique is especially useful if a professional resistance welder is not locally available. Remember that each time a blade is rewelded this way it becomes shorter by the length of the bevel, so too much rewelding eventually will make the blade too short for your saw. You can also silver-braze your own blades from coil stock.

Silver alloy for brazing is also called silver solder and must not be confused with the soft solder used for plumbing. Although brazing and welding are similar, there are important differences. Because the material to be joined is not melted in brazing, the metal is not distorted and its original metallurgical properties are preserved. Silver brazing generally can be done at low temperatures (below 450 degrees C or 850 degrees F), and it does not produce as strong a joint as welding. Welding is a high-temperature process in which the metal actually melts and fuses.

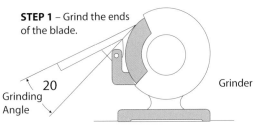

STEP 1 – Grind the ends of the blade.

20

Grinding Angle

Grinder

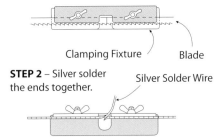

Clamping Fixture

Blade

STEP 2 – Silver solder the ends together.

Silver Solder Wire

Figure 3.43. Silver brazing is a two-step process. First the matching blade ends are ground at an angle. Then, the two ends are held in a vise while the metal is heated with a torch until the silver solder melts into the joint.

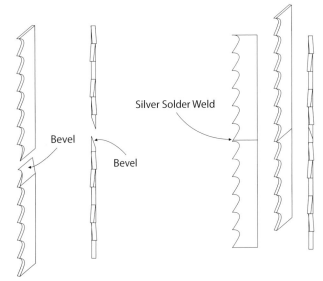

Bevel

Bevel

Silver Solder Weld

Figure 3.44. To increase the surface area of the weld, the blade ends are ground to a 20-degree bevel. Silver brazing is easier to do with large blades than with small blades.

In the brazing process, the molten solder is drawn into the joint by capillary action. Thus, it is particularly important to maintain the correct amount of space between the blade ends, which is the job of the blade-holding fixture. You want a space in the range of .001 inch to .005 inch, about the thickness of a piece of paper. Wider spacing will result in a weaker joint. The irregularity of the grinding process usually provides enough space when brazing band saw blades. A small clamp may help to keep the two band saw ends together and prevent them from bending away from each other as they are heated. It is also important to remember that metals expand and contract at different rates when heated and cooled. Let the joint cool completely before removing it from the fixture.

The joint area must be clean. The silver solder will not flow properly if grease, dirt, or rust blocks its path. Joints to be brazed should be coated with flux, a chemical paste that helps prevent oxidation when the metal heats up, protects the braze alloy, and improves its flow. As heat is applied to the joint, the flux will dissolve before the silver solder melts. A variety of fluxes are available for use at different temperatures, with different metals, and for a variety of environmental conditions. Silver solder usually is sold with a tube of the appropriate flux.

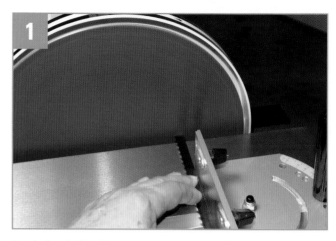

Cut the band with a large shear or a bolt cutter. Square the cut ends with a belt or disk sander. Use a fixture to hold the blade.

Use a combination square with a carbide scribe to mark the length of the bevel on both blade ends. Remember that the bevels are on opposite sides of the blade.

I find that I have more control grinding if I use the corner of the wheel and rotate the blade to be about 15 degrees to the edge of the wheel.

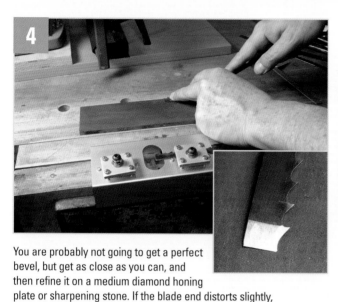

You are probably not going to get a perfect bevel, but get as close as you can, and then refine it on a medium diamond honing plate or sharpening stone. If the blade end distorts slightly, the side of the blade opposite the bevel can also be honed.

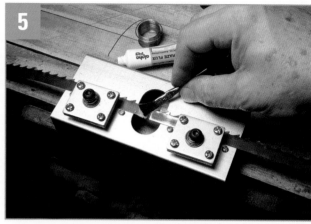

Apply the flux to the bevel ends with a small brush.

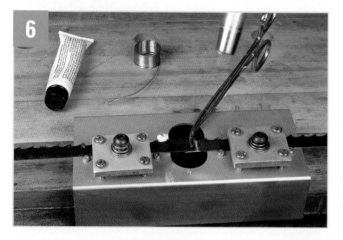

Before applying heat to the blade ends, make sure they are properly positioned and secured to remain in proper alignment. For the strongest braze joint, the metals that are being joined together need to be at close to the same temperature. Slow heat cycles generally produce better results than fast heat cycles. Hold the tip of the torch 3 to 4 inches from the blade, and move it back and forth to gradually heat up the whole blade.

When the blade is hot, remove the torch and feed the solder into the opening. The temperature of the blade will melt the solder, and capillary action will pull the material into the gap. Don't use too much solder because it is very hard when it cools and then requires a lot of work to remove the excess.

After the solder cools, remove the excess with a file or by sanding. I have found that a random orbit sander works best.

FOLDING THE BLADE

The blade should be handled with care when it is off the saw. Be sure to wear gloves when handling the blade. If the blade is to be stored in a humid place, it should be wiped with an oily rag to retard rusting. If a blade has become rusty, wipe it with an oil rag to remove as much rust as is possible. If it is very rusty, try steel wool.

You can hang up a blade in an unfolded position, but it will take up a lot of space on the wall. Some people find it difficult to fold a blade into three loops. It is not hard. The principle is you hold the blade and make one twist; then, you make another twist, which creates the three loops. There are two techniques and each takes a little practice. The two-hand approach works well for small blades. The blade is held with both hands grasping it with your thumbs pointing in opposite directions. The blade is then folded into three loops, as shown in **Figure 3.45**. For larger blades, it works best if you use your foot to secure the blade to the floor. Then, twist the blade once and then again into three loops (see **Figure 3.46**).

When unfolding a blade, be very careful, especially when using wide blades, because they have a lot of spring. Wear safety glasses and gloves. Always hold the blade away from you; never try to catch or control it with your body. Hold one loop with one hand, and let the blade recoil at arm's length. Always turn your face away from an uncoiling blade. After you unfold the blade, inspect it. Avoid using blades with cracks, bends, or kinks.

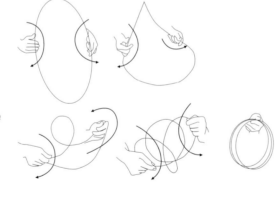

Figure 3.45. For compact storage, fold the blade into three loops. Hold the blade with your thumbs pointing in opposite directions. Then, make one twist, then another twist.

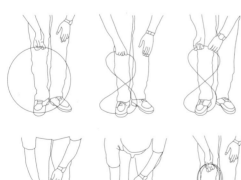

Figure 3.46. For larger blades, use your foot to secure the blade to the floor. Then, twist the blade once and then again so it forms three loops.

Blade maintenance

Care and attention can extend the life of the blade. The condition of the band saw itself makes a big difference. If the machine vibrates or has out-of-round wheels, blade life will be shortened. Vibration may be decreased by installing a good, balanced pulley and aligning the drive belts carefully. Quality cast-iron pulleys and a high-quality belt often make a great improvement, especially on low-priced saws.

Proper saw adjustment also prolongs the life of the blade. Saw alignment and the tracking and adjustment of the guides and thrust bearings are very important. Poorly adjusted metal guides can damage the blade teeth. The new nonmetal guide blocks prevent tooth damage and also prolong blade life by decreasing the heat from friction between the blade and the blocks.

Over-tensioning and under-tensioning can also shorten blade life. It is a good idea to decrease the tension after using the saw. This is also good for the wheels and the tires. When decreasing the tension, use the same number of turns of the knob each time. Then, when it comes time to increase tension again, you can do it quickly and accurately. Tensioning is discussed fully in Chapter 4, "Adjusting the Band Saw," page 69.

Keep the blade clean. With green woods and pitchy woods like pine and cherry, residue can build up on the face of the tooth. The effect is that the blade will cut as if it were dull, when in reality it is only packed with residue. This is especially true with fine-pitched saw blades. Cherry residue can actually become baked onto the front of the tooth.

To clean coarse-tooth blades, use a stiff bristle or fine wire brush. To clean fine-tooth blades, soak the blade in a cleaning solution, and then clean it with a very fine wire brush. A number of solutions, such as cleaning ammonia, oven cleaner, or turpentine, work well.

Stoning the Side of the Blade

The ⅛-inch and ³⁄₁₆-inch blades are often used for scroll sawing where a fine surface finish is desired. Even with these small blades, excessive tooth set or a bent tooth can cause a rough surface. If you notice the cut is rougher than you expect, a way to fix it is to remove the blade and flip it inside out so that it is positioned on the saw with the teeth upside down, as shown in **Figure 3.47**. Touch the sides of the teeth with a fine, dry stone while the saw is running. Then, return the blade to its normal position to resume sawing. Before you try this, clean the saw and disconnect dust collection so sparks don't ignite sawdust. Stoning the side of the blade makes the set on the teeth more uniform, creating a smoother surface, as shown in **Figure 3.48**. However, after the stoning process is complete, the saw will cut slower and not make as tight a turn, so there is a trade-off.

Sharpening a Blade

A dull blade should be replaced or resharpened. There are two means of sharpening: filing and grinding. Professional sharpeners use a grinding machine that indexes itself from one tooth to the next. Filing is the traditional method you can do yourself on softer blades, such as spring steel. Fine-pitch carbon blades with a standard tooth form can be refiled. Harder blades such as hardened spring steel and carbon blades are often too hard to file except with a diamond rod, as shown in **Figure 3.49**.

Most people feel that it is not economical to sharpen a band saw blade since most blades have several hundred teeth. However, if you are patient and you make a fixture to hold the blade in position, you will find that it is quite possible, and it can produce superb results.

Figure 3.47. Excessive tooth set or a bent tooth can cause a rough surface. You can dress the blade by removing it from the saw, flipping it inside out, and replacing it so the saw teeth are upside down; then, lightly stone the side of the blade.

Figure 3.48. Stoning the side of the blade makes the set on the teeth more uniform, creating a smoother surface. After stoning, replace the blade in its normal position. The smooth surface on the top piece of walnut was made after stoning the side of the blade.

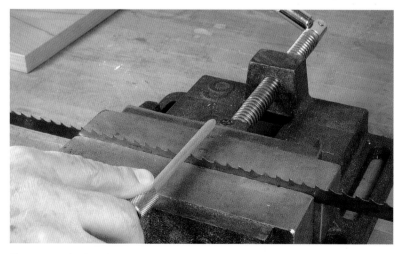

Figure 3.49. Hard blades such as hardened spring steel and carbon steel blades are often too hard to sharpen except with a diamond rod.

CHAPTER FOUR

Figure 4.1. Aligning the band saw wheels enables the blade to find its own equilibrium and essentially track itself. This is called coplanar tracking.

Adjusting the Band Saw

To get the best performance from your band saw, it has to be properly tuned and adjusted. If you've selected the correct blade for the material and the task, if the saw blade is tracked and tensioned, and if the guides are properly adjusted, the saw will work fine and behave predictably. That being said, the band saw does have a reputation as a troublesome tool because most saws are not adjusted properly. The problem with the band saw is that most people either don't know how to adjust the machine correctly or lack the patience to learn. Once you learn, however, adjustment takes only a minute or two. It is kind of like playing the guitar: The musician can't help but pay attention to how his instrument sounds and tune it as he plays.

Having a well-tuned and adjusted band saw in your shop has many benefits. It will greatly increase your confidence and your cutting options. It makes woodworking more efficient and much more enjoyable. In addition, a well-tuned band saw can prevent accidents. You can even rip small pieces on a band saw that would be dangerous to cut on table or radial arm saws. However, the band saw is unique. Unlike the miter saw or table saw, where you simply install the blade and you're ready to cut, each band saw blade has to be individually adjusted on the machine. A poorly adjusted band saw wanders, vibrates, breaks blades, and will be very frustrating to use. Therefore, all the attention you give to properly adjusting your saw is certainly worth the effort. In this chapter, I'll show you the techniques for doing it right every time.

Take it in steps

Tuning and adjusting the band saw is a logical process that you can divide into stages.

The first stage is when you acquire the saw and begin to consider what you will do with it. You will consider whether its existing guides are adequate or whether you should replace them with aftermarket guides. This is also the time to decide whether or not to use what I call coplanar tracking (tracking wide blades with the wheels lined up with each other in the same vertical plane), and if so, to adjust the position of the wheels on their axles in order to make coplanar tracking possible (see **Figure 4.1**).

The second stage is when you change the band saw blade. Each blade is different and requires you to make a number of adjustments. First, you will install the blade on the saw and tension it; then, you will observe and adjust how it is tracking on the band saw wheels. Once the blade is under tension and tracking correctly, you can adjust the thrust bearings and side guides. Close observation during this process may lead you to do additional work on the blade or the guides until it is running smoothly and well.

The third stage is when you are using the saw. As you gain experience with your band saw, you will learn how to observe the blade in relation to the machine's wheels and guides and how to continue to adjust it as you work. The heat generated by sawing will affect the blade's tension and the saw's adjustments, as will the pitch and dust generated by cutting the wood.

As in most things, the proof is in the pudding—how well does the band saw cut? Is the cut square to the surface, flat, and relatively smooth (depending, of course, on the coarseness of the blade's teeth)? Does the cut belly, does it show a pattern of diagonal lines, does it lead in one direction or another? The skilled operator absorbs all of this information and pauses as necessary to readjust the saw.

FACTORS AFFECTING BAND SAW PERFORMANCE

Saw quality—In woodworking machinery, you generally get what you paid for, and a bargain-price saw may turn out to be no bargain at all (see page 11).

Operator's adjustment skill—It takes practice to become a skillful band saw operator. Pay attention and give it time (see page 71).

Wheel shape (crowned versus flat)—Most small saws have crowned wheels, which track small blades well. Large saws that can take wide blades should have flat wheels (see page 73).

Tracking the blade—An incorrectly tracked blade may damage the blade guides and is at risk of coming off the wheels or breaking (see page 75).

Correct blade choice—Match the blade to the work. You need three saw teeth in the thickness of the material at all times. Narrow blades can make tight turns. The heavier the work, the wider the blade should be, but don't exceed the limitations of your machine (see page 46).

Guide adjustment—Poorly adjusted guides allow the blade to twist inaccurately and may damage the saw teeth (see page 82).

Blade tension—Over-tensioning will damage the saw and risks breaking the blade. Under-tensioning causes the blade to steer off the cut and to barrel in thick wood (see page 78).

Blade sharpness—Don't push a dull blade; you'll only damage the workpiece and the machine. Replace it (see page 56).

The band saw is like a good soup—all of these ingredients play a role. The operator's adjustment skill and attention to detail are very important, and there is no magical product or silver bullet. Because the band saw is so mercurial, there is a lot of mystery, suspicion, myth, and certainly sales hype surrounding it—but study and common sense are always better than snake oil.

ADJUSTMENT SEQUENCE

The band saw can seem bewildering and capricious to adjust, and it is if you get the adjustments out of order (see **Figure 4.2**). Each adjustment depends on the one before. Furthermore, the saw changes as you use it due to the inconsistency of the material you are sawing, the heat generated by sawing, and the progressive dulling of the saw blade. Although the sequence is logical, remember to observe the saw cut and respond accordingly. The logical sequence is:

1. You just acquired the saw

- Level the machine, clean up the metal and remove rust, brush and vacuum away old sawdust.
- Plug it in and confirm that the motor runs.
- Examine the guides and decide whether you can use them, or replace them (see page 82).
- Align the wheels for coplanar tracking (see page 76).

2. Every time you mount a new blade

- Tension the blade (see page 75).
- Track the blade (see page 75).
- Square the table to the blade and set the 90-degree stop (see page 84).
- Adjust the thrust bearings (see page 87).
- Adjust the side guides (see page 91).
- Stone the corners off the back of the blade (see page 59).

3. Preparing to cut wood

- Install an appropriate blade (see page 73).
- Tension and track the blade (see page 75).
- Adjust the side guides and thrust bearings (see pages 87 and 91).
- Tilt the table to the angle you want (see page 6).
- Adjust the guide post to the workpiece (see page 85).

4. While you are sawing wood, observe and adjust as necessary

- Blade tension and tracking (see page 75).
- Thrust bearings and side guides (see pages 87 and 91).
- The straightness and smoothness of the saw cut (see page 78).

5. Troubleshoot and adjust as necessary

- Does the table rock? Tighten the trunnions (see page 5).
- Does the thrust bearing continue to spin when you pause sawing? Check the blade tracking and readjust the bearing (see page 87).
- Do you hear a rhythmic ticking or clicking from the guide assembly? Check the blade weld and stone or grind it smooth (see page 59).
- Is the cut straight and parallel from end to end? Check the blade for lead (see page 99).
- Is the cut straight or does it lean or belly in the thickness of the wood? Check the blade tension (see page 78).
- Does the blade leave a smooth surface or are there diagonal striations? Check the side guides and the blade tension (see pages 75 and 91).
- Do you find yourself forcing the feed? Slow down, and check to see if the blade is loaded with pitch or has become dull (see page 56).

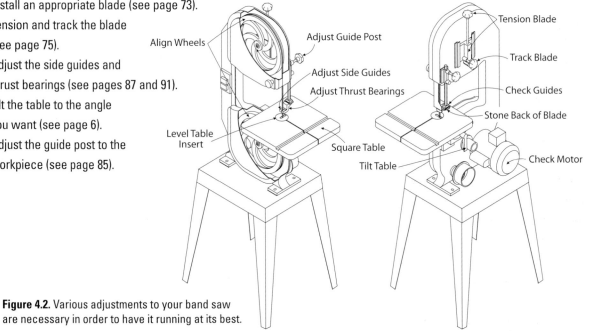

Align Wheels

Adjust Guide Post

Adjust Side Guides

Adjust Thrust Bearings

Level Table Insert

Square Table

Tilt Table

Tension Blade

Track Blade

Check Guides

Stone Back of Blade

Check Motor

Figure 4.2. Various adjustments to your band saw are necessary in order to have it running at its best.

Adjustment controls

Each machine is a little bit different, but most have a common anatomy. When you look at the saw, there are a number of knobs, as shown in **Figure 4.2**. On the back of the saw is the horizontal tracking knob, which is used to tilt the top wheel, as shown in **Figure 4.3**. The vertical tension knob applies tension to the blade by raising the top wheel. The tension knob connects to a shaft leading to a box containing the tension spring and tension gauge, as shown in **Figure 4.4**.

Most machines have a tension gauge to indicate the compression of the spring. As the tension knob applies tension to the blade by raising the top wheel, the spring is compressed. A red washer on the bottom of the spring rises against a scale of blade width numbers. Narrow blade widths are on the bottom because it takes less compression of the spring to tighten small blades. Tension gauges don't register anything until the blade is relatively taut, so variations in blade length do not affect it.

The saw tension gauge is an adequate indicator for most work. When resawing, make a test cut in scrap. I usually use a ½-inch-wide blade for resawing and get good results with the tension gauge at the normal ½-inch mark. If the blade is not sharp or if the material is especially thick, I increase it to the ¾-inch mark.

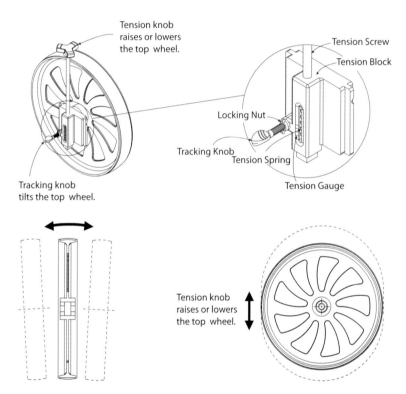

Figure 4.3. On the back of the saw is a horizontal tracking knob, which is used to tilt the top wheel, and a vertical knob for adjusting the blade tension.

Figure 4.4. The tension gauge is located at the bottom of the tension shaft. A red washer on the tension spring rises as the spring is compressed. The blade width scale indicates where to locate the washer.

Safety Tip: Gloves and Goggles

Be sure you wear gloves and safety glasses when you uncoil a band saw blade, and hold the coil so the teeth point away from your face and body.

INSTALLING THE BLADE

All band saw adjustments begin with installing a blade. The blade must be under tension and tracked or else the adjustments will change once you do tension it. All blades are installed in the same way.

Step 1: Start by loosening the blade side guides and then retract them.

Step 2: Uncoil the blade. Remember to wear gloves and safety glasses. If it is a new blade, it may have oil or dirt on it, which you do not want touching the workpiece, so wipe it off with a rag or a paper towel. Pull the blade through the rag backward so that the teeth don't catch.

Step 3: Hold the blade up to the saw to check which way the teeth are pointing. They should point downward as the blade runs down toward the saw table. If the teeth are pointed in the wrong direction, turn the blade inside out by holding the blade with both hands and rotating it, the same way you would turn a sock inside out.

Step 4: Slide the blade through the table slot and place it on the top wheel; then, fit it over the bottom wheel. Loosely position the blade where you want it on the wheels before you proceed to the tensioning and tracking adjustments.

Understanding blade tracking and tensioning

The term "tracking" refers to positioning or balancing the band saw blade on the wheels. Every time you put a new or different blade on the saw, you have to track it. There is no external agent holding the blade on the wheel. It is held on by a combination of two factors: One factor is the outside shape of the wheel, the second is the angle of the top wheel. Both are discussed below.

Tensioning the blade makes it taut between the wheels and keeps the blade straight. Tension is applied when the saw's adjustable top wheel is moved away from the fixed bottom wheel, mediated by the saw's tension spring. The greater the tension, the greater the resistance to side pressure or blade deflection. If the tension is too low, the blade may flex or belly in the cut, and the force of feeding the wood into the blade could even push the under-tensioned blade off the wheels. Blade tracking and tensioning go hand in hand.

Wheel Shape

The shape of the wheel is determined by the shape of its cast metal rim, as shown in **Figure 4.5**. The outside rim of the wheel is covered with a piece of rubber called a tire, which is between ⅛- and ¼-inch thick. The tire acts as a blade cushion and a shock absorber. Wheels are either flat or curved (crowned). Which kind of wheel your saw has determines what you have to do to track the blade, though currently you cannot buy a 14-inch saw with flat wheels, only crowned.

The curved profile, or crown, causes the blade to ride near the middle of the wheel rim. The advantage of the crowned wheel is that it is easy to track small blades. The disadvantage of the crowned wheel is that it provides minimal surface area between the blade and the tire, making it more difficult to track wide blades.

If crowned wheels are not perfectly aligned

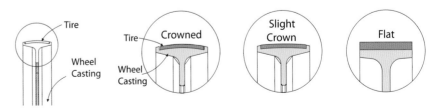

Figure 4.5. The shape of the wheel is determined by the shape of the metal casting on the rim of the wheel. Wheels are either flat or crowned. The blade rides near the middle of a crowned wheel, but can be tracked anywhere on a flat wheel. Wide blades run best on flat wheels.

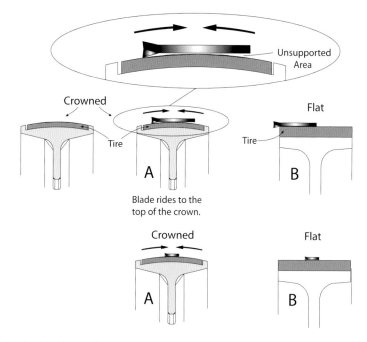

Figure 4.6. A wide blade will track close to the middle of the tire as at A. Narrow blades can be tracked just about anywhere on flat tires, as shown at B.

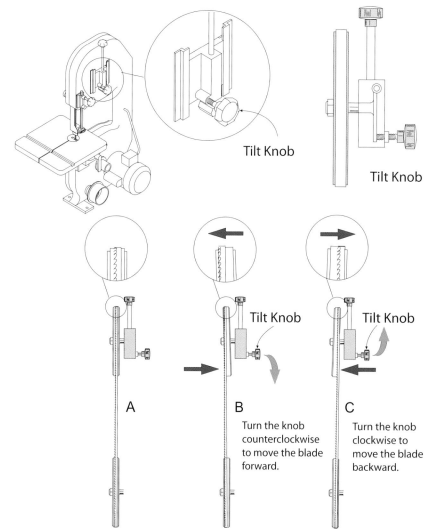

Figure 4.7. A tilt knob on the back of the saw tilts the top wheel. The angle of the top wheel steers the blade in the direction of the tilt.

with each other, the crowns on each wheel will compete for control of the blade. This causes vibration and shortens the life of a blade. Bringing crowned wheels into alignment is discussed on page 76.

Flat wheels give wide blades good support, as shown in **Figure 4.6**. Narrow blades can be tracked just about anywhere on flat wheels (see **Figure 4.6**). A wide blade can be tracked close to the middle of the tire or with the teeth off the front of the tire. If the blade is coarse or has carbide or bimetal teeth, it is better to have the teeth run off the front edge of the tire so they don't damage the rubber material.

When the band saw tires start to wear, a depression or groove forms, making blades harder to track. You can dress the tires with sandpaper so that there is a crown of about .020 inch, or the thickness of five pieces of paper. When that fails, you can replace the tires.

Top Wheel Angle

The second factor that affects the tracking of a blade is the angle of the top wheel. A tilt knob on the back of the saw tilts the top wheel, as shown in **Figure 4.7**. The angle of the top wheel steers the blade in the direction of the tilt.

The usual approach is to tilt the top wheel, usually backward, until the blade tracks in the center. This approach works best with narrow blades ¼ inch and under. These blades are flexible, and any misalignment of the wheels doesn't harm their performance or life expectancy. However, wider blades are not as flexible and may require a more thorough approach that includes aligning the saw's wheels.

Tensioning the blade

After you have installed a blade and positioned it loosely on the saw wheels, slowly raise the top wheel with the tension knob. Start to rotate the top wheel by hand in the normal direction while the blade is still slack. As you do this, watch to determine where the blade wants to track. If the blade is tracking too far forward or backward, adjust the tilt mechanism. As you rotate the wheel with one hand, increase its tension, or tautness, with the other, as shown in **Figure 4.8**. Continue to do this until you have adequate tension, shown on the tension gauge.

A blade cannot be correctly tracked until it is under tension. Never tension the blade with the saw running.

Figure 4.8. Slowly raise the top wheel with the tension knob while you rotate the wheels by hand in the normal direction. Note where the blade wants to track, and center it by adjusting the tilt mechanism.

Tracking the blade

After the blade has been tensioned, replace the cover and the blade guard. Plug in the electrical cord. Turn the saw on for a second, and then turn it off again. Watch to see how the saw runs. If the blade seems to track well, run it under full power. If there is a problem, you will know it since the blade is likely to slip off the wheels—turn off the power, allow the machine to coast to a stop, and investigate what happened. Below are the specific tracking instructions for different width blades.

Tracking Small Blades

If you are using narrow blades (up to ¼ inch wide and particularly with ³⁄₃₂-inch to ³⁄₁₆-inch blades), you can use center tracking. This method uses the wheel crown, if any, and the top wheel tilt mechanism to position the blade on the wheels. Rotate the wheel by hand, and tilt the top wheel until the blade is tracking in the middle of the top wheel. Make several revolutions of the blade to make sure that the blade stays in the same place on the wheels. Lock the tilt knob. Turn the saw on for a second, and then turn it off again. Watch to see how the saw runs. If the blade seems to track well, run it under full power.

If there is a window in the top cover, as is common on European saws, you will be able to see where on the wheel the blade is tracking. If not, observe it in relation to the top guides— the blade should run in a straight line, without moving forward or backward. This indicates it is remaining in position in the center of the top wheel. If it does seem to be moving, shut off the saw and adjust the tilt of the top wheel, and repeat the procedure until the blade runs smoothly and in one position on the wheels.

Tracking Large Blades

If you intend to run blades ¼ inch and wider on your saw, you should take the time to adjust the wheels for what I call coplanar tracking (see the Aligning Band Saw Wheels section on this page). This means you will track wide blades with the wheels lined up with each other and lying in the same vertical plane, rather than with the top wheel tilted.

While coplanar tracking works best with wide blades, it will not cause any problems with narrow blades. Since it may require removing the band saw wheels in order to insert shims, the saw should be set up for coplanar tracking when you first acquire it, or when you first decide you need to run wide blades.

When the wheels are in the same plane, the blade will find its own equilibrium and essentially track itself. One of the things you will notice when you are using coplanar tracking is that the blade may track slightly toward the front of the wheels. This is because the front edge of the blade is minutely shorter than the back edge. When the blade was manufactured, the teeth were first ground and then hardened, causing the metal there to shrink in relationship to the unhardened back.

Make several revolutions by hand to make sure that the blade stays in the same place on the wheels. Lock the tilt knob. Tilt the top wheel slightly backward if the blade starts to move forward or comes off the front of the saw.

Place the metal guide blocks about .004-inch away from the blade. This is the thickness of a piece of paper, so you can use a dollar bill as a spacer. The distance between the gullet and the front of the guide block should be about $1/_{64}$ inch because the blade will flex backward during the cut.

Aligning band saw wheels

Wheel alignment is important if you have a saw with crowned wheels but not important for saws that have flat or almost flat wheels. The goal is to allow the blade to run as straight as possible. If the wheels are crowned, each wheel exerts a pulling force on the blade, and the wheels are essentially competing with each other for control. Wheel misalignment is not problematic for small blades, but it is important to avoid for larger blades, especially when making demanding cuts like resawing. Unless you are certain you will only ever run small blades on your saw, it makes most sense to align the wheels in the first place when you acquire the machine.

Aligning band saw wheels is a simple procedure that should take only a couple of minutes. Since it may require removing the wheels from their axles, it is not something you want to do every day. The wheels might already be aligned, so the first thing to do is find out.

Begin by installing and tensioning the blade. Alignment without the blade on the saw doesn't mean anything. Tension the widest blade that you can use on your saw. Use the tension scale on your band saw. On a 14-inch saw, use a ½-inch x 3 TPI hook tooth blade because that is the coarsest blade the machine can accept.

Safety Tip: Unplug It

When you want to work inside the saw, whether for adjustments or repairs, unplug it or throw its circuit breaker so it can't possibly start up with your hands inside. Don't rely on the on-off switch because you might accidentally bump it to the on position.

Figure 4.9. With the blade under normal tension and the saw table out of the way, check the saw's wheel alignment with a long straightedge.

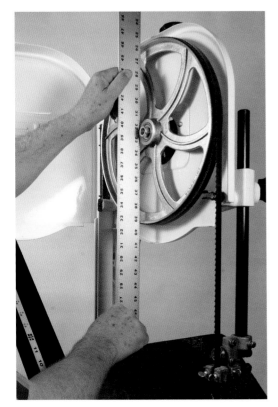

Figure 4.10. Hold the straightedge near the middle of the wheels. If it touches the top and bottom of both wheels, they are parallel and in the same plane, that is, coplanar.

Disconnect the power from the saw (you wouldn't want to accidentally hit the on button while you were working inside it). Tilt the saw table to get it out of the way; on some saws, it will be easier to unbolt it from the trunnions and remove it.

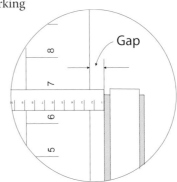

Now use a long straightedge to make sure that the wheels are parallel to each other, as shown in **Figure 4.9**. You may have to fiddle with the tilt adjustment on the top wheel to get them parallel. Put the straightedge near the middle of the wheels. If it touches the top and bottom of both wheels, the wheels are not only parallel but also in line or coplanar, as shown in **Figure 4.10**.

If you are lucky, the wheels are already coplanar and you will not have to align them. However, the wheels can be parallel without being coplanar. If the wheels are not coplanar, the straightedge will not touch the top and bottom of both wheels. Instead, it will either touch the top and bottom of the top wheel or the top and bottom of the lower wheel. In either case, you will have to move one of the wheels on its axle to bring it into alignment.

Since the method of alignment is to add or remove washers from the axle behind the wheel, you need to measure the misalignment. The misalignment is the gap at the top and bottom of the wheel that is not touching the straightedge, as shown in **Figure 4.11**.

Coplanar alignment is the situation where the straightedge touches both the top and bottom of both wheels, with the saw tensioned

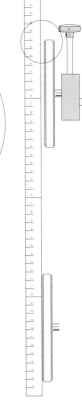

Figure 4.11. If the straightedge does not touch on the rims of both wheels, measure the wheel misalignment with a small ruler. This tells you what thickness of washer(s) to add or remove.

using its widest blade. On 14-inch Delta saws, washers are usually added behind the top wheel, as illustrated in **Figure 4.12** (B). With imported band saws, the bottom wheel usually needs to be moved forward, as shown in **Figure 4.12** (C). Each saw is a little different. You can buy suitable washers at the hardware store. After the first alignment, rotate the wheels several times to make sure the blade is tracking; then, recheck the alignment.

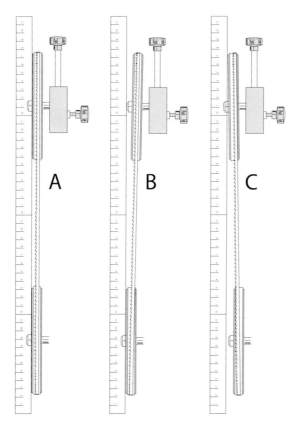

Figure 4.12. The straightedge should touch the top and bottom of both wheels, as shown at A. On the Delta saw, shown in B, adding washers behind the top wheel would align it with the bottom wheel. With Asian manufactured saws, such as in C, the washers usually go behind the bottom wheel.

The role of blade tension

It is essential that there is enough tension on the blade to prevent it from flexing during the cut. Once the blade starts to flex, it is very difficult, if not impossible, to correct the cut. The blade follows its wayward path. But how much tension is needed? Simply put, enough to keep the blade from flexing inside the workpiece and to keep it cutting in a straight line without wandering from side to side. The greater the tension, the greater the resistance to side pressure or blade deflection.

While there must be enough tension to ensure a good cut, you don't want so much that the saw or blade is damaged. Consideration must be given to the whole range of factors, including the type of blade being used, the feed rate, and the thickness and hardness of the material being cut. For example, more tension is needed when wide blades are being used; hard, thick stock is being cut; or material is being cut with a dull blade and at a fast feed rate. Decreasing the feed rate decreases the drag on the blade, thus lessening the need for tension.

If the band saw blade isn't under enough tension, it will flex during the cut, causing what is called a barrel cut, until it tensions itself. The blade will follow the path of least resistance and deflect at the point of greatest stress, which is where it enters the wood.

This self-tensioning phenomenon is evident in experiments. A slightly under-tensioned blade will make a slightly barreled cut. A grossly under-tensioned blade will make an extremely barreled cut. If the operator were to stop the saw before the very end of a barrel cut and check the tension in the distorted blade, it would be close to the proper level. This is not, however, an experiment you should try in your shop since it would be very difficult to get the blade moving again.

A barrel cut commonly occurs when resawing or cutting thick stock with an under-tensioned blade, as shown in **Figure 4.13** and discussed fully on page 38. The blade flexes sideways in the work, progressively straying from the desired line and making a curved cut. This is very frustrating and wasteful. The operator will feel the blade pulling the wood to one side, which indicates that something is going wrong. When this happens, you must be sure your fingers are not on the side of the workpiece nearest the blade since it can flex enough to come out of the side of the board.

When a barrel cut has been made, three things are noticeable. First, the cut will not be straight from front to back. Second, the cut will curve (barrel) through the thickness of the workpiece from the top to the bottom. Third, by the end of the cut, the blade will be very hot because it has flexed enough to rub hard against the guides, causing friction and heat. This can all contribute to blade breakage.

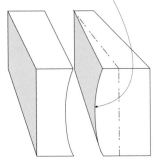

The barrel cut is caused by blade deflection.

Figure 4.13. When thick stock is cut with an under-tensioned blade, a barrel cut occurs.

DIAGNOSING THE CUT

If wandering or barrel cuts are the result, how does the operator know for sure that the cause is an under-tensioned blade? The first and simplest test is to increase the tension and make another cut. If this doesn't help, there may be one or more other factors responsible, including:

1. Dull blade.

2. Poorly set guides and/or thrust bearings. Poor wheel alignment and tracking.

3. Not enough of a tooth set. This will give the same slow, labored cut as a dull blade.

4. Uneven set or sharpening. This will cause the blade to lead, which means that the blade will cut faster on one side and pull in that direction.

5. Blade speed too slow. Correct this by feeding the material more slowly or, on saws that have a variable speed motor, increasing the blade speed.

6. Poor operator technique. Find out if this is the problem by experimenting with different feed speeds. A slower feed will often improve the blade's cutting performance.

Another condition called blade lead occurs when a blade pulls to one side without barreling. Blade lead can be caused by a number of things other than insufficient tension, including:

1. Poor wheel alignment, poor tracking.

2. Uneven teeth, or uneven sharpening.

When curves are being cut in relatively thin material, it isn't difficult to compensate for blade lead. It is more of a problem when you are trying to cut a straight line. Compensating for blade lead is discussed in Chapter 5, "Sawing Straight Cuts," page 97.

The tension gauge box fits into two grooves in the cast-iron saw frame, as shown in **Figure 4.14**. Inside the tension gauge is a smooth shaft with a threaded end, which is the top wheel axle, as shown in **Figure 4.15**. The plate that holds the top wheel axle pivots on the pin, shown in **Figure 4.16**. The tracking knob threads into the back of the tension gauge box and adjusts the angle of the top wheel. The hinge bracket is the weak link on 14-inch saws, and, if the saw is over-tensioned, it will either bend or break (see **Figure 4.17**).

Myths about blade tensioning

Until about 20 years ago, band saw blade tension was not a big deal, and there was no disagreement about how to tension a blade. Then, an article by the late Jim Cummins about the popular 14-inch Delta band saw appeared in the influential magazine Fine Woodworking and asserted the following:

1. The tension gauge on most saws was inaccurate, and an expensive aftermarket strain gauge was more accurate.
2. The tension on most saws was inadequate, and the blades needed to run with higher tension than the reading on the gauge.
3. The saw's tension spring should be replaced with something stiffer to provide higher tension.

I do not agree with any of the above assertions. In my experience using over a hundred different band saws of various types, I have always used the standard gauge and gotten good results. To my knowledge, Delta did not respond to the article, although at the time, knowledgeable people in the industry disregarded the article. Nevertheless, some authors and persuasive retailers continue to advance the same inadequate gauge/ replacement spring theory. Some authors have also claimed that over time, the tension spring

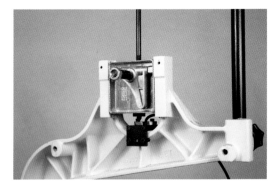

Figure 4.14. The tension gauge box fits into two grooves in the cast-iron frame.

Figure 4.15. Inside the tension gauge is a smooth shaft with a threaded end, which is the top wheel axle.

Figure 4.16. The plate that holds the top wheel axle pivots on a hinge. The tracking knob adjusts the angle of the top wheel.

Figure 4.17. The hinge is the weak link. This Taiwan-made hinge broke after the owner replaced the spring to increase the tension on the blade.

somehow weakens so that it must be replaced, which is simply not true. Springs do not weaken except under extraordinary conditions that induce extreme heat or work-hardening metal fatigue and ultimately breakage, and this is not likely to happen in your band saw. When this information is combined with some very persuasive sales literature, consumers are falsely led to believe that they cannot trust the saw gauge.

More recently, some retailers have emerged on the opposite side of the equation, recommending that you tension the saw on the low side, using the phenomenon of blade flutter as a guide. With these contradictory opinions and sales hype on both sides, it is easy to see why there is a lot of confusion about the subject of blade tension.

I use the tension gauge on the saw and set the blade at the recommended setting. Occasionally, if I'm cutting thick material or if the blade is not super sharp, I'll increase the setting to the next blade width setting, which means increasing the tension from the 1/2-inch mark to the 3/4-inch mark. My observation over many years of woodworking is that the manufacturer's gauge and spring are adequate, and this is the easiest way to achieve good results. One problem with replacing the original spring with a stiffer spring is that the gauge is no longer functional, so the operator is on his or her own for figuring out the tension. When I contacted Delta, they would not comment on the tension/spring replacement controversy, but I received this comment from John Otto at the Jet/Powermatic group: "We see no reason for replacing the tension springs in the Jet or Powermatic band saws. Our tests show that the tension spring provides enough tension and that our tension scales are accurate. It is a myth that the spring deteriorates and needs to be replaced."

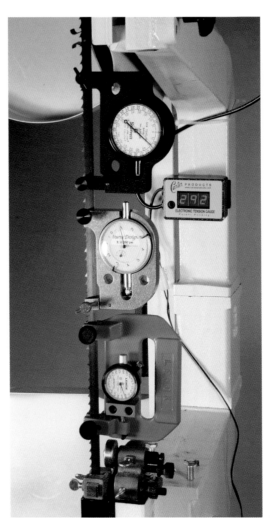

Figure 4.18. These three aftermarket mechanical tension gauges each show a different reading. The electronic Carter gauge is the most accurate and is in agreement with the built-in saw gauge, confirming its adequacy. The readout shown on the column shows the wheel load in pounds. Of the mechanical gauges, the Starrett is the most accurate, and the Ittura the least accurate and the least consistent.

To help sort out the confusion about aftermarket gauges (some of which cost over $300), I acquired all of the aftermarket tension gauges available (see **Figure 4.18**) and had a metallurgical engineer test the gauges and do a report. He confirmed my experience, which is that the tension gauge on the saw is quite adequate. Would you spend several hundred dollars to upgrade the gas gauge in your car? Probably not, because you have learned that, although it is a rough indicator, it is adequate for the purpose. I hope this discussion helps clarify the controversy over blade tension and gives readers useful, common-sense information.

Since then, Aaron Gesicki, the metallurgical engineer, and I did a number of additional tests of these gauges, some of which were published in an article about blade tension in the February 2007 issue of *Woodworker's Journal.*

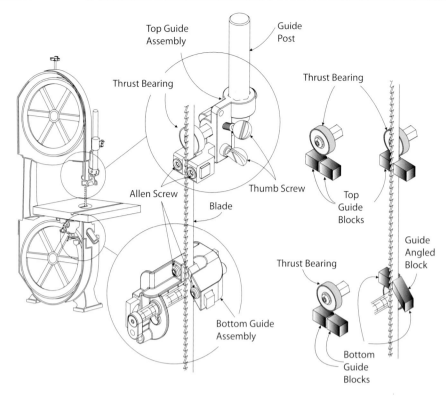

Figure 4.19. Two sets of guides are located above and below the table. The thrust bearing prevents the blade from being shoved off the wheels while cutting. The side guide blocks or guide bearings prevent side deflection or rotation of the blade.

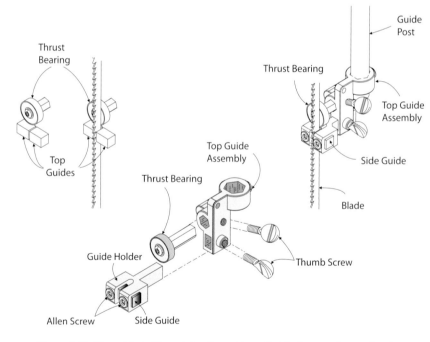

Figure 4.20. The guide holder retains the guide so that both move forward and backward in unison; they are locked in place with a thumbscrew.

The blade guide system

Two sets of guides are located above and below the table, as shown in **Figure 4.19**. Each set of guides is a two-part system of support for the blade. One part, the thrust bearing, supports the back of the blade during the cut and prevents the blade from being shoved off the back of the wheels under the pressure of wood being fed into the blade. The guide blocks or guide bearings prevent side deflection or rotation of the blade.

The two thrust bearings must be aligned with each other so that the blade is supported equally above and below the table. The two thrust bearings should be positioned just behind the blade. When the cut begins, the blade moves backward and contacts the thrust bearings. When the cutting stops, the blade moves forward again, and the thrust bearings stop rotating.

Guide blocks or bearings are located on either side of the blade and are fitted to a guide holder, as shown in **Figure 4.20**. Both guides are held in line with each other by the guide holder so they move forward and backward in unison. Each guide is locked in place with a setscrew. Both the thrust bearing and the guide block holder are held in place by thumbscrews in a cast piece of metal called a guide assembly, shown in **Figure 4.21**.

The top guide assembly is mounted on the guide post, which the operator can move up and down to adjust it to the thickness of the workpiece, as shown in **Figure 4.22**. A lock screw locks the guide post in position. The post is usually set for about ¼-inch clearance between the top guide assembly and the workpiece. This not only prevents the operator's finger from coming into contact with the blade, but also minimizes the blade span between thrust bearings and decreases the likelihood of blade deflection.

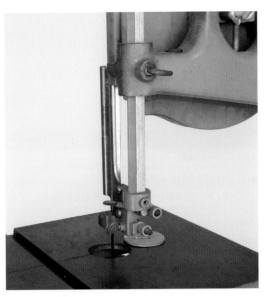

Figure 4.22. The top guide assembly is attached to the guide post, which is adjustable up and down to the thickness of the workpiece.

The guide assembly below the table is stationary. On some saws, the adjustments for the guide holder and thrust bearing are made through the hole in the table, and some models are easier to adjust through this opening if the table is first tilted to one side. On other saws, the adjustments are made from underneath the table.

Adjusting the guides requires attention to detail but no specialized tools (see **Figure 4.23**). I like to use a dollar bill as a gauge for spacing the guide adjustments.

Figure 4.23. Adjusting the guides requires an Allen wrench and attention to detail. A folded dollar bill is a useful gauge.

Figure 4.21. This is the guide assembly on the popular 14-inch Delta saw, with the thrust bearing positioned above the two side guide blocks.

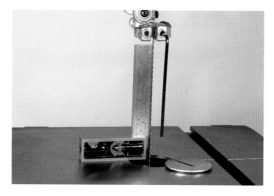

Figure 4.24. After you have tensioned and tracked the blade, adjust the table so that it is square to the blade. Back off the guides and bearing so nothing interferes.

Figure 4.25. The table should be square to the blade in two directions, from the side and from the back.

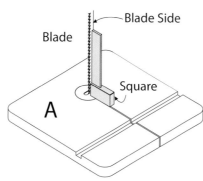

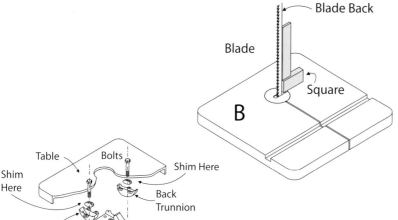

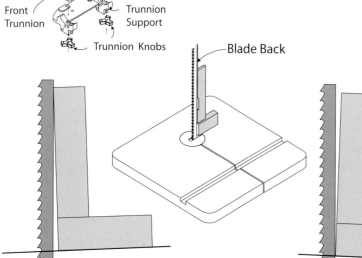

Shim the front trunnion.   Shim the back trunnion.

Figure 4.26. The table is adjusted square to the back of the blade by placing shims between the table and one of the two trunnions.

Square the table to the blade

For accuracy, it is important that the saw table be square to the blade. Back off the guides and bearing so nothing touches the blade. After you have tensioned and tracked the blade, adjust the table so that it is square to the blade using a high-quality square, as shown in **Figure 4.24**. Many saw models have an adjustable bolt mechanism for returning the table to its square position, such as a bolt on the bottom of the table. Adjust the bolt by trial and error until the blade and table are square.

The table should be squared to the blade in two directions (see **Figure 4.25**). Making the blade back square to the table is a subtle adjustment. This adjustment is not important for straight cuts, but it is important for cutting curves and deep circles. Make the adjustment by placing shim material such as plastic or brass shim stock between the table and the top of the table trunnion, according to the drawings in **Figure 4.26**. First use coplanar tracking, as described on page 76, to tension and track a ½-inch blade. Check the back of the blade with an accurate square, and gauge the gap between the square and the back of the blade. A gap at the top of the square indicates that the back of the table should be raised by shimming the rear trunnion. A gap at the bottom of the square indicates that the front of the table should be raised by shimming the front trunnion.

Table insert

The removable table insert surrounds the blade. Removing it allows you to see the bottom guides and thrust bearing. If the blade is running too close to one side of the slot opening in the insert, you can reposition the tabletop by loosening the bolts that secure it to the trunnion. During the cut, if the blade twists too much, it can chew into and damage the table insert. On some saws, the table insert should be filed so that it isn't too close to the blade. American band saws usually have metal inserts, which are more likely to damage the blade. Plastic inserts, which are a good idea, are now available at an inexpensive price. Of course, you can also make a new insert yourself.

So that the stock doesn't hang up on either the hole or the insert, the front edge of the insert should be very slightly lower than the table surface. File the bottom of the insert to remove excess material. The back of the insert should be just a hair higher than the table. If it is low, raise it by adding a layer of masking tape to the bottom of the insert. By having the front a little low and the back a little high, you will not have to worry about the workpiece binding on either the table or the insert.

Guide post alignment

The top guide assembly, which contains the top thrust bearing, is secured to the bottom of the guide post, which is adjustable up and down to accommodate different thicknesses of workpieces. A lock knob secures the post in position. If the two thrust bearings, which support the back of the blade, are not perfectly aligned with each other, the blade will touch one first and bend or deflect until it touches the other bearing. This deflection or twisting of the blade has a negative effect on the ability of the blade to cut straight. Thrust bearing misalignment is a very subtle but serious problem with band saws. The backward

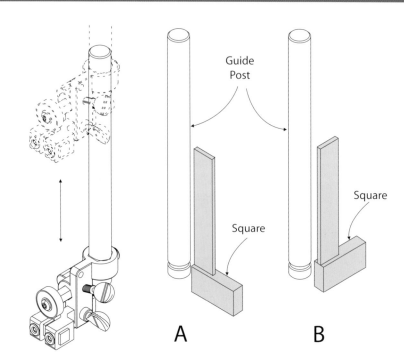

Top Guide Assembly

twisting isn't good for the blade either.

Part of the problem with bearing misalignment is with the guide post itself. Unfortunately, you cannot assume that the guide post will go straight up and down and stay square to the table. If it is out of square, and most are, the adjustments may be correct at one height and not correct at another. If it is out of square from front to back, it will affect the alignment of the thrust bearings. If it is out of square from side to side, it will affect the accuracy of the top guide blocks or side bearings. The guide post should be checked in both the side orientation and the front-to-back orientation, as shown in **Figure 4.27**.

Before you attempt to evaluate the guide post, tension and track a ½-inch blade without the guides or thrust bearing being in contact with it. Check the blade to table relationship with an accurate square (see **Figure 4.24**). After squaring the table to the blade, check to see if the top guide assembly goes straight up and down. One way to do this is to locate the square against the top guide assembly and then check for contact at a low and also at a high position, as shown in **Figure 4.28**. Another way is to remove the top guide assembly and check

Figure 4.27. The guide post should be checked for squareness in both the side orientation and the front-to-back orientation.

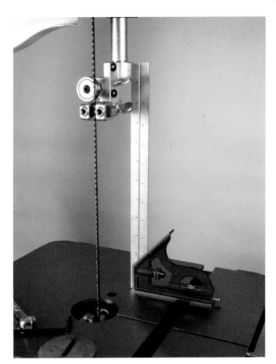

Figure 4.28. Contact the square against the top guide assembly, and check for squareness at a low and then a high position.

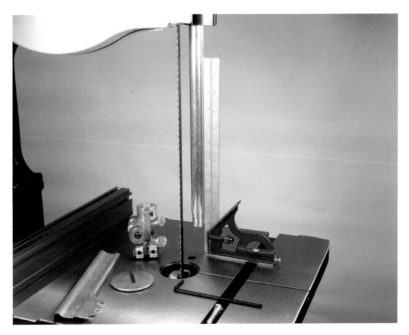

Figure 4.29. Another way to check for squareness is to remove the top guide assembly and check against the post itself.

with a square against the post itself, as shown in **Figure 4.29**. Remember that the check is for the bottom end of the post going straight up and down, not for whether it is square to the table. It may be square to the table at the bottom position but not go straight up and down, so check it at a high and a low position.

Because the groove for the locking mechanism is often in the back of the guide post, it may not be possible to take an accurate reading there. However, you should be able to position the square at a slight angle to the blade and thus contact the front of the post.

If the guide post, and thus the top guide assembly, goes straight up and down in both the side orientation and the front-to-back orientation, thank your lucky stars. If it doesn't go straight up and down, make a mental note (or write a note with a diagram) and be aware of the fact that, for accuracy, you will need to readjust the top thrust bearing and/or side guides every time you move the post to a different height. Moving the top guide an inch or two will not make a lot of difference, but moving it from top to bottom will. Any misalignment problem is usually made worse by the 6-inch riser block commonly installed on 14-inch band saws.

Some saws have adjustment mechanisms for aligning the post so it goes straight up and down. If your saw doesn't have an alignment mechanism, you can make your own by using brass shim stock or by drilling and tapping adjustment screws into the casting that holds the post.

Larger saws and the European saws have a rack-and-pinion mechanism for raising and lowering the post, as shown in **Figure 4.30**. These saws may also have a hinged blade guard, a nice feature when changing blades. The rack-and-pinion mechanism has recently been added to some 14-inch saws as well (see **Figure 4.31**).

The thrust bearings

The thrust bearings are round bearings placed to stop the backward movement of the blade. If the thrust bearings weren't in place, the blade could be shoved off the wheels. There are usually two thrust bearings, one above and one below the table. For blades ³⁄₁₆ inch wide and wider, the two thrust bearings should be positioned about ¹⁄₆₄ inch (.015 inch) behind the blade, or the thickness of a twice-folded dollar bill, as shown in **Figure 4.32** (A). When the cut begins, the blade moves back and contacts the thrust bearings, as shown in **Figure 4.32** (B). When the cutting stops, the blade should move forward again, and the bearings should stop rotating. If the blade and bearings are always in contact, both will wear prematurely.

When properly aligned, the thrust bearings support the back of the blade and keep it in a straight line. If both thrust bearings are not accurately aligned, the back of the blade will contact one bearing before the other, and it will not be equally supported by both bearings. Under sawing pressure, the blade will twist or deflect sideways until the back contacts both bearings. This twist causes the blade to cut at a slight angle, decreasing the likelihood of a straight cut. The better the bearing alignment, the straighter the cut and the longer the blade will last.

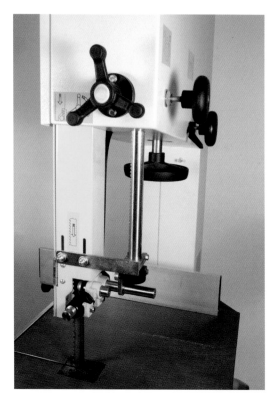

Figure 4.30. The guide post on this Italian saw is a machined rod with teeth cut into the front of it, for a rack-and-pinion adjustment mechanism.

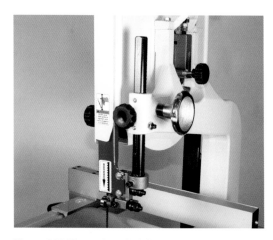

Figure 4.31. The rack-and-pinion mechanism has recently been added to some 14-inch saws, such as this Shop Fox.

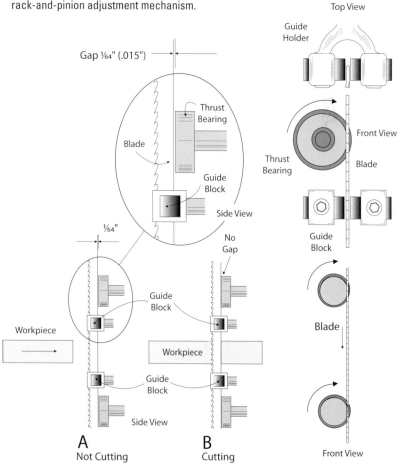

Figure 4.32. For blades ¹⁄₄ inch wide and wider, the thrust bearings should be positioned about ¹⁄₆₄ inch (.015 inch) behind the blade, as shown at A. When the cut begins, the blade moves backward and contacts the thrust bearings, as shown at B.

Figure 4.33. Paper money is .004-inch thick so folded twice it is about the desired .015 inch needed to set the space between the back of the blade and the face of the thrust bearing.

Track and tension the blade before adjusting the thrust bearings. To adjust the thrust bearings, use the blade as a straightedge. Remembering that the weld is the least straight part of the blade, rotate the weld to be opposite the bearings. Some bearings are moved manually, and others are moved by rotating a knob. The thrust bearings should be positioned about 1⁄64 inch (.015 inch) behind the blade.

You can use a number of means to accurately make this measurement, including a feeler gauge or paper, as shown in **Figure 4.33**. A dollar bill is .004 of an inch thick, so folded

twice it is about the .015 inch needed. A feeler gauge, the tool commonly used to measure the space between two machine parts, consists of many small leaves of metal, each of a different thickness. It gives a more certain measurement than the dollar bill because, unlike paper, the gauge leaves don't compress. After you have adjusted the bearings, rotate the wheels by hand and listen for any noise. If you hear a noise, retract the bearing back another 1⁄64 inch (.015 inch), check again, and continue until the noise stops.

Thrust Bearing Adjustments

The back of the blade should contact the outside edge of the thrust bearing, as shown in **Figure 4.34**. On most saws, the bearing is eccentrically mounted on a six-sided shaft, which can be removed and rotated to adjust its position, as shown in **Figures 4.35** and **4.36**.

If the blade has a rough spot or a bad weld, it can scar the thrust bearing. If this is the case, you will hear a distinct ticking sound when the saw runs. The blade digs into the thrust bearing, starting a groove or a scar. The bearing will rotate, but it will stop at the scar. As the saw runs, the scar becomes deeper. Eventually the bearing stops rotating and the blade runs in the scar, destroying the bearing, as shown in **Figure 4.37**. The metal-to-metal contact between the blade and the bearing also heats up the blade, which shortens blade life.

Sharp corners on the back of the blade contribute to bearing wear; grinding the blade back round is covered in Chapter 3, "Band Saw Blades," page 37. The round back cannot dig into the thrust bearing the way that sharp, square corner can. Some retailers are now selling ceramic guide blocks and

Figure 4.35. The thrust bearing mounts off-center on a six-sided shaft.

Figure 4.36. The six-sided bearing shaft can be removed and rotated to adjust the bearing in relationship to the blade. The thumb knob on the right of the photo moves the shaft forward and backward.

Figure 4.34. The back of the blade should contact the outside rim of the thrust bearing. This location is ideal. If it is too close to the edge, the blade could slide off the bearing.

Figure 4.37. If the blade has a rough spot or a bad weld, it can scar the thrust bearing and eventually will destroy it, as shown on the left.

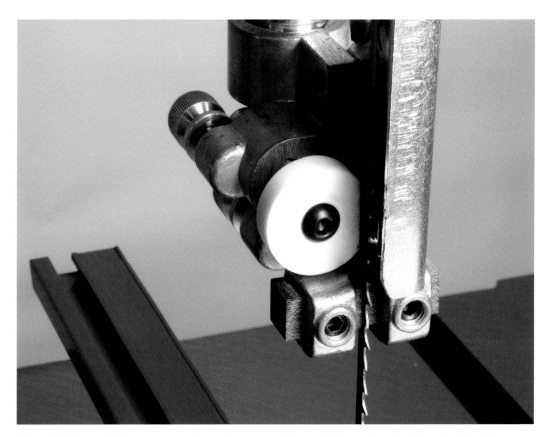

Figure 4.38. Some retailers are now selling a piece of round ceramic that can function like a thrust bearing.

a piece of round ceramic that can function like a thrust bearing, as shown in **Figure 4.38**. Maybe I'm old-fashioned, but watching sparks at the back of the blade doesn't seem right to me. I usually consider sparks a bad thing when I'm using woodworking equipment. However, if you have a blade with a bad weld, replacing the regular thrust bearing with a ceramic one would provide a way to smooth the back as you were working. If you do use ceramic as the thrust bearing, spend time rounding the corners of the blade so that the back doesn't get too square. After the back of the blade has been cleaned up with the ceramic, I would replace the ceramic with the standard thrust bearing.

It is a good practice to observe the thrust bearing often during the sawing process to make sure that both bearings are rotating. It is not unusual to discover, after blades have been breaking, that one of the bearings is damaged. The thrust bearing below the table is often the problem; replacing it may require taking the bottom guide assembly off the machine.

The surface of the thrust bearing should be smooth and show no signs of scarring. It should also rotate smoothly. Some bearings can be rejuvenated by being pressed off their shafts and then pressed back on in a reversed position. Thrust bearings should be considered a wear item, so keep one or two spares on hand.

Adjusting the side guides

With the table square to the blade and the thrust bearings aligned, the next step is adjusting the side guides. These may be solid metal guide blocks or bearing guides. They prevent side deflection or rotation of the blade. The side guides are held in place by a guide holder and are located on either side of the blade. Both guides are held in line with each other so that both move forward and backward in unison.

There are two side guide adjustments. The first is the forward/backward adjustment, as shown in **Figure 4.39**. The distance between the bottom of the blade gullet and the front of the side guide should be the same as the distance between the back of the blade and the thrust bearing, usually about $1/64$ inch. This adjustment allows the blade to move back during the cut without the set of the teeth touching the guide block or bearing.

The second adjustment is the setting of the distance between the blade and the side guides. Locate the side guides about .004 inch away from the blade on either side. This is the thickness of a dollar bill, so paper money can be used as a gauge, as shown in **Figure 4.40**.

Although it is easy to adjust the upper guides with an Allen wrench, the bottom guides below the table are not easily accessible. On the 14-inch saw, I like to tilt the table about 40 degrees to have better access to the bottom guides, as shown in **Figure 4.41**.

The guides should be checked often for wear. It is very important that the blade teeth do not accidentally touch the guide. If there is contact between the teeth and the metal guide, the teeth will be damaged and the blade ruined. The metal guide will also suffer damage and will have to be resurfaced with a file or, better yet, a belt/disk sander. Guide blocks also can be rotated or reversed to expose a new surface.

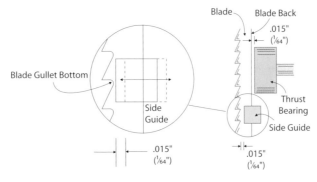

Figure 4.39. The distance between the bottom of the blade gullet and the front of the side guide should be the same as the distance between the back of the blade and the thrust bearing, usually about $1/64$ inch.

Figure 4.40. Locate the solid metal guide blocks or bearings about .004 inch away from the blade. This is the thickness of a dollar bill.

Figure 4.41. Tilt the saw table about 40 degrees to improve access to the bottom side guides.

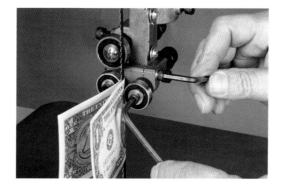

Figure 4.48. The Shop Fox 14-inch saw has three diagonal bearings. The two side bearings are on a camshaft, so they are rotated for the adjustment to the blade.

Figure 4.49. This guide system, a European standard, consists of a casting with two holes on top for the mounting rod and the thrust bearing. The side bearings are parallel to the blade and can be adjusted without a tool.

Figure 4.50. For very small blades, replace the metal guide blocks with nonmetal blocks to avoid damaging the teeth. Place the blocks just behind the blade's gullets, directly in contact with the blade.

Fox 14-inch saw has three diagonal bearings. The two side bearings are on a camshaft so they can be rotated for the adjustment to the blade, as shown in **Figure 4.48**. Most European saws have a guide system consisting of a casting with two holes on top for the mounting rod and the thrust bearing, as shown in **Figure 4.49**. The side bearings are parallel to the blade and can be adjusted without a tool, a handy feature. All of these bearings can be adjusted using a dollar bill as a gauge.

Guides for Small Blades

The versatility of the band saw is increased by its ability to run small blades. Small blades are useful for making tight turns, and those with fine teeth are extremely handy for accurately cutting dovetail joints. For small blades such as the ³⁄₃₂ inch or ¹⁄₈ inch, you must replace the metal guide blocks with phenolic blocks such as Cool Blocks. Set the blocks just behind the blade's gullets and directly in contact with the blade, as shown in **Figure 4.50**. This decreases blade twist and deflection and improves the accuracy of the saw to the point where it can cut a dovetail gauge line in half.

The guide and thrust bearing setups are a little different for ³⁄₃₂-inch and ¹⁄₈-inch blades. These blades work better and last longer if the thrust bearings are advanced at least ¹⁄₆₄ inch past the point of initial contact with the back of the blade. Bringing the bearings forward gives the blade body more support, as shown in **Figure 4.51**. You may want to experiment with increasing the backward angle on the top wheel, but be sure you do not track the blade over the centerline of the top wheel.

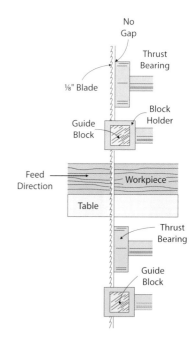

Figure 4.51. Very small blades work better and last longer if the thrust bearings are advanced ¹⁄₆₄ inch past the point of initial contact with the back of the blade.

COOL BLOCKS: FULL DISCLOSURE

Nonmetallic replacement guide blocks called Cool Blocks are widely available. Cool Blocks are phenolic fiber blocks containing a dry lubricant that greatly decreases the friction with the blade. This decreases the heat generated and thus increases the life of the blade. Cool Blocks are currently manufactured by Olson Saw, under license from the patent holder, who happens to be me. I hold patents on a number of woodworking machinery innovations, and naturally I believe my inventions to be real improvements over standard equipment. In the interests of full disclosure, however, I will be sure to tell you whenever I am recommending one of my own inventions.

CARTER GUIDES

Carter Products from Grand Rapids, Michigan, makes a number of guide systems that are popular as aftermarket replacement products, particularly for industrial saws. If you come across a large industrial saw that is in good shape except for the guides, one option is to purchase the Carter 500 series bearing guides, as shown in **Figure 4.52**. These guides are designed to mount to just about any saw, with a number of different mounting options. A good share of Carter's business is retrofitting old saws, so they have a lot of expertise in that area.

Figure 4.53. The Carter Zefyr guide, featuring a huge thrust bearing, is standard on some of the best American-built saws, such as the Northfield.

Figure 4.52. Carter Products from Grand Rapids, Michigan, makes a number of guide systems as aftermarket replacements for industrial saws. This is the Carter 500 model.

The Carter Zefyr guide is used as the standard guide on some of the best American-built saws like the Northfield. The design features a huge diagonal thrust bearing with an adjustable solid block side guide, as shown in **Figure 4.53**. The Carter Stabilizer is an optional blade support system used for making turns with an 1/8-inch or 3/16-inch blade. The Stabilizer, which is made in a number of configurations to suit different brands of saw, fits in the guide assembly opening and replaces the original guide holder, as shown in **Figure 4.54**. The Stabilizer will support the small blades for tight turns but will not deliver the straight-line accuracy of solid phenolic blocks for tasks like cutting dovetails.

Figure 4.54. The Carter Stabilizer is an optional blade support system used for making turns with a 1/8-inch or 3/16-inch blade.

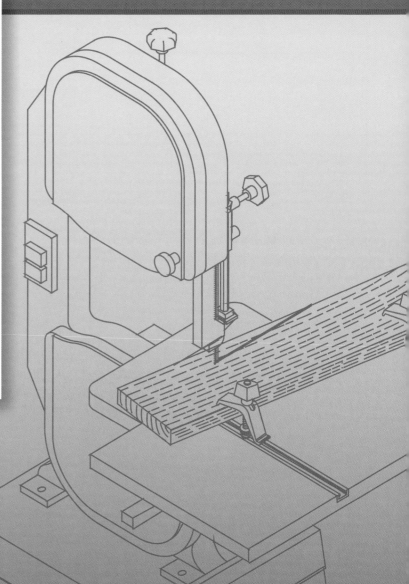

Figure 5.1. The band saw excels at making straight cuts, especially in thick wood. This quality makes it ideal for resawing, or cutting wood through its width.

Sawing Straight Cuts

5

The band saw excels at making straight cuts in thick or thin wood. It can cut thicker stock than either the radial arm saw or the table saw. This makes it the machine of choice for making straight cuts in thick material (see **Figure 5.1**), though for accuracy the saw must be well adjusted with the correct blade for the job. In this chapter, I'll discuss how to take advantage of the band saw's design, accessories, and fixtures to get the most accurate cuts possible.

There are two techniques for making straight band saw cuts. One technique is to feed the workpiece into the blade freehand, following a layout line by eye and adjusting for the saw's tendency to lead. The other technique is to use a jig or fixture such as a fence to control the workpiece. The jig or fence must include a method or mechanism to compensate for lead. To maintain consistency and accuracy, you should use a fence jig or fixture whenever possible. The fixtures most often used are the miter gauge, the rip fence, and the taper jig. A sled that slides in the miter slot is also useful.

One advantage in using the band saw for straight cuts is the fact that it is safer than either the table saw or the radial arm saw, particularly with small pieces of wood, as shown in **Figure 5.2**. The one disadvantage of the band saw is that the wood is not left as smooth as it is by the table saw or the radial arm saw. However, most of the time the band-sawn edge can be planed or jointed straight and smooth. One problem with ripping on the band saw is the tendency of many blades to lead, or steer the workpiece, one way or the other. The skilled operator learns to anticipate lead, and there are a number of ways to compensate for it, discussed later in this chapter on page 99.

Figure 5.2. For straight cuts, the band saw is safer than either the table or radial arm saw, particularly with small workpieces. This eighth grader is using a rip fence to help saw the board straight.

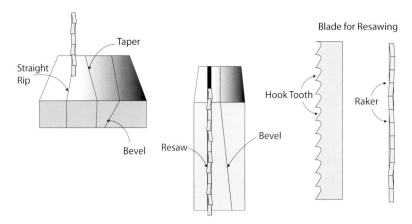

Figure 5.3. A rip is a cut made with the grain of the wood. The four most common cuts made with the grain are straight rip, taper, bevel, and resaw, or cutting a board along its width. The best blade for ripping and resawing has hook teeth with a raker set.

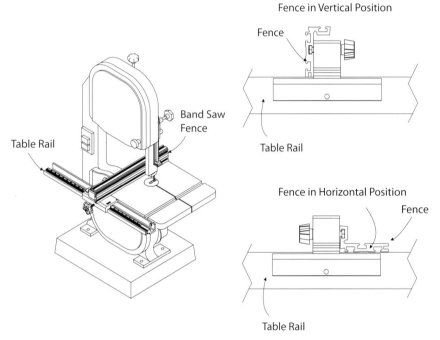

Figure 5.4. The band saw fence guides the workpiece parallel to its face, similar to a table saw fence. This is an aftermarket fence designed by the author and marketed by Kreg Tools.

Ripping

Rip cuts are made with the grain of the wood. The four most common ripping cuts are straight rip, bevel, taper, and resaw, as shown in **Figure 5.3**. As special blades have been developed for ripping and resawing, the use of a fence on the band saw has become more common. If you are going to do a lot of ripping, it is more efficient to use a fence versus cutting freehand.

Band Saw Fence

The band saw fence is an accessory used to guide the workpiece parallel to the blade. Most saws come with a fence that is similar in function and appearance to a table saw fence, as shown in **Figures 5.4** and **5.5**, with the additional ability of being slanted one way or the other to compensate for blade lead (see page 99). A high-quality fence not only is an aid to ripping but also introduces the level of accuracy needed for such tasks as making tenons and dovetails.

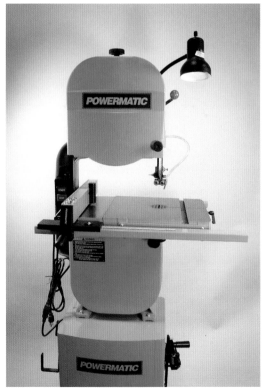

Figure 5.5. This Powermatic machine comes with an adjustable rip fence that includes a removable point fence for resawing. The fence rides, and locks, on the square rail bolted to the front of the saw table.

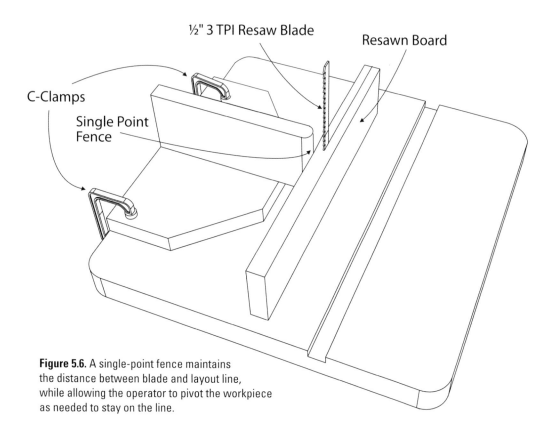

½" 3 TPI Resaw Blade

Resawn Board

C-Clamps

Single Point
Fence

Figure 5.6. A single-point fence maintains
the distance between blade and layout line,
while allowing the operator to pivot the workpiece
as needed to stay on the line.

Some craftsmen prefer to rip using a single-point fence with a rounded tip. It usually consists of a vertical piece of wood screwed onto a flat base piece that can be clamped to the band saw table. This shop-made accessory helps maintain a fixed distance between blade and layout line, while allowing the operator to pivot the work in order to stay on the layout line (see **Figure 5.6**). Recently, aftermarket fences that operate in the same way as the shop-made fence have appeared.

Blade Lead Adjustment

When ripping with the band saw, you may notice that the band saw doesn't usually cut perfectly straight but instead tends to cut at a slight angle. This is referred to as blade lead, or drift. Since lead is caused by blade and tooth geometry and tracking position, and perhaps by uneven tooth sharpness, it will be different for each blade. Rather than fighting the tendency of the blade to lead, one can easily learn how to compensate for it, either by sawing by eye or by adjusting the rip fence angle to match the angle at which the saw cuts best.

A number of things can be done to minimize blade lead, including using a sharp coarse blade like a 3 TPI hook tooth, using coplanar tracking (see page 76), and adjusting the top wheel angle. Changing the top wheel angle will often (but not always) change the blade lead angle.

If you are doing a lot of ripping, it is best to change the rip fence to match the cutting angle of the blade that is on the saw. Although it may sound complicated, this is quite simple to do and well worth the minute or two that it takes. Adjusting the fence will allow the user to align the fence to match a saw blade's lead angle, sometimes called its drift angle. You set the fence to compensate for the drift angle by deliberately adjusting the fence out of square. Here is the method:

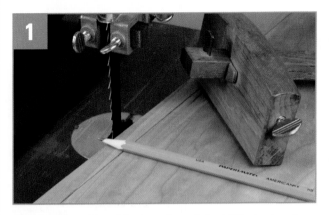

Machine a flat and straight piece of wood about 20 inches long to use as a test workpiece. The width of the piece doesn't matter, but make sure its edges are parallel. Mark a line along the edge of the test board with a pencil.

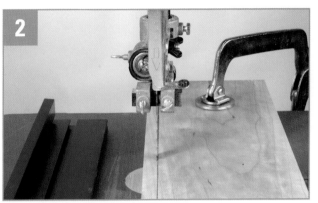

Feed the wood into the blade as you cut the edge of the pencil mark. If the blade is leading, you will have to angle the wood slightly to keep it cutting along the pencil line. Cut to the middle of the test workpiece, and then stop cutting halfway through the board. Turn off the saw, and hold the workpiece firmly while the saw coasts to a stop. Either mark the angle of the workpiece on the table with a pencil, or clamp the wood to the tabletop.

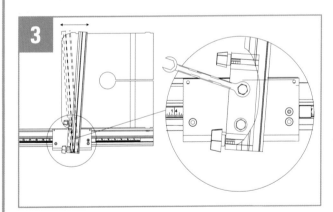

The test workpiece now indicates the angle at which the blade is leading (the drift angle). Thus, you have discovered and marked the best angle at which to feed work into this particular blade. Most band saw fences can be adjusted to match the drift angle. Loosen the fence bolts with a wrench, and change the angle of the fence so that it corresponds to the angle of the test cut.

Start the saw and use the fence to complete the test cut. Observe to see if the cut followed the pencil mark. At this newly adjusted angle, the saw should cut straight without the workpiece pulling to one side or the other. If the fence angle is adjusted correctly and you use the proper sawing technique, the result will be a rip cut of uniform width. At the end of the cut, the workpiece should just touch both the blade and rip fence.

If the ripped piece is narrower or wider than the distance between the blade and the rip fence, the cut has veered away from the fence. This means the fence is not angled correctly. Repeat the procedure until you get it right. Each time you change the blade, it is a good idea to check and possibly adjust the angle of the fence.

KREG FENCE

The aftermarket Kreg fence, another of my patented inventions (see Cool Blocks: Full Disclosure on page 95), has a scale and lens cursor similar to the one found on a professional table saw, an optional microadjuster, and a heavy-duty L-shaped fence extrusion that accepts stops. The L-shaped, blue-colored fence extrusion can be mounted in a vertical or horizontal position. A handy feature of the Kreg fence is that it can easily be lifted off the saw rail and the fence extrusion can be rotated to lie flat on the table. The fence is adjustable in two dimensions for ease in setting it parallel to the blade.

The Kreg resaw guide is either 4½ inches high or 7 inches high for a wide resaw. It bolts or clamps to the standard fence on the saw, as shown in **Figure 5.7**. The middle of the curved fence should be positioned about ¼ inch in front of the blade, as shown in **Figure 5.7**. The workpiece rests against the high point of the curve before the cut is started (see **Figure 5.8**).

I think my curved fence is easier to use than a shop-made single-point fence because it supports the board better and allows for very slight angle adjustments.

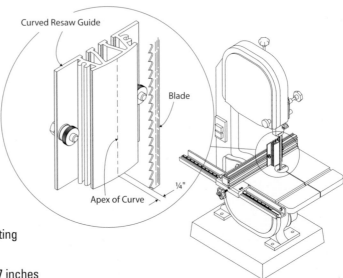

Figure 5.7. The curved resaw guide can be bolted or clamped to a standard fence. The apex of the curve should be about ¼ inch in front of the blade.

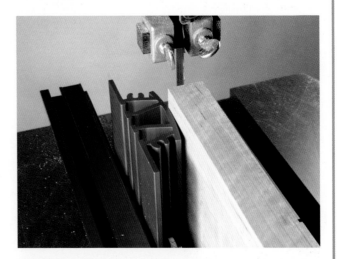

Figure 5.8. The Kreg resaw guide allows the operator to steer the wood to compensate for blade lead.

Resawing

Resawing is the process of cutting a board through its width, making it into two thinner boards.

Resawing exposes the two inside surfaces of the board, as shown in **Figure 5.1**. The two surfaces are mirror images of each other. When the two matching halves are glued together, it is called bookmatching, as shown in **Figure 5.9**. Bookmatching greatly enhances the character of a piece and is useful on all surfaces that are flat, such as tabletops and doors. Resawing thick wood into a number of thin veneers is a great way to get the most out of rare or valuable wood, such as the piece of crotch walnut shown.

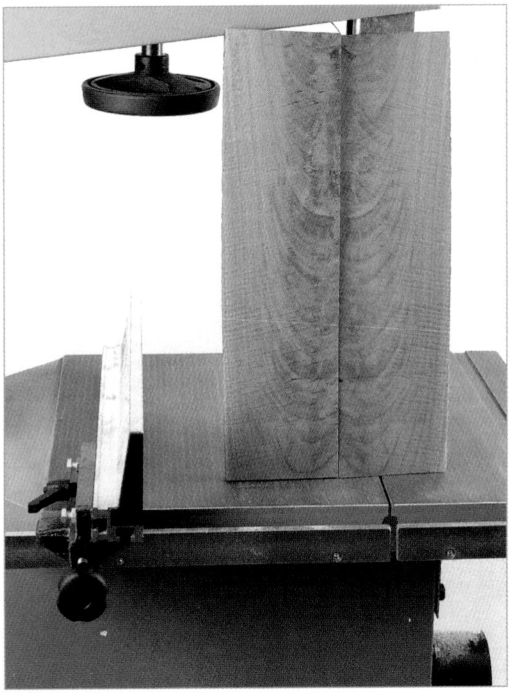

The ability to slice thick stock—resawing, making veneers, bookmatching, and cutting boards from small logs (see **Figure 5.10**)—has broad appeal to the experimental woodworker because it greatly enhances your design abilities without requiring extra tools or accessories.

Blades for Resawing

Cutting thick stock puts maximum strain on both the blade and the machine. The blade used should be the largest hook tooth blade that your saw can handle. For a band saw with 14-inch or smaller wheels, the largest recommended blade is a ½-inch x 3 TPI hook tooth, as shown in **Figure 5.11**. Hook tooth blades are available in a number of materials. It's also possible to find a ⅝-inch blade, which, at .025 inch thick, is thin enough for small saws and has somewhat more beam strength than the ½-inch blade. For more information on blades, review Chapter 3, "Band Saw Blades," page 37.

Hook teeth cut aggressively, and their large gullets have the capacity to carry the waste through the stock. The blade has to be sharp, so start with a new blade or a newly resharpened one. As the blade dulls, the cutting speed will slow, and the tendency to wander or lead will increase; increasing the tension from the ½-inch to the ¾-inch level may help for a while (see page 104), but, when resawing, there is no substitute for a new, sharp blade.

Figure 5.9. Resawing a piece into veneers is one good way to get the most out of a piece of rare or valuable wood such as this crotch walnut, shown here bookmatched.

Figure 5.10. The band saw is capable of making premium boards from small logs, as with this quarter-sawn oak. A sharp blade is a must.

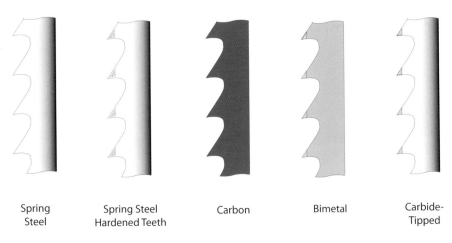

Spring
Steel

Spring Steel
Hardened Teeth

Carbon

Bimetal

Carbide-
Tipped

Figure 5.11. Cutting thick stock puts maximum strain on both the blade and the machine. The blade used should be the largest hook tooth blade that your saw can handle.

Resawing Technique

Before resawing, check to ensure that the table is square to the blade and that the face of the resaw fence is also square to the table. If the blade and the fence are both square to the table, they should be parallel with each other.

There are three frequently used techniques for making straight band saw cuts. One technique is to use the rip fence as a guide, provided it has been set to compensate for blade lead, as discussed earlier in this chapter. Another technique is to use a single-point fence to help guide the work freehand. The technique that I prefer and think is the easiest to use is a curved resaw guide attached to the standard rip fence, which is a hybrid of the two techniques. It offers the advantages of the single-point fence and the rip fence (see the Kreg Fence sidebar on page 101).

When you are using a shop-made point fence or an aftermarket resaw fence, the middle of the fence should be positioned about ¼ inch ahead of the blade, as shown in **Figure 5.7** on page 101. The workpiece rests against the apex of the curve before the cut is started.

Begin feeding the wood slowly, while exerting light pressure against the guide just ahead of the blade, as shown in **Figure 5.12**. Continue to feed slowly, but, for safety reasons,

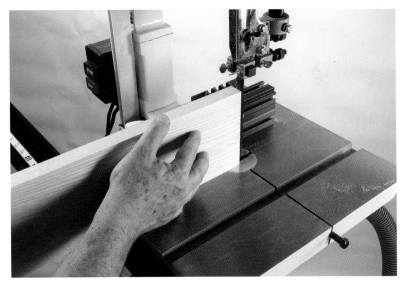

Figure 5.12. As you feed wood into the blade, exert light pressure against the resaw guide at a point just in front of the blade. Keep the cut on track by shifting the back end of the board from side to side.

never apply pressure right next to the blade because the blade could deflect and cut through the side of the workpiece.

The feed rate is very important—as a rule, the slower, the better. It is imperative that the blade not begin to deflect or twist because once the blade starts on a wayward path, it is virtually impossible to get it straight again.

The point fence (see **Figure 5.6**, page 99) or resaw fence allows you to steer the wood as needed to keep the blade on the layout line. As the cut progresses, a slight change in angle is easily accomplished by moving the back of the board toward one side or the other. Keep the pressure on the wood just ahead of the saw teeth and remember that, to steer the cut, it must also be advancing at the same time. At the end of the cut, pull the wood through the blade, as shown in **Figure 5.13**.

The advantage of the shop-made point fence and the aftermarket curved fence is that you can fine-tune the feed direction during the cut. This is necessary not only to compensate for lead or drift, but also because each board has a different density and may require a slightly different feed direction.

Figure 5.13. At the end of the cut, pull the wood through the blade.

Figure 5.14. Good resawing requires proper machine alignment, good blade choice, and a slow, steady feed rate to yield uniform pieces of wood.

These fences also avoid the annoyance of having to check for drift and adjust the fence angle each time you change a blade.

As with all new techniques, some experimentation is suggested. Good resawing results from a combination of factors, including proper machine alignment, good blade choice, and a slow, steady feed rate. **Figure 5.14** shows a nicely resawn piece of wood. The stripes across the wood mark where the operator paused during the cut.

Resaw Troubleshooting

Occasionally when resawing, the board separates and starts to spread apart. The point fence and the curved fence allow room for the expansion, whereas the standard straight fence does not. Rarely, the saw kerf closes up when resawing, possibly pinching the blade and stalling it. In that situation, you should stop the saw and free the blade by inserting a slender wooden wedge into the kerf. If the blade sticks but does not actually stall, back up and make multiple short cuts to clean out the material.

Resawing thick material may require some special techniques. For tough woods like hard maple, I prefer a ½-inch x 3 TPI bimetal blade, tensioned at the ¾-inch setting. With this setup, I can get uniform cuts, as shown in **Figure 5.15**. If you are making a number of thin pieces from one plank, it is a good idea to

Figure 5.15. For resawing tough woods like hard maple, I use a ¹/₂-inch x 3 TPI bimetal blade tensioned at the ³/₄-inch setting.

plane the surface after each cut to establish one smooth side for the next cut. This also makes the resawn material easier to work with since each piece has one planed side and one sawn side.

One option when resawing thick and hard material is to make table saw cuts into the edge of the board to remove waste and decrease the amount of wood that has to be removed with the band saw, as shown in **Figure 5.16**. This technique does result in extra material being lost in the saw kerf, and by burying the circular saw blade in the wood, it also increases the risks of binding and burning, especially in pitchy woods like cherry.

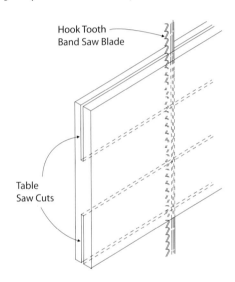

Figure 5.16. On an underpowered saw, make table saw cuts on the edge of the board to remove waste and decrease the amount of material that has to be cut with the band saw blade.

Special cuts

There are a number of special sawing operations that are closely related to ripping and resawing. These include bevel cuts, where you want the edge of the board to be some angle other than 90 degrees to the face, slicing dowels and circular rods, sawing tapers, and putting a square edge on irregular pieces of wood.

Bevel Cuts

Bevel cuts are made with the band saw table tilted. It is best to use the rip fence on the downhill side of the blade so that gravity cannot slide the workpiece away from the blade or off the table (see **Figures 5.17** and **5.18**).

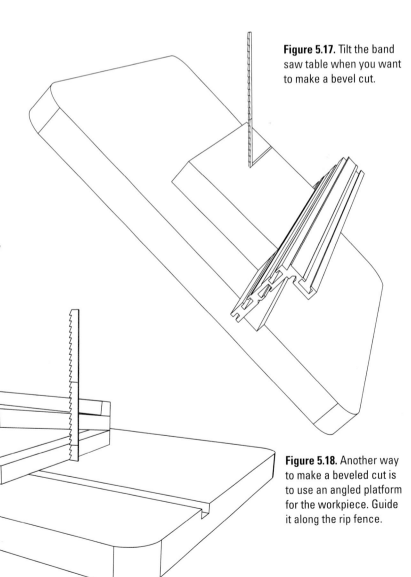

Figure 5.17. Tilt the band saw table when you want to make a bevel cut.

Figure 5.18. Another way to make a beveled cut is to use an angled platform for the workpiece. Guide it along the rip fence.

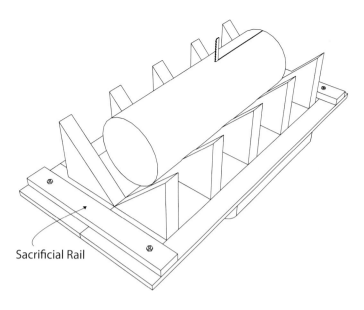

Sacrificial Rail

Figure 5.19. Use a V-block to hold and guide awkward pieces, such as cylinders being sliced into half-rounds. This V-jig is made in two parts, connected by a sacrificial rail.

Cutting Round Stock

When splitting dowels and round stock into half-rounds, it is important that you make the cut through the middle of the workpiece. If the cut is located anywhere but the middle, the downward pressure from the blade will cause the workpiece to rotate. This rotation is liable to break the blade. A V-block can be used to support the workpiece during the cut, as shown in **Figure 5.19**. You also can use the V-block to hold a cylindrical workpiece for other cuts, such as using the band saw to whittle a round tenon on the end, as in **Figure 5.20**.

Figure 5.20. The V-jig holds the cylindrical piece while band sawing a tenon on the end.

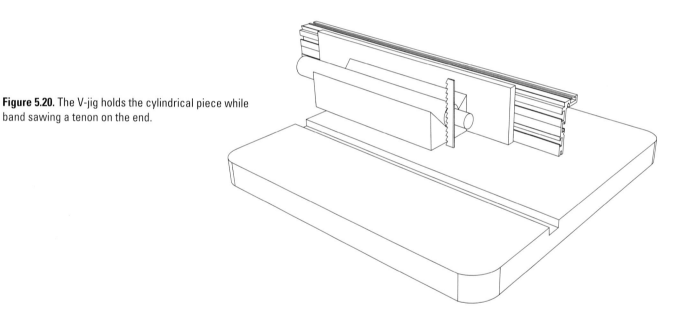

Tapers

Most tapers are angled cuts made along the grain of the workpiece. Tapers are often used for chair and table legs. The taper can be on one, two, three, or four sides, as shown in **Figure 5.21**. Tapers may also be combined with bevels for making staved containers such as butter churns.

When making tapered cuts on a long piece, use a jig. You can make your own or buy one. The step jig is often used to make a taper on one side, opposite sides, or adjacent sides of a workpiece. A step jig, as the name implies, is a fixture with three notches or steps. The jig rides against the rip fence of the saw. The first cut is made with the workpiece resting on the middle or second step. To make a taper on the opposite side of the workpiece, use the third step on the jig, as shown in **Figure 5.22**. To make a taper on the adjacent side, rotate the workpiece 90 degrees.

The sled jig, **Figure 5.23**, is a safe choice for making tapers because the operator doesn't have to get close to the blade. This jig will securely hold the workpiece while you make a straight cut on either the band saw or the table saw. You can also use the sled jig to saw a straight edge on an irregular board.

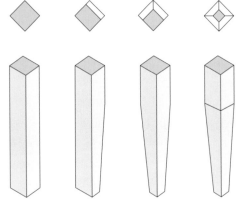

Figure 5.21. Tapers, which are angled cuts made along the grain of the workpiece, are often used for chair and table legs. The taper can be on one, two, three, or all four sides.

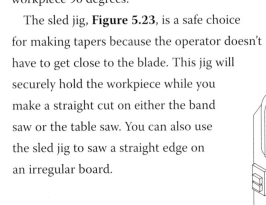

Figure 5.22. The step jig for tapering has three notches or steps. The jig rides against the rip fence of the saw. Make the first cut with the workpiece resting on the middle or second step. To taper the adjacent side, use this same step; to taper the opposite side, use the jig's third step.

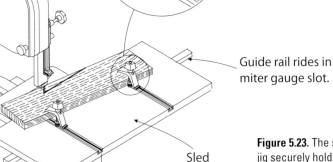

Guide rail rides in miter gauge slot.

Sled

Mini Track

Figure 5.23. The sled jig securely holds the workpiece for making a straight cut with either the band saw or the table saw. The sled jig can be used to make tapers or to put a straight edge on a board.

CLAMPS FOR JIGS

Sled jigs and many other kinds of jig will be more versatile if they have clamps built into them. One method is to screw a cam clamp or a quick-action clamp to the jig. Be sure the clamp's attachment plate does not interfere with the cut you intend to make. DeStaCo is one common brand of quick-action clamp.

Another method is to install a couple of pieces of ³/₈-inch-by-³/₄-inch minitrack in the top of the jig. The Kreg Fast Trak Clamp, another of my inventions, shown on the sled in **Figure 5.24**, was designed to be mounted on these tracks. Be sure to have the base of the clamp seated on the track to avoid pulling the track out of the jig surface.

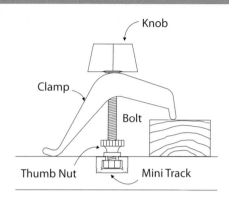

Figure 5.24. This aftermarket clamp mounts on a length of minitrack cut into the surface of the jig. Now that you can see how it works, you'll be able to make your own version.

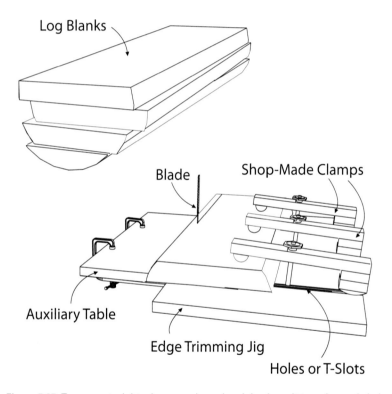

Figure 5.25. To saw a straight edge on an irregular slab, clamp it to a plywood sled jig that can be guided against the saw fence or along the edge of an auxiliary table, as shown here.

Irregular Slabs

There are a number of techniques for cutting a straight edge on large and odd-shaped pieces of wood with the band saw. A large version of the sled taper jig is one option. Many skilled operators prefer to simply snap a chalk line onto the workpiece and saw to it by eye (see page 109). It's important that the slab sits flat on the saw table because, if it rocks during the cut, it's likely to bind the blade, and it might break the blade. A straightforward technique for avoiding this problem is to clamp or screw the slab onto a sacrificial plywood sled or to a two-part sled jig, as shown in **Figure 5.25**, making sure that one edge of the sled remains entirely clear of the slab. Steer this edge of the sled against the rip fence or against an auxiliary table, thus sawing a parallel edge on the workpiece. There's more on making the two-part sled jig in Chapter 8, "Jigs and Fixtures," page 145.

Figure 5.26. The ability to resaw, make veneers, bookmatch, and cut flitches from small logs greatly expands the options for any woodworker.

Sawing a log by eye

"Sawing by eye" means sawing to a layout line without any fence, jig, or sled. It is a particularly useful technique for sawing boards out of a small log, such as the rough cherry log shown in the following photos.

There are several different ways to saw a log, each of which exposes the wood figure from a different orientation. If the cut exposes a surface from the pith to the bark, it is referred to as a radial cut, and the resulting board is said to be quarter sawn. When the cut is at a tangent to the growth rings, it is called a tangential cut, and the wood is flat sawn (in softwood) or plain sawn (in hardwood). I use the term "plain sawn" in this book because I work primarily with hardwood.

Quarter-sawn boards expose each growth ring and give a uniform pattern of closely spaced lines. The pattern of the plain-sawn board reveals a few widely spaced lines or long arches, with growth rings that are nearly parallel to the face of the board. Many boards will be neither quarter sawn nor plain sawn but

will have growth rings that are about 45 degrees from the face of the board, called rift sawn.

If you own land or have access to wooded land, harvesting your own lumber may be a realistic option. If the log will fit under your guides, you can rip it on the band saw. The step-by-step sequence on pages 110 and 111 shows you how.

Once you can resaw a log into useful boards, you will also be able to saw your own veneers from interesting logs or from rare and valuable wood, such as the crotch walnut shown in **Figure 5.26**. The photo shows that the three pieces cut from the side of the chunk of firewood have a very similar and quite lovely grain pattern. My 20-inch Italian-made Agazzani band saw is fitted with a variable pitch 1-inch blade, which will make an extremely clean cut in a variety of wet or dry woods. It is a wonderful experience to be able to effortlessly slice off pieces of wood that are 12 inches wide.

STEP-BY-STEP: SAWING A LOG INTO BOARDS

Begin by jointing one surface of the log to create a stable resting surface. You can do this on a jointer, with a power plane, or with a hand plane.

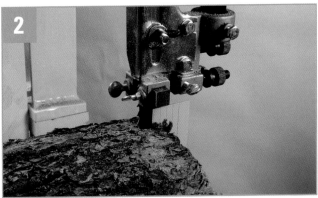

Start the cut in the center of the log, and fold a brightly colored 3 x 5 card the long way and place it in the saw kerf. Feed the wood into the blade, trying to keep the kerf in line with the brightly colored 3 x 5 card.

Try to sight down the side of the blade and keep the chalk line, the colored card, and the saw kerf visible.

Stop occasionally to check your progress. As the cut progresses, the kerf usually expands, making it easier to see. The folded 3 x 5 card will expand with it and remain in the kerf.

The Jet 14-inch band saw handled this rough log without any difficulty. The cut is flat within 1/8 inch of the line.

To further process the log, the rip fence technique is used to divide each half of the log. It is easier to cut half the log because there is less material to saw through.

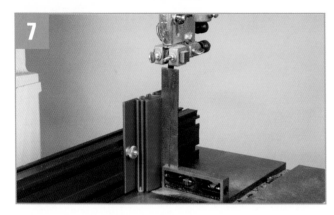

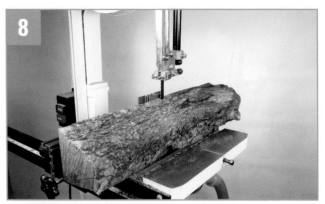

After the log has been cut into quarters, its surfaces should be hand planed or jointed flat and square. Make sure that the fence or resaw guide and the blade are square to the table.

Slicing the quarter of the log will produce some pieces of quarter-sawn wood. The quarter of the log is easy to handle using the fence or resaw guide. Because this piece of cherry is close to being quarter sawn, it will dry and remain straight. Chunks of firewood are often beautiful and useful if processed correctly.

The wood dries quickly if it is cut into narrow thicknesses. The first and second strips of wood cut from the quarter log are quarter sawn.

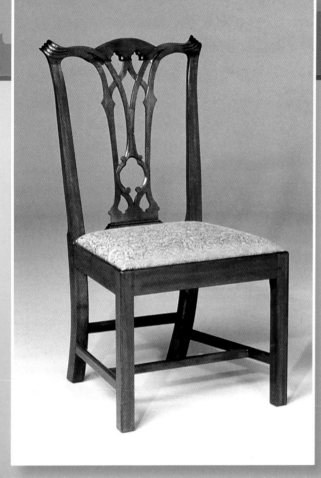

Figure 6.1. Complicated chair parts, such as the back of this chair, are made with a curved cut on one surface of the material and another on the adjacent surface.

Sawing Curved Cuts

A band saw excels at cutting curves in both thick and thin wood. A curved cut is possible because the workpiece can be pivoted around the narrow blade, and the blade is thin so it saws with a minimum of effort and waste. Curves are commonly used as decorative elements, as shown in **Figure 6.1**. Curves are also used as a functional design element, such as a curved chair back or bottom, as shown in **Figure 6.2** and **Figure 6.3**. Complicated chair parts, such as the back of a traditional chair, are made with a curved cut on one surface of the material and also on the adjacent surface.

Cutting curves with the band saw is not difficult and is a lot of fun. Many first-time users get acceptable results right away, especially if they don't try to make complicated or difficult cuts. With practice, it does not take long to become proficient; you will soon develop a slow, smooth rhythm that works with your saw, not against it. This chapter will look in-depth at the techniques used for cutting curves, how to plan your project and the correct sequence of cuts, and the precautions you should take to keep your curves smooth and accurate and avoid common pitfalls. It will even take you step-by-step through the process of crafting a cabriole leg used in fine pieces of furniture.

Figure 6.2. The curves in this Adirondack chair are all band sawn.

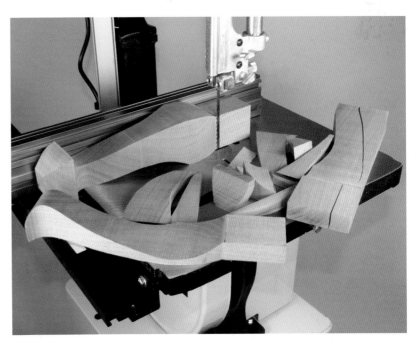

Figure 6.3. Here is a curvy cabriole leg and all of its waste pieces, sawn out of a block with a ¼-inch x 6 TPI blade on the band saw.

Blades for curves

To use the band saw efficiently, you have to use the correct blade, as discussed in Chapter 3, "Band Saw Blades," page 37. To decide which size blade to use, you have to evaluate the work correctly (see **Figure 6.4**). At least three teeth must be in the thickness of the material throughout the saw cut, so thin materials require fine-toothed blades. The coarser the blade, the faster and rougher the cut, but thick materials require coarse-toothed blades so they don't clog with sawdust. More teeth create a smoother cut, but too many teeth will overheat and cut slowly.

Overheated teeth dull quickly, and the blade may also break. Too few teeth produce extremely rough cuts, stalled cuts and blade breakage. There are a number of blade options, as shown in **Figure 6.5**; Chapter 3 contains a larger chart relating blade width to the smallest radius the blade can cut (see page 40).

You can easily determine the appropriate blade width for curves by using two coins and a pencil, as shown in **Figure 6.6**. A ¼-inch blade can make a turn that is roughly the size of a quarter. A ³⁄₁₆-inch blade can make a curve the size of a dime. The smallest curve that a ⅛-inch-wide blade can make is the size of a pencil eraser.

Figure 6.4. This monkey-riding-a-tricycle pull toy has a lot of curves of different sizes.

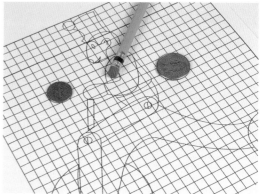

Figure 6.6. Use two coins and a pencil to size the curves. A ¼-inch blade can make a turn about the size of a quarter. A ³⁄₁₆-inch blade can make a curve the size of a dime. The smallest curve that a ⅛-inch-wide blade can make is the size of a pencil eraser.

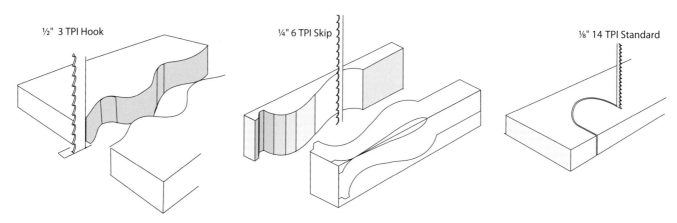

½" 3 TPI Hook   ¼" 6 TPI Skip   ⅛" 14 TPI Standard

Figure 6.5. The blade should be appropriate for the task. The most commonly used blades are the ½ inch, ¼ inch, and ⅛ inch.

When the workpiece is turned sharply, the back of the blade rubs against the saw kerf. This is what limits the smallest turn that the blade can make. If you rotate the workpiece past this point, the blade body will start to twist. This should be avoided if possible because twisting the blade shortens its life. To prevent the blade from twisting, make sure that you feed the workpiece forward into the blade while you are making a sharp turn and that you use a blade of the appropriate width. The best way to assess what the cutting characteristics of a blade are is to test it or to keep pieces of scrap from various projects, as shown in **Figure 6.7.**

Plan your saw cuts

Although the band saw is easy to use, it does require thinking ahead. There are some situations that are best to avoid, such as having to back the blade out of long, curved cuts. This can cause the blade to move forward off the saw wheels. If you must back out, turn off the saw first. You can also tilt the top wheel backward slightly. This will decrease the likelihood of the saw blade coming forward off the wheels when you back out.

The pivot point for any curve is the front edge of the blade, where its teeth are, so practice steering the workpiece around that point and all of your curves will come out better. Whenever possible, rotate the workpiece away from the column rather than into the column. This may require that you plan the sequence of cuts or that you cut off the bulk of the waste before you saw precise curves.

Sometimes, especially if you try to cut too tight a curve, the saw blade will bind or the kerf may close, pinching the saw blade. Avoid stalling the saw if you can because it will be difficult to get it started again. Stop trying to turn the workpiece and pause to let the saw get back up to speed. Sometimes you can insert a slender wooden wedge to open it

up. If the blade does not stall, back up if you can and make multiple short cuts to clean out the material.

Know Where to Saw

The usual practice is to draw the cut line on the workpiece. Pencil lead is often used because it can be erased and because it doesn't leave a permanent mark. Another option is to tape or rubber cement a paper pattern onto the workpiece.

Saw near the outside of the line, but not on it. This way, the line will still be intact if you decide to sand or plane the edge, and you can still see the desired shape. If you are going to sand the edge smooth, be careful that you don't sand too much. Sanding about $1/16$ inch is ideal—depending on whether you are sanding by hand or with a power tool. If you are using a spindle or a disc sander, you may want a little more material between the edge of the cut and the finish line.

Hand Position

The hand position that you use is important for both comfort and safety. Use both hands to feed the wood into the blade and keep them on opposite sides of the workpiece. Never cross your hands. Using a gentle, smooth rhythm will give the best results. Do not force the work or bend or twist the blade. Remember that you

Figure 6.7. The best way to know the cutting characteristics of a blade is to test it or to keep a piece of scrap that it cut. This $1/4$-inch blade was used to saw a cabriole leg; the scrap of walnut is from the leg.

Figure 6.8. Curved pieces of a uniform width are easily cut using the fence. The desired curve is first cut by eye, and then the curved surface contacts the fence during subsequent cuts.

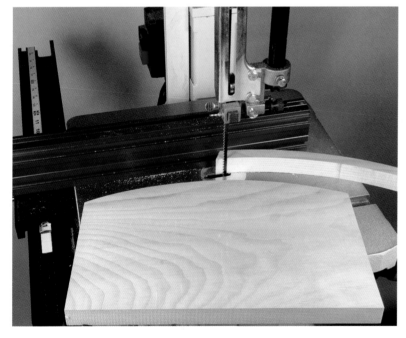

Figure 6.9. At the end of the cut, the piece should contact both the blade and the fence.

must be feeding the wood forward when you are making a turn, especially a tight turn. If you try to pivot the workpiece without moving into the blade, it will twist the blade and possibly break it.

When you are sawing, you must have good control of the workpiece. Hold the workpiece securely with both hands. Most people find that standing slightly to the side of the blade is the most comfortable way to work. Remember that eye protection is important, so be sure to wear safety glasses or goggles. If you are in an awkward position, keep one hand on the work and move the other hand.

Cutting Sequence

The sequence of the cuts is important. It is easiest to maneuver a small piece, so it is best to cut off the largest pieces of waste first. As the larger pieces are cut off, the more delicate cuts are left. On the other hand, cutting very small pieces might put your fingers dangerously close to the saw blade. In that case, it's safest to form the small piece on the end or edge of a larger piece of wood and to saw it free as a last step.

Cutting multiple pieces

When cutting multiple pieces with gentle, parallel curves, it is possible to use the rip fence to space the width of the cuts, as shown in **Figures 6.8** and **6.9** and discussed more fully in Chapter 5, "Sawing Straight Cuts," page 97. This technique allows you to make multiple pieces that are exactly the same size with very little effort. It works on small and large workpieces. The workpiece should contact the fence about ¼ inch ahead of the saw teeth. For efficiency, you can stack several thin pieces of wood and saw them all at once.

Single-point fence for curves

If the piece curves in several directions, you can use a point fence instead of the rip fence to guide the workpiece through the band saw, as shown in **Figure 6.10**. The single-point fence can be as simple as a pointed stick or a round-head bolt. If the curve to be cut is a gentle curve, use a stick with a rounded point. Hold the edge of the workpiece against the point. You have to angle or fishtail the workpiece into the blade at the correct angle. This technique does require some skill and concentration, but it is quite easy to make pieces with multiple curves that are almost identical, as shown in **Figure 6.11**. It is particularly useful on pieces with multiple curves, such as chair backs. It is also useful on small objects with multiple curves, such as band-sawn boxes.

Sawing guidelines for curves

Projects with curved parts can get you into a lot of tricky situations. In this section, I'll address some of them.

Small Pieces

Use a jig or clamp to hold odd-shaped or small pieces during the sawing process. Small pieces are more dangerous to cut than large pieces because your fingers are closer to the blade. One way to minimize the risk is to form the small part on the edge of a larger piece of wood and to sever it as a last step. When you are cutting very small pieces, you may see them disappear down the blade slot in the table insert. Train yourself not to reach for them, but to let them go.

Figure 6.10. Cut multiple curved pieces that have a double curve by using a single point about 1/4 inch in front of the blade. The rotation point can be a bolt, as shown here.

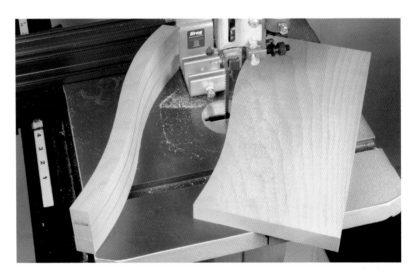

Figure 6.11. Using this single-point technique, it is easy to make pieces with multiple curves that are almost identical.

Release Cuts

It is not only possible to paint yourself into a corner, but also possible to band saw yourself into a corner. A release cut is used to prevent such a situation from occurring. It is made to meet with the end of a long cut so that the waste piece can be easily separated from the workpiece, as shown in **Figure 6.22** on page 121. Of course, you have to anticipate the need for the release cut and make it before you make your next cut along the project lines.

Curved surfaces can be laminated—that is, glued together in layers—for a number of interesting design elements, such as the cutting board shown in **Figure 6.12**. The cherry, maple, and walnut boards are secured one atop the other, and the saw cut is made along a gentle curve, as shown in **Figure 6.13**. This allows the pieces to be reassembled and glued to each other to create three different cutting boards. This technique is similar to the scroll saw method of stack sawing for making intarsia and marquetry projects.

Jeff Kurka's moon face tables are an example of a sophisticated curved lamination technique, as shown in **Figure 6.14**. Tables like these will challenge your woodworking skills with the band saw and the router. The maple and cherry tabletops are cut in half with a ⅛-inch band saw blade and then matched with the opposite pieces to form the face of the man in the moon on the edge of the seam. The curved legs complement the round tabletop and the curves of the face.

The process of joining two pieces of wood on a curved line can be intimidating. Like any other acquired skill, understanding the process and experimentation with scrap wood are good ideas. A very accurate template is made of the curve profile. The template is clamped to the tabletop and trimmed with a router and a guide bushing set. When the two halves are glued together, the glue line is almost invisible, as shown in **Figure 6.15**.

Figure 6.12. The band saw can make decorative curves such as those in this cutting board of cherry, maple, and walnut.

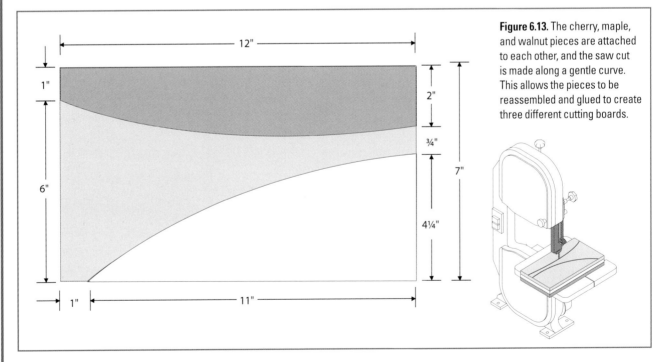

Figure 6.13. The cherry, maple, and walnut pieces are attached to each other, and the saw cut is made along a gentle curve. This allows the pieces to be reassembled and glued to create three different cutting boards.

Figure 6.14. Jeff Kurka's moon face tables demonstrate a sophisticated curved lamination technique. Photo courtesy of Jeff Kurka.

Figure 6.15. When the two halves of the moon face are glued together, the glue line is almost invisible. Photo courtesy of Jeff Kurka.

Band saw boxes are popular band saw projects and can be decorated in a number of ways. There is no end to the design variations using lamination techniques. The boxes shown here were made by Illinois box maker Larry Anderson. His boxes display a creative and artistic use of the curved lamination technique.

The box in **Figure 6.16** is a split-top design made up of a lamination that includes dark and light woods. The split top is hinged on each corner with a brass pin. The box is finished on the inside with a dark brown spray-on suede.

Figure 6.17 is a line and dot box. These boxes can be made from a solid piece of wood or from two different species of wood. The box in the photograph has a dark walnut base and a light-colored top.

The curved checkerboard design in **Figure 6.18** is a lamination of walnut and maple. The two species of wood are attached to each other and then sawn on a long, gentle curve, similar to the technique shown in **Figure 6.13**. After the curved pieces have been glued together, a series of curved cuts is made in the opposite direction. The sawn pieces are then laminated together to create the checkerboard effect.

One option is to include part of the checkerboard design in the design for the top of the box, as shown in **Figure 6.19**. The checkerboard design is laminated to walnut, which was cut and reglued with a light veneer strip.

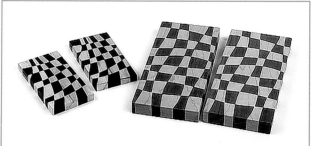

Figure 6.18. This design is a lamination of walnut and maple sawn in both directions. Photo courtesy of Larry Anderson.

Figure 6.16. This box design is a lamination including dark and light woods. Photo courtesy of Larry Anderson.

Figure 6.19. Part of the checkerboard design can be included in the top of the box. Photo courtesy of Larry Anderson.

Figure 6.17. This box has a walnut base and a light top. The top was sawn, and then walnut veneers were glued in between the pieces. The black walnut dots were made with a plug cutter. Photo courtesy of Larry Anderson.

Turning Holes

Turning holes help to cut out complex patterns more quickly. Turning holes are drilled at key locations to give the operator more space to rotate the workpiece around the saw blade. Turning holes, like release cuts, also make it easier to remove waste wood. The holes and the straight cuts are made first, then the curved cuts.

Another advantage to drilling turning holes is the consistency and quality of the curves that are created. For best results, use a rim-cutting drill bit since they make the smoothest holes. Because the holes are smooth, this technique saves the time that you otherwise would spend sanding the inside corners.

Turning holes work extremely well with a project that has holes that match the size of drill bits, such as the Scandinavian-style corner shelf shown in **Figure 6.20** and fully detailed on pages 138 and 139. The holes are drilled at various locations along the edge of the sides, as shown in **Figure 6.21**. The two sides should have the joints, such as dadoes, cut first; then, they can be fastened together to be drilled and sawn simultaneously.

The first cut is a release cut that divides the waste material in half, as shown in **Figure 6.22**. The first cut along the edge of the pattern cuts through the drill holes and removes the top half

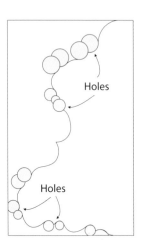

Figure 6.21. Turning holes are drilled at key positions in the workpiece. The turning hole can serve as a smooth curve in a pattern. Turning holes also give the operator more space to rotate the workpiece around the saw blade.

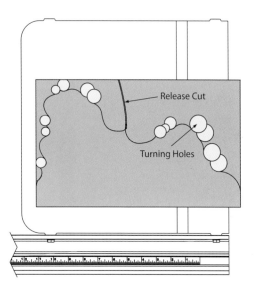

Figure 6.22. The first cut is a release cut that divides the waste material in half.

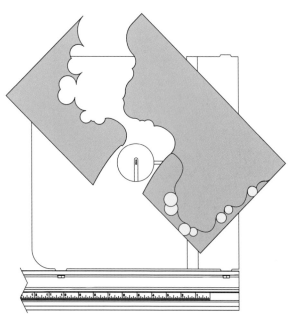

Figure 6.23. The first cut along the edge of the pattern cuts through the drill holes and ends at the release cut, removing the top half of the waste.

Figure 6.20. The Scandinavian-style corner shelf has curves that match the size of drill bits. Using drill holes and release cuts helps create this project quickly and accurately. For more on this project, see pages 138 and 139.

Curves are usually made by sawing into a square blank of wood. However, curves also can be made by gluing thin pieces of wood together on a curved form or by steaming them to soften the fibers and then bending and clamping them around a form. A good example of a steam-bent curve

is the bow of a Windsor chair, as shown in **Figures 6.24** and **6.25**. Chair maker Jeff Trapp of Madison, Wisconsin, then uses hand tools to refine the shape of the steamed bow. This technique might seem far afield for a book on band sawing, but note that the bending form Trapp uses was first band sawn to shape. The Shakers used a similar technique to make curved boxes and carriers, as shown in **Figures 7.9** and **7.10** in Chapter 7, "Patterns and Templates," pages 140 and 141, and in **Figures 6.26** and **6.27**.

Figure 6.24. The bow of this Windsor chair was made by steaming the wood to soften it, then bending it around a band sawn form. Photo courtesy of Jeff Trapp.

Figure 6.25. The bending form for the chair bow was cut on the band saw. The chair maker uses wooden wedges to hold the steamed wood on the form to dry. Photo courtesy of Jeff Trapp.

Figure 6.26. This Shaker carrier is made of wood that was band sawn thin and then steam bent around a band sawn form. There's a similar project on page 140.

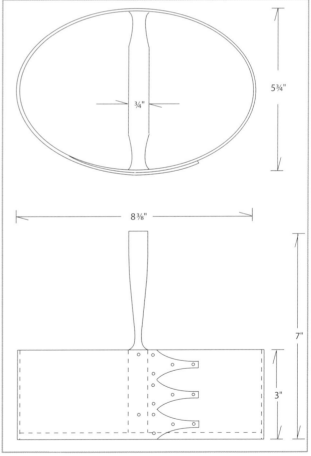

Figure 6.27. These dimensions will make a nice Shaker carrier. The three overlapped tongues are for copper rivets.

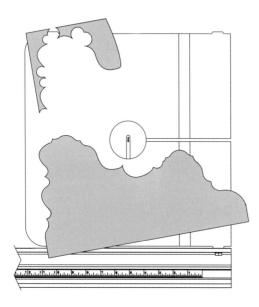

Figure 6.28. The second cut along the edge of the pattern cuts through the drill holes and removes the bottom half of the waste.

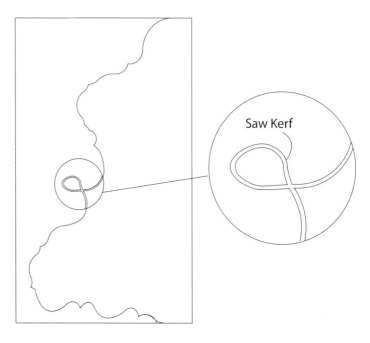

Figure 6.29. One way to make a sharp curve is to continue past the corner and make a circular release cut in the waste area; then, back up the workpiece and continue.

of the waste, as shown in **Figure 6.23**. This first edge cut ends at the release cut. The second cut is along the bottom edge of the pattern through the drill holes. It removes the two bottom pieces of the waste, as shown in **Figure 6.28**.

Cutting Past the Corner

When making a sharp curve or a point, it is often useful to cut past the corner and make a circular cut in the waste area. Continue the cut into the corner. This cut will function like a release cut. Then, back up the workpiece and make another cut along the opposite side. This cut will release the waste, as shown in **Figure 6.29**.

Nibbling

Nibbling is using the band saw blade to remove small pieces of material. It is often used on tight curves. Small pieces of the material are cut away. This creates room for the blade so that you can rotate the workpiece without having to twist the blade body. You can nibble a tight curve as well as a small straight-sided cutout, like the notch shown in **Figure 6.30**.

Figure 6.30. Another way to make a tight curve or a small notch is to nibble at it with multiple short cuts.

STEP-BY-STEP: MAKING A CABRIOLE LEG

One technique that is often intimidating for beginners is the making of a cabriole leg. The cabriole leg is actually quite simple to make if you follow the correct sawing sequence.

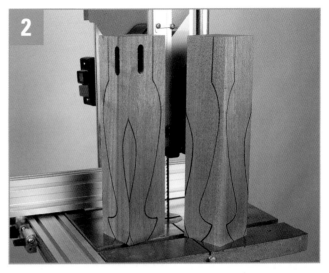

The knees and feet on adjacent sides of the blank should be pointing toward each other on the front corner and away from each other on the back of the leg. Make joints such as mortises on the back of the leg before sawing the curves because it is much easier to cut joints while the material is square.

Mark the pattern on two adjacent sides of the legs. Laying out the pattern correctly is critical. Since for most projects you will be making a set of four legs, it can get very confusing.

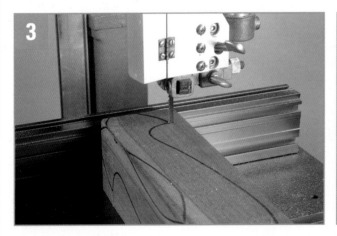

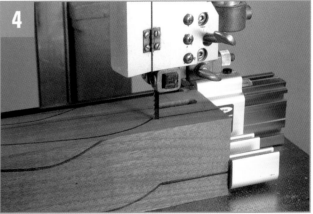

Saw the straight lines first. It is important to align the two crosscuts on the top of the foot, so use the rip fence to space the cuts an equal distance from the bottom of the leg.

Use the rip fence and a stop to make the rip cuts parallel to the edge on the top of the leg.

Saw the bottom of the foot. After removing the piece, rotate the leg and replace the removed piece so that you can continue to use the pattern that you cut off. Hold the pattern in place while making the cut.

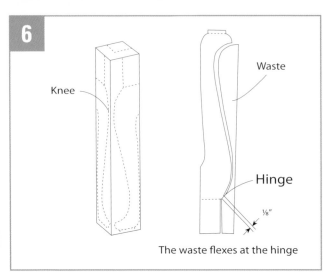

Knee

Waste

Hinge

⅛"

The waste flexes at the hinge

It is advantageous to be able to keep the waste in place on the blank because the pattern is drawn there. Do it with a hinge cut. Make the cut as usual, but leave about 1/16 inch or 1/8 inch of material; this is the hinge.

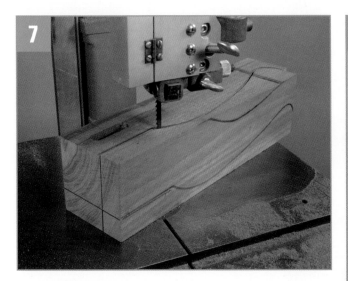

The hinge allows the waste to flex so you can withdraw the blade.

After making all of the long cuts, saw through the hinge and remove the waste. The completed leg is shown here.

Scroll sawing

Until recently, the narrowest blade that was available for the band saw was ⅛ inch wide. For a while a 1/16-inch blade was available, but it was discontinued. Recently, blades that are ³⁄₃₂ inch wide have appeared on the market. When the ³⁄₃₂-inch blade is combined with lubricated, nonmetallic side guide blocks, it becomes possible to do scroll saw work with a band saw. These blades makes fairly tight turns, similar to those made by a scroll saw blade. In some instances, it is very hard to tell the difference between work done with a band saw and that done with an expensive scroll saw (see **Figure 6.31**).

Figure 6.31. These cuts were made with the same blade. The smoother cut on the top piece was made after the blade was turned upside down and the teeth were lightly stoned to remove the excessive set. Even one bent tooth can create a rough cut.

Figure 6.32. To stone the side of the blade, flip it inside out and track it on the saw in the usual way. Then to gently stone the side of the blade, run the stone back and forth on both sides of the blade. Running the blade upside down also works well for cutting thin brass and aluminum sheet material.

The advantage of the band saw is that it will cut faster and also has the ability to cut thick material. A ³⁄₃₂-inch band saw blade has many teeth per inch so that the final cut will be smooth. It can also make very accurate straight cuts that would be extremely hard, if not impossible, to do with a scroll saw.

The disadvantage of the band saw is that you cannot make an inside cut, except by sawing through the wood from an edge and then gluing it back together (see page 127). The scroll saw allows you to undo one end of the blade, thread it through a drilled hole, and reattach it to the saw. On the band saw, you would have to cut and reweld the blade. Metalworkers sometimes do this when sawing complex patterns, but it is not really practical for scroll sawing.

To use the smaller blades successfully, you will have to make some changes in the standard adjustment procedure. It is necessary to replace the metal side guides. Lubricated phenolic guides such as Cool Blocks (see page 95) seem to work best. Place these blocks in contact with the blade, just behind the gullets. Be sure to round the back of small band saw blades (see **Figure 6.32**), as discussed on page 59, and, if the cut is rough, touch up the sides of the reversed blade with the stone, as discussed on page 67.

Also, use center tracking to track the blade. Keep the top guide assembly about an inch above the work. This will allow the blade to flex slightly backward during the cut and eliminates the possibility that the blade will be forced to make a sharp angle under the top thrust bearing. For added support, the thrust bearing should rest against the back of the blade with no space between the bearing and the blade.

Making inside symmetrical cuts with a narrow blade

You can use a narrow blade on a band saw to make inside cuts. To do this, divide the pattern in half, prepare blanks for both halves, stack and cut them both at once, and then glue them together. We will refer to this technique as the cut-and-glue technique.

The cut-and-glue technique has several advantages. Both sides of the pattern are sawn at the same time, which means they will be symmetrical and you will save time. The more complex the pattern, the greater the saving in time. No matter how good you are at scroll sawing, it is extremely difficult to cut two halves of a pattern exactly the same. The cut-and-glue technique can be used for decorating just about any type of object, such as the letter holder and the small bookshelf shown in **Figure 6.33**.

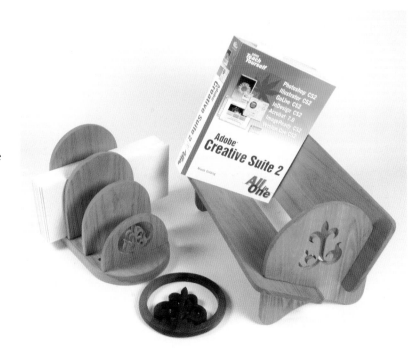

Figure 6.33. The cut-and-glue technique allows you to band saw inside curves, such as on this letter holder and small bookshelf.

To try the cut-and-glue technique, machine material for the two halves of the project and make a clean half pattern.

Drive screws in the corners help to locate the two halves in relation to each other. Glue the pattern onto the wood with rubber cement.

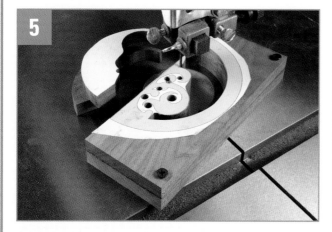

Drill turning holes at key positions in the workpiece. The cleanest holes are made with brad point bits or rim-cutting Forstner bits.

Saw right up to the edge of the pattern line. Make sure that the nonmetal guides are close to the workpiece and that they are close to the blade to prevent it from wandering.

Remove the bulk of the waste with the first cuts.

After sawing away all the waste, glue the two halves together to create the fleur-de-lis design. Clean up the outside edge with a round-over router bit.

Band saw boxes

Band saw boxes are made using narrow band saw blades. The outside of the box can be a decoration such as a leaf pattern or any other type of pattern, as shown in **Figure 6.34**. One style of box has a removable top with a plug on the bottom of the cover that fits the inside box cavity, as shown in **Figure 6.35**. The sequence is to saw the outside of the box, slice off the top and bottom, and then saw out the inside. As with the cut-and-glue technique, you'll have to locate an entry kerf somewhere in the pattern in order to get at the inside. Then, glue the box bottom back in place. The plug for the lid is sawn off the waste you cut out of the inside of the box. Another method is to make a band saw box with a key that has to be removed before the top of the box can be slid off the bottom, as shown in **Figure 6.36**.

Figure 6.34. Make band saw boxes using narrow band saw blades. The outside of the box can be any shape you like.

Figure 6.35. These boxes have a design based on a leaf. This style of box has a removable top with a plug on the bottom of the cover that fits the cavity. The box bottoms and the plugs are made from the interior waste pieces.

Figure 6.36. These band saw boxes are made with a removable key. The key is to be removed before the box can be opened.

Table tilt designs

By making the band saw cuts with the table tilted, a number of interesting effects can be created, as shown in **Figure 6.37**. The oak leaf pattern was cut with the table slightly tilted, and then the inside cutout was sawn from the opposite side. The tilted table technique can be use for a number of different designs, as shown in **Figure 6.38**.

Figure 6.37. By making the band saw cuts with the table tilted, a number of interesting effects can be created. The oak leaf pattern was cut with the table slightly tilted, and the inside cutout was then sawn from the opposite side.

Figure 6.38. The tilted table technique can be used for a variety of designs.

Figure 6.39. This box is decorated with an intarsia flower, made by band sawing several pieces of wood and fitting them tightly together. Photo courtesy of Barbara Reifschneider.

Intarsia

Two different species of wood are often placed next to each other to create a decorative design. When thin veneer is used, the technique is referred to as marquetry. When thicker pieces of solid wood are used, it is called intarsia, as shown in **Figures 6.39** and **6.40**.

To use the techniques of marquetry or intarsia, you usually have to cut the two mating pieces simultaneously. When the cuts are long or have gentle curves, the two pieces will fit exceptionally well if the blade and table are at 90 degrees to each other. Place one piece on top of the other, and cut both at the same time.

However, when the curves are tight or the design is small, the fit between the matching pieces will be better if the table is slightly tilted. The angle helps to compensate for the wood lost to the saw kerf. You will have to experiment with scrap wood to get the right angle. The angle will depend on the blade thickness and the wood thickness.

Figure 6.40. Here is a close-up of the flower intarsia. Photo courtesy of Barbara Reifschneider.

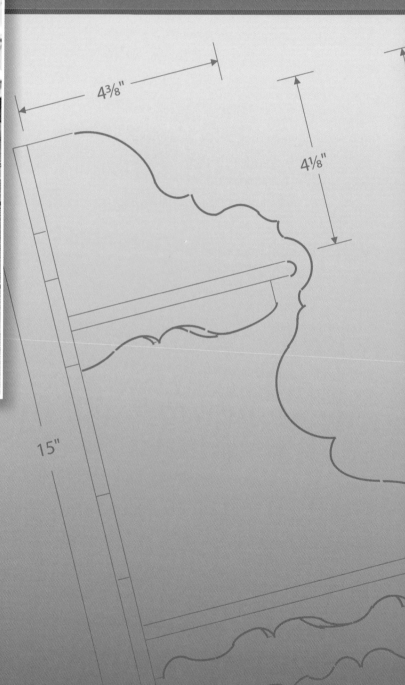

CHAPTER SEVEN

Figure 7.1. The pattern for guiding the band saw is drawn directly on the workpiece. The usual practice is to saw next to the pencil line, not directly on it.

4³⁄₈"

4¹⁄₈"

15"

7³⁄₈"

Patterns and Templates

Several previous chapters have referred to patterns and templates as being useful tools in certain situations. They are particularly valuable when your project design includes intricate or asymmetrical curves, or when you need to produce duplicate pieces of work. This chapter will address the most common types of patterns, when to use them, how to create templates from your patterns, and the basics of template sawing and routing.

Before we begin, let's take a quick look at the difference between a pattern and a template. A pattern is the shape of the item that you plan on cutting out. It can be drawn directly on the workpiece, as shown in **Figure 7.1**, or drawn on paper and taped or glued to the workpiece. When you want to fasten a paper pattern to the workpiece, you'll find that adhesives like rubber cement and double-sided tape both work well.

A template is a thin, solid piece of material that is exactly the size of the pattern. Templates are used to draw, to guide the saw cut using a jig that follows the template edge, or to guide a flush-trimming router bit.

Figure 7.2. A template is a solid piece of thin wood or clear plastic that is exactly the size of the pattern. Templates are used to draw the pattern onto the workpiece, to guide the saw blade, or to guide the router bit.

When to use a template

If you are going to only make the item once, it doesn't make sense to go through the trouble of making a template. When you are planning to make multiple pieces, it is worth your effort to make an accurate template out of a durable material such as high-density fiberboard (Masonite is a common brand), thin plywood, or plastic. Then, you can use the template to trace the pattern directly onto the workpiece. If you label it and hang it on the shop wall, you probably will still have it, perhaps many years later, when you need to make the same piece again.

My favorite template material is an acrylic plastic such as Plexiglas (see **Figure 7.2**).

Clear plastic works well because you can see the figure of the wood through it and shift the pattern on the wood accordingly.

Templates are especially useful on workpieces such as cabriole leg blanks, where parts of the pattern need to be drawn on different sides of the wood block, as shown in Step 1 on page 124. When you are making complex pieces such as the Shaker stand in **Figure 7.3**, joints generally should be laid out and cut before sawing the part on the band saw. In this example, you would make the sliding dovetails on the leg pieces before sawing their curved shape.

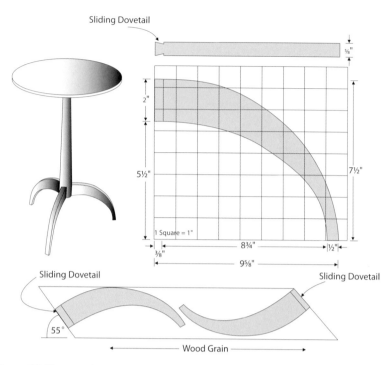

Figure 7.3. Use templates to lay out the pattern on the workpiece. Joints such as sliding dovetails should be positioned close to the edge and cut before the piece is sawn on the band saw. This is the pattern for a Shaker three-leg table.

Types of patterns

Not all patterns represent the entire piece to be made. In addition to full patterns, you are likely to encounter half patterns, quarter patterns, double patterns, and compound patterns. It is important to consider the direction of the wood's grain when laying out a pattern on the piece of wood. In most cases, the wood's grain should run the length of the pattern.

Full Pattern

The full pattern is used when the shape of the object is not symmetrical. Sometimes full patterns are broken into a number of smaller patterns corresponding to different parts or subassemblies. The Scandinavian shelf, drawn in **Figure 7.8** on page 139, is a good example of a full pattern with a number of subsidiary patterns.

Half Pattern

When the object is symmetrical, a half pattern is the best pattern to use. A half pattern is only half of the shape. You use the same pattern for both halves of the object by drawing one side and then flipping the pattern over. When you are using half patterns, be sure you mark a clear centerline on the workpiece to help you align the two parts. The fleur-de-lis project, shown on page 128, was made using a half pattern.

Quarter Pattern

When the object has four corners that are the same, such as an ellipse, a quarter pattern is useful. The pattern is flipped left to right and then top to bottom, as shown in **Figure 7.10** on page 141. This is the pattern for a Shaker box.

Double Pattern

When a three-dimensional object has the same profile on two adjacent sides, the pattern can be used twice. An example of this is the pattern for a cabriole leg, as shown in **Figure 7.2** on page 134. When there is a pattern on adjacent sides of the block, such as the cabriole leg or the toy boat hull in **Figure 7.4**, you will need to make two series of cuts to release the workpiece.

Compound Pattern

Patterns often provide a front, side, top, and bottom view, as shown in **Figure 7.8** on page 139, which is for the small Scandinavian-style corner shelf shown in **Figure 7.6**. An enlarged grid section, to show details full size, is sometimes included in a pattern, as shown in **Figure 7.7** on page 138.

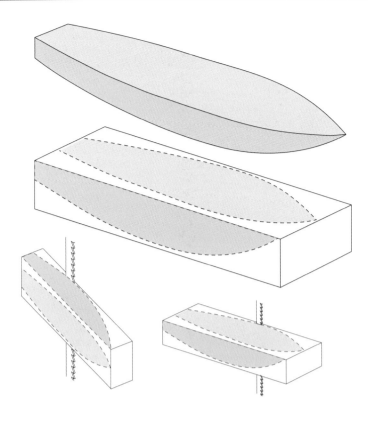

Figure 7.4. A double pattern has elements drawn on adjacent sides of the workpiece, like this toy boat hull. You need to make two series of cuts to release the object.

Sources of patterns

Patterns commonly are found in books or magazines. They also can be ordered from a variety of sources. You may use the exact pattern, or you may want to change it slightly. Usually when you build something from scratch, it does not turn out the way that you would like it to. The advantage of using a pattern is that you know exactly what the project is supposed to look like. There are a number of ways to make patterns. If you have good drawing skills, you can draw the pattern and then revise the drawing as it suits you.

Enlarging Patterns

If you decide to use a pattern from a book or a magazine, you will have to transfer the shape to your workpiece, and you probably will have to enlarge it first. Most page-size patterns are printed on a uniform grid as an aid to enlargement. Typically each grid square is meant to be 1 inch at full size. To enlarge the pattern, you can either make a full-size 1-inch grid on a piece of paper or use a sheet of graph paper that already has grid lines. Stationery stores sell large pads of paper that are ruled with a 1-inch grid. Using the intersecting lines as references, transfer the pattern one square at a time, as shown in **Figure 7.5**. It may be helpful to number the lines in both directions on both the large and the small pattern. Use a French curve, profile gauge, or curved rulers to connect the dots forming the lines of the desired pattern.

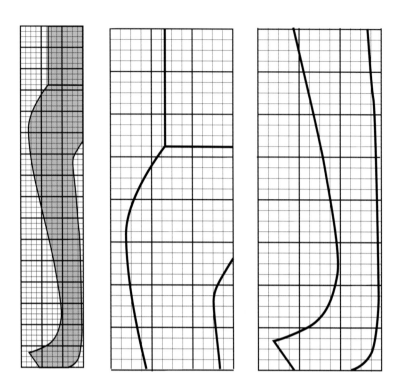

Figure 7.5. Small patterns printed in books can be enlarged using a grid. You can transfer the pattern to a full-size grid, or you can work with the enlarging feature of a copy machine.

Another way to enlarge a pattern is with a copy machine. Most copy machines are capable of enlarging, though you may need to enlarge in several stages before you reach full size, and you'll be piecing the result together from many pieces of paper. This is another situation where it will help to number the grid lines before you start. Some copy shops have large-format copying machines so they can serve the local construction industry. They may be able to enlarge your pattern onto a single sheet of paper.

This little Scandinavian-style corner shelf (see **Figure 7.6**) offers an excellent exercise in using patterns (see **Figure 7.8**) and band sawing various kinds of curves. The flat side pieces have a curved pattern sawn in them, which is best accomplished by first drilling a series of turning holes, as shown in **Figure 7.7** (for more on turning holes see page 121). The shelves are circular arcs, best made using a quarter circle jig, as described on page 148.

The shelf aprons combine both kinds of curves—they're sawn to a broad radius, and they're also scalloped in tight curves on the bottom edge. You can saw the blanks for the shelves out of a 6/4 plank. Then, take a double pattern off the drawing, and glue it onto the inside of the curved blank so you can see it as you saw. When you saw this pattern, you'll have to roll the blank as you proceed so the place where you are doing the cutting is on the saw table.

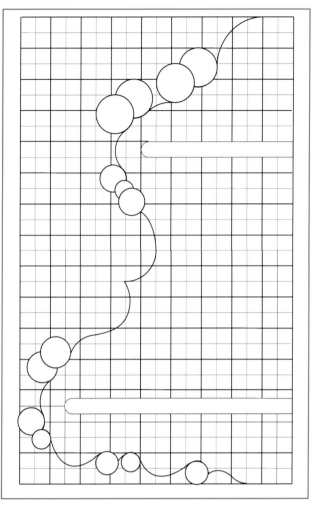

Figure 7.7. An enlarged grid pattern is sometimes included in a plan. This is the side view of the Scandinavian-style corner shelf, with turning holes (see page 121) indicated.

Figure 7.6. This Scandinavian-style corner shelf offers a good exercise in working with patterns.

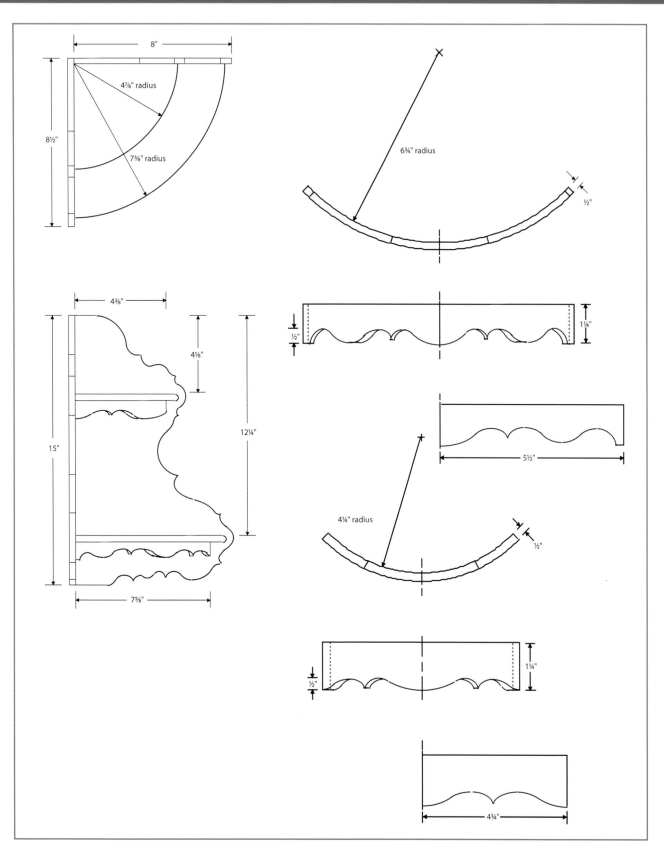

Figure 7.8. This full pattern, which includes a number of secondary patterns, was used to make the small Scandinavian-style corner shelf.

This beautiful Shaker-style oval box with lid, **Figure 7.9**, combines a number of important pattern-making and band saw techniques. The box sides are made by resawing a thin piece of wood from a thick plank of maple (see page 102). After resawing the material, cut it to length so you can lay out and band saw the tongue pattern on one end. Then, bend the sides around an oval-shaped form and retain by setting copper rivets through the overlapped ends. Sometimes soft maple will bend easily to a curve like this, but usually the wood must first be bathed in hot steam for 20 minutes to soften it. Clamp it onto the form, and let it dry before you rivet it.

To make the oval-shaped form, take a quarter pattern off the drawing in **Figure 7.10**, and flip it left to right and top to bottom. That way, all four quadrants of the ellipse will be the same. The same quarter pattern can be used to lay out and saw the oval-shaped pine blank for the inset lid and box bottom.

Figure 7.9. When the object has four corners that are the same, like this Shaker oval box, a quarter pattern can be used.

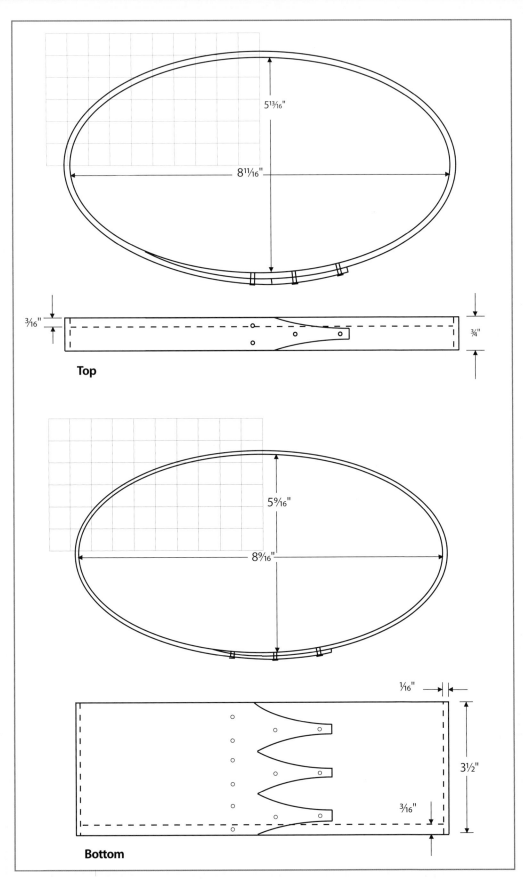

Figure 7.10. The Shaker box has a pine lid and bottom with maple sides. The thin maple was resawn using the band saw.

$5^{13}/_{16}$"

$8^{11}/_{16}$"

$3/_{16}$"

$3/_4$"

Top

$5^{9}/_{16}$"

$8^{9}/_{16}$"

$1/_{16}$"

$3^{1}/_2$"

$3/_{16}$"

Bottom

Template sawing

Template sawing is a way to make multiple pieces that are identical, such as parts for making multiples of the chair shown in **Figure 7.11**. A solid template is attached to the workpiece, as shown in the step-by-step sequence below. The waste material is removed by band sawing while guiding the template against a rub block, which is a very common and useful kind of band saw jig. The rub block keeps the band saw blade near the template without quite touching it. The last bit of the waste, right up to the template, can then be removed with a bearing-guided router bit.

Figure 7.11. The closely related techniques of template sawing and template routing can help you make multiple pieces that are identical, such as parts for a set of chairs.

STEP-BY-STEP: TEMPLATE SAWING THE CHAIR BACK

A good example of template sawing and routing is the chair's back rail (see **Figure 7.11**). The rail is curved on its front and back, and it also has a curve on the top. Take your time and make a good template. It works best if the template is made of plastic or plywood because these materials, unlike solid wood, do not shrink or expand.

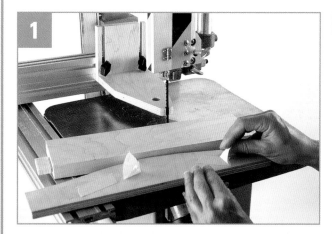

Attach the template to the workpiece with double-sided carpet tape. It is strong enough that you don't need any other means of attachment. Make the joints while the workpiece is square—here, the tenon has already been sawn on the end of the workpiece. Notice also that the blank is thick enough to accommodate the front-to-back curve.

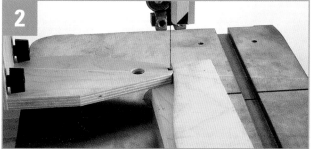

Make the rub block. The rub block should have a curved end with a notch in it, called a follower. The notch fits over the blade, extending past it by about $1/16$ inch. Clamp the rub block to the saw table or to the saw fence at the height where it will contact the template but not the workpiece. For more on making the rub block, see Chapter 8, "Jigs and Fixtures," page 154.

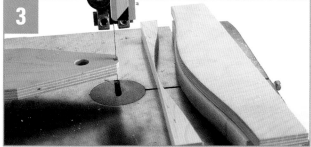

When you guide the template against the follower, the band saw cuts a duplicate shape in the wooden blank. The template contacts the rub block throughout the saw cut. Because the blade is about $1/16$ inch short of the template, the sawn workpiece will extend past the template by about $1/16$ inch. You'll see how to rout the workpiece back to the template in the next section.

Template routing

Template routing with a flush-cutting router bit (also called a flush-trimming router bit) is the complementary technique to template sawing. It allows you to trim the workpiece right up to the template. A flush-cutting router bit has a bearing on the top or the bottom of the cutting edge. The bearing rubs against the template as the cutter trims the waste. The router leaves a smooth finish that requires little sanding.

If you are going to be making a lot of duplicate parts, it is worthwhile to make a sled jig. When you want to rout a symmetrical part, use a half-template jig, like the one shown in **Figure 7.12**. You don't need to make a template for the whole shape.

The sled jig that is used to hold the chair back has the half-template shaped on its front edge. The workpiece is held in place against stop blocks with two fast-action clamps. Half of the template is routed; then, the piece is unclamped and reversed, and the other half is routed. The advantage of this approach is that the router bit is always cutting with the grain, avoiding tear-out and chipping, as shown in **Figure 7.13**. There's more on jigs and fixtures in the next chapter.

Figure 7.12. The workpiece is clamped on a half-template sled jig. The bearing on the bottom of the flush-cutting router bit rides against the curved template on the jig. The workpiece is flipped over and end for end to cut the second part of the curve.

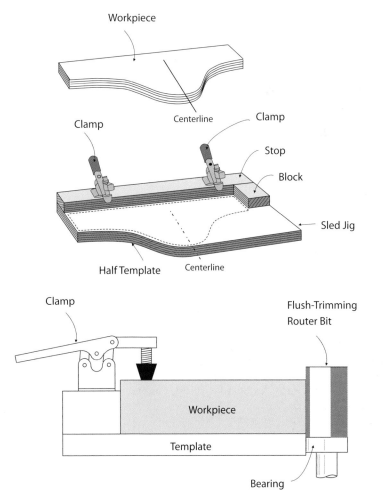

Figure 7.13. Details of the half-template jig.

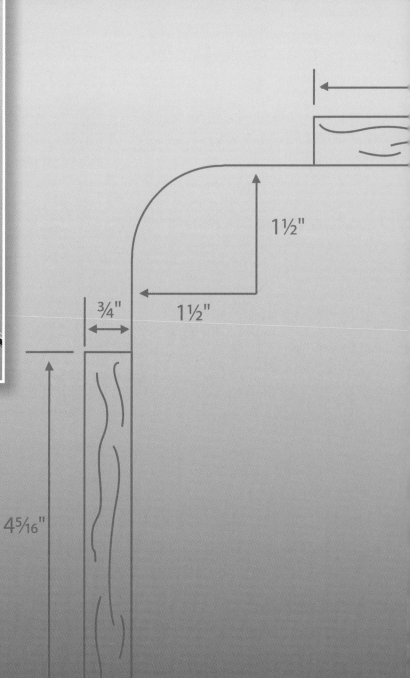

CHAPTER EIGHT

Figure 8.1. This bowl-forming jig consists of the regular circle cutting jig combined with the tilted band saw table (see page 150 for more information).

1½"

¾"   1½"

4⁵⁄₁₆"

Jigs and Fixtures

A fixture is a device that positions or holds the workpiece. A jig is a fixture that also serves as a tool guide. The terms "jig" and "fixture" are often used interchangeably or together to define a store-bought accessory or something that you can make yourself for your shop. The idea behind jigs and fixtures is that they can help you work more efficiently and more accurately. The most common kind of band saw jig is for cutting circles and parts that include part-circular arcs, such as the bowl-forming jig shown in **Figure 8.1**.

The one drawback of the band saw is that the cut is often too rough for the desired purpose. Template routing, shown on page 156 (see **Figures 8.21** through **8.23**), is a technique for cleaning up the sawn edge with a flush-trimming router bit. The band saw and the router are an extremely effective combination in the workshop. The second part of this chapter will focus on jigs and fixture techniques that can be used after the band saw has been used.

The jigs and fixtures shown in this book are very basic with no attempt at anything but pure function. Many woodworkers get very involved in designing and making elaborate jigs with a high degree of detail and finish. That is not my objective here. The purpose of this chapter is to give you some ideas for jigs and fixtures that can speed your work and make it more accurate. The best jig is the one that you don't need, meaning that you can often do the job with what you already have, such as the miter gauge or the rip fence.

Designing and building jigs and fixtures is an acquired skill—the more you do it, the easier it will be. The trick is to see the big picture. If you can find and define the real problem, you're halfway to designing a good solution.

Taper jig

The very simple taper jig, shown in **Figure 8.2**, is used in conjunction with the rip fence. Just make a piece of wood longer than the tapered parts you want, and saw it to the taper you want. Then, drill and install the dowel stop, as shown. Set a rectangular blank against the jig, stopped by the dowel, and propel the assembly past the band saw blade, along the rip fence—the taper in the jig is reproduced in the workpiece. You will have to experiment to get the rip fence in exactly the right place for the parts you want to reproduce.

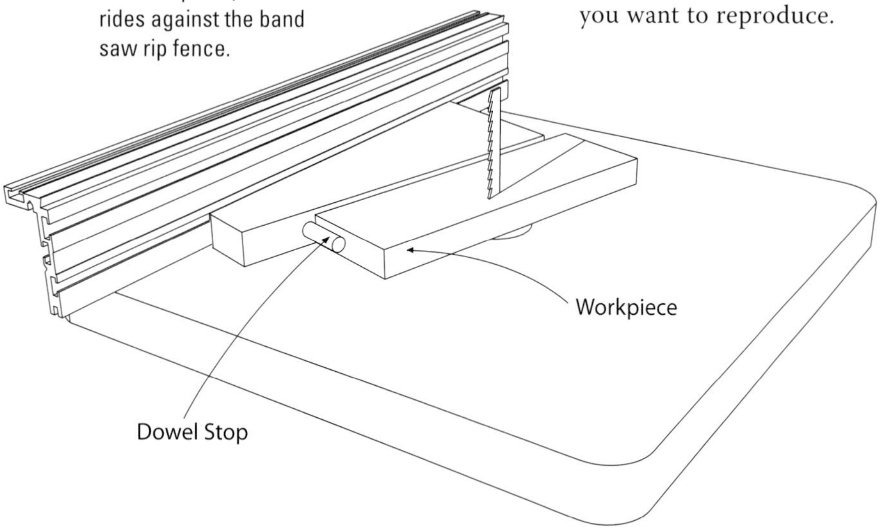

Figure 8.2. The taper jig has a dowel stop for the workpiece, and it rides against the band saw rip fence.

Workpiece

Dowel Stop

Micro-adjustable fence

Now that you know how to saw a nice taper, you can use two identically tapered wedges of wood to make a micro-adjusting fence for your band saw (see **Figure 8.3**). This fence can be nudged and tightened in very small increments for when you really want to saw right on your layout line.

To make the jig, first taper the two wedges of solid wood or MDF (medium-density fiberboard); then, make the slotted block. Screw the block to one of the wedges, and mount the locking knob and bolt in the other wedge. Glue a straight fence onto the non-tapered edge of the wedge with the locking knob, and set the whole thing up, as shown in **Figure 8.3**. Clamp the wedge with the slotted block on it to the band saw table.

To use the micro-adjusting fence, loosen the lock knob and slide it along the slot to shift the fence toward the blade or away from it. The amount of motion is governed by the tapers sawn into the two wedges. For finer adjustments, make a steeper taper.

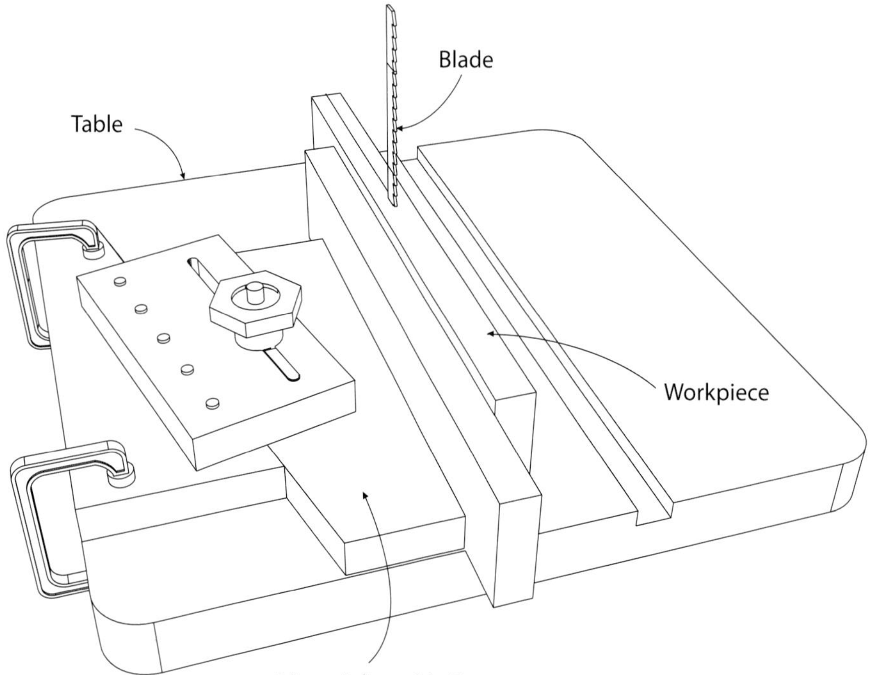

Figure 8.3. You can make a micro-adjusting band saw fence using two identically tapered blocks of wood.

Blade

Table

Workpiece

Micro-Adjustable Fence

Circle cutting jigs

Many projects require either complete circles or a portion of a circle. Although it is possible to cut a circle freehand, it would be a lot more accurate to use a circle cutting jig. The basic idea is the same as drawing a circle with a compass. First you locate a rotation point at a given distance from the blade and center the workpiece on it. As you rotate the workpiece on the point, the band saw cuts the circle. The distance between the point and the blade determines the radius of the circle. The jig locates and holds the rotation point and also supports the workpiece. To start the cut, the jig slides forward in the saw's miter slot until it hits a stop.

Circle cutting jigs are commercially available or can be shop-made, as shown in **Figure 8.4**; both work the same way. To set the size of the shop-made jig, you just measure the radius along the rotation point line shown in the drawing, drill a pilot hole, and drive a sharp-pointed screw through from the bottom side. Center the workpiece on the screw point, and saw it (see **Figure 8.5**), as shown in the Sawing a Circle step-by-step sequence on page 148. Commercial jigs are usually adjustable so that you can easily change the radius of the circle. The rotation point can be either above the workpiece or below it. Having the rotation point on the bottom has some advantages, especially if you use the jig for cutting half and quarter circles.

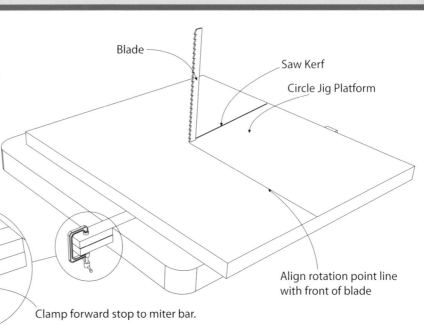

Blade
Saw Kerf
Circle Jig Platform
Clamp forward stop to miter bar.
Align rotation point line with front of blade

Figure 8.4. A circle cutting jig is straightforward to make, using a piece of plywood as the jig base and the tip of a screw for the rotation point.

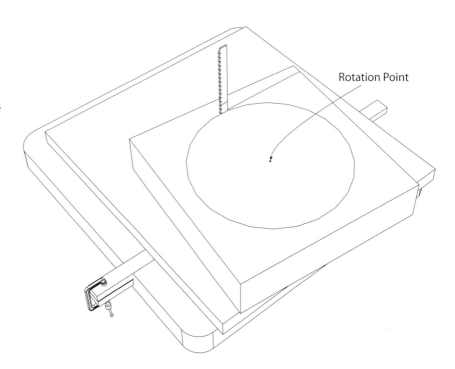

Rotation Point

Figure 8.5. To use the shop-made jig, center the blank on the point, push the jig platform straight into the blade until the stop contacts the table edge, and pivot the blank to saw it out.

This commercial circle cutting jig has a center point mounted on a block that slides in a track. To use the jig:

Make a small hole in the center of the workpiece, which you'll use for mounting the workpiece on the jig's center point.

Position the stop nut on the jig at the appropriate radius.

Locate the jig's center point in the center of the workpiece.

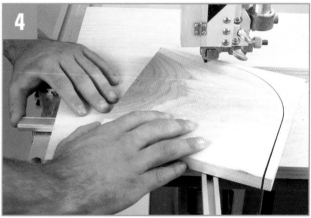

Set the stop so that the jig stops moving forward when the blade is lined up exactly with the center point. Move the jig and the workpiece into the blade until the stop touches the table. The stop has to stay in contact with the table or the cut will not be round. Slowly rotate the workpiece.

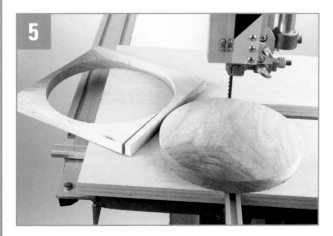

Here is the finished circle.

Radius Jigs

Radius jigs are useful for making parts of a circle, which you would need for projects like the ones shown in **Figures 8.6** and **8.7**. Once you have made one part with a half-round end, you can use the part to make a radius jig by attaching a strip of wood to each side of the part. The radius jig sits on top of the circle cutting jig's rotation point. The side strips locate the workpiece and hold it in place.

Half Circle Jig

A half circle jig is very useful for production items. It will save the effort of having to mark, punch, and locate each corner. Simply hold the workpiece against the jig sides (see **Figure 8.8**), and rotate the jig into the saw blade, as shown in **Figure 8.9**. It is important that the jig does not move during this operation, and, for this reason, you should clamp it to the table. After the half circle is done, you can also use this jig in conjunction with a flush-trimming router bit by advancing the workpiece in the jig about $\frac{1}{16}$ inch.

Figure 8.6. The half circle pieces in this letter holder were made with a half circle cutting jig.

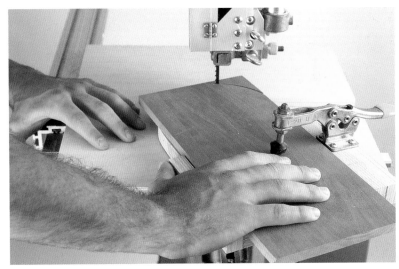

Figure 8.8. The half circle jig is made of plywood with two side pieces and a quick-action clamp. It rests on the rotation point of the regular circle cutting jig.

Figure 8.7. These clocks were sawn and then sanded with a half circle jig.

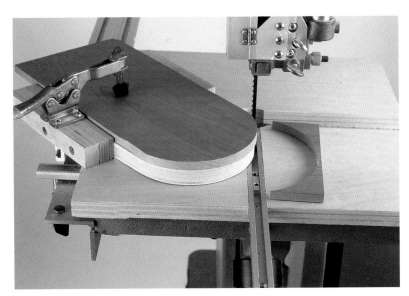

Figure 8.9. The workpiece is secured to the jig as it is pivoted into the blade.

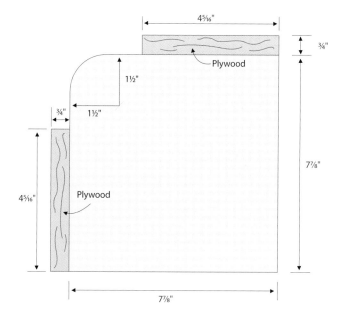

Figure 8.10. A corner sawing jig is easy to make because the workpiece can be held in the corner of the jig without the need for a clamp.

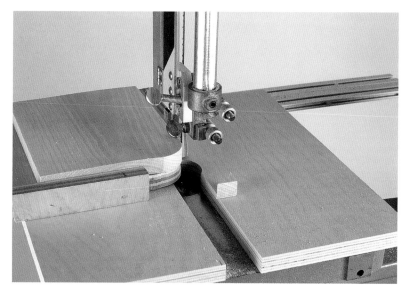

Figure 8.11. The workpiece rests in the corner of the jig as it is pivoted into the blade.

Corner Sawing Jig

A corner sawing jig is easy to make and mount on the circle cutting jig because the workpiece can be held in the corner without the need for a clamp, as shown in **Figures 8.10** and **8.11**.

Jig for Turning Blanks

A circle cutting jig is particularly useful for woodturners. The closer a workpiece is to a circle, the less material has to be removed with the turning tools, saving time and energy. Starting with a round workpiece also decreases the amount of vibration on the lathe, which is much safer than attempting to turn a large, unbalanced workpiece. The step-by-step sequence on the next page shows how to use the circle cutting jig to band saw a turning blank.

STEP-BY-STEP: SAWING A TURNING BLANK

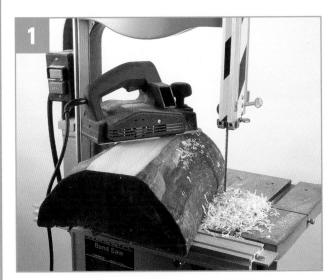

1

To begin, flatten the bottom of a rough board with a hand plane or power plane.

2

Mount the workpiece on the circle cutting jig with the table tilted at the desired angle.

3

Try to center the workpiece on the jig. Ideally the saw blade should trim off the edge.

4

The completed bowl blank will have a smooth side wall and will be well balanced, with only the top retaining its rough character.

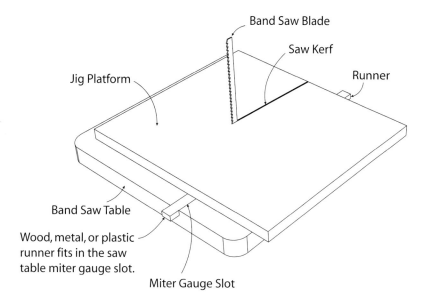

Band Saw Blade

Saw Kerf

Jig Platform

Runner

Band Saw Table

Wood, metal, or plastic runner fits in the saw table miter gauge slot.

Miter Gauge Slot

Sled jigs

The circle cutting jig, discussed earlier, and many other band saw jigs are specific examples of sled jigs. The workpiece mounts on the sled, and the sled then is guided by the saw's rip fence or miter gauge slots. Sled jigs are ideal for managing large and irregular workpieces on the band saw table, such as slabs of wood with irregular edges that you want to saw straight or big planks that you want to taper. They're also a good way to mount a platform and a high fence that can carry a rough log into the blade for sawing it into boards and veneer.

The idea behind the universal sled jig shown here is that you make a plywood or MDF platform and screw a runner to it that will fit and slide in the miter gauge slot in the band saw table. After you have mounted the runner, slide the whole platform through the saw to cut it off at the blade. This way, the platform ends right at the saw blade, and the edge of it shows exactly where the blade is going to cut (see **Figure 8.12**). In many situations, a sled jig supports the workpiece best if there's no drop at its blade edge, so clamp a second piece of plywood or MDF of the same thickness as the platform onto the table on the other side of the blade, as shown in **Figure 8.12**, to act as an auxiliary support table.

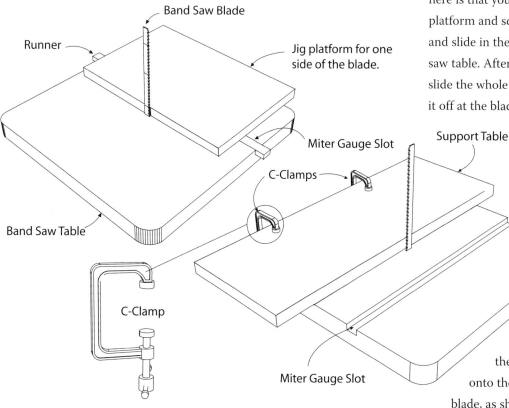

Band Saw Blade

Runner

Jig platform for one side of the blade.

Miter Gauge Slot

Support Table

C-Clamps

Band Saw Table

C-Clamp

Miter Gauge Slot

Figure 8.12. The sled jig consists of a workpiece platform that slides in the miter gauge slot, plus an auxiliary support table clamped to the band saw table on the opposite side of the blade.

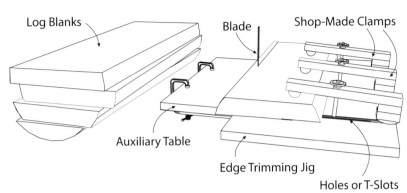

Log Blanks

Blade

Shop-Made Clamps

Figure 8.13. The edge trimming jig for cleaning up slabs of log is a good example of a sled jig.

Auxiliary Table

Edge Trimming Jig

Holes or T-Slots

Add clamps, high fences, or other work-holding apparatus to the jig platform to suit the job you want to accomplish. You can screw the clamps to the platform, you can mill slots for mini-track, or you can mount shop-made clamps in holes. You can see these different approaches at work in the illustrations: **Figure 8.13** shows an edge trimming jig for squaring up planks band sawn from a small log; it has shop-made clamps mounted on the jig platform. **Figure 8.14** shows a sled jig set up for tapering, with mini-track routed into its surface for some quick-mount clamps. **Figure 8.15** shows a sled jig set up to slab planks off a small log; it carries a moveable high fence fastened to the sled with bolts in T-slots.

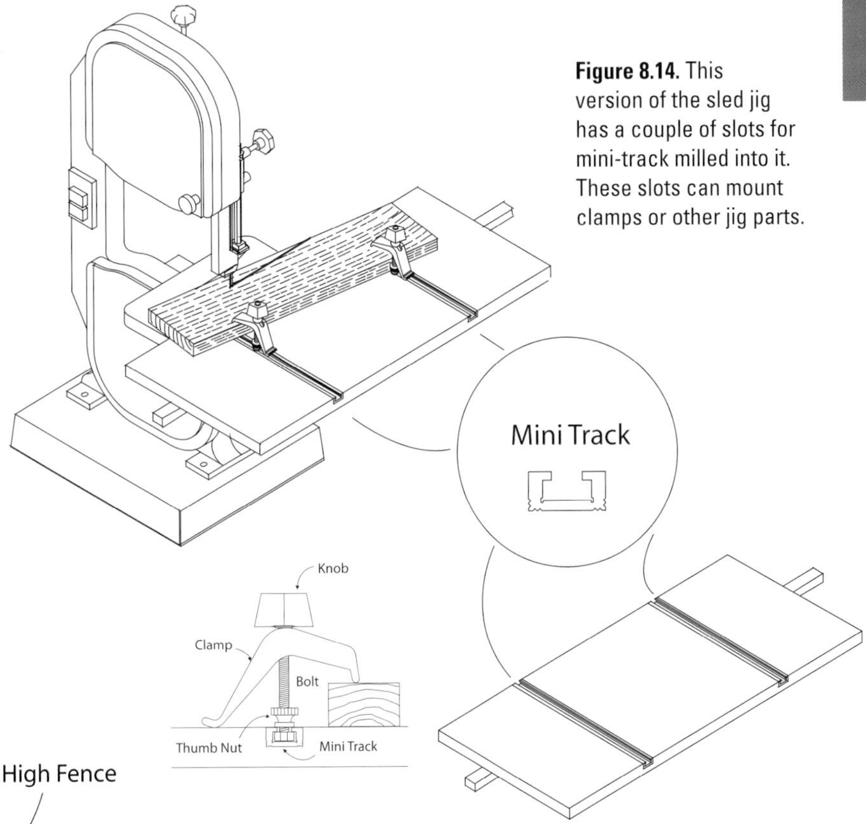

Figure 8.14. This version of the sled jig has a couple of slots for mini-track milled into it. These slots can mount clamps or other jig parts.

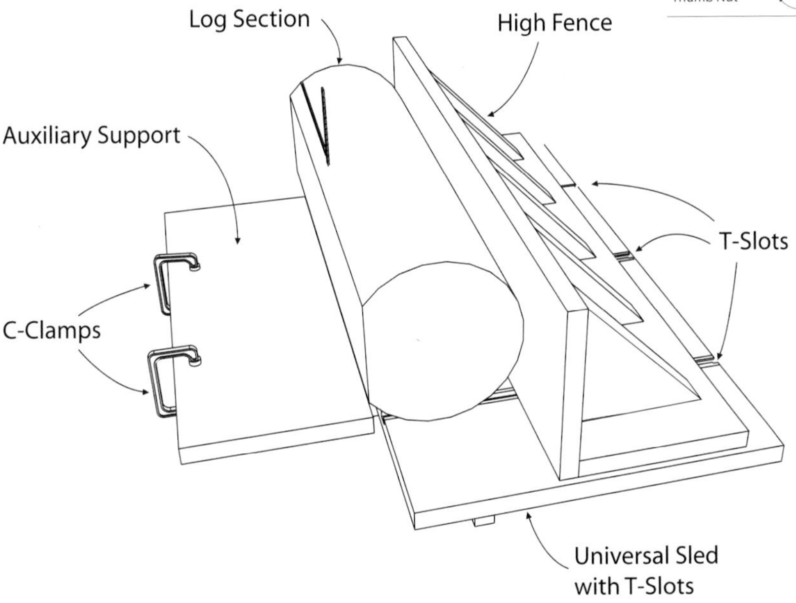

Mini Track

Knob

Clamp

Bolt

Thumb Nut   Mini Track

Log Section

High Fence

Auxiliary Support

T-Slots

C-Clamps

Universal Sled with T-Slots

Figure 8.15. The shop-made high fence has mounting bolts that allow it to move in the T-slots milled into the sled jig platform. Here it is set up for slabbing a small log.

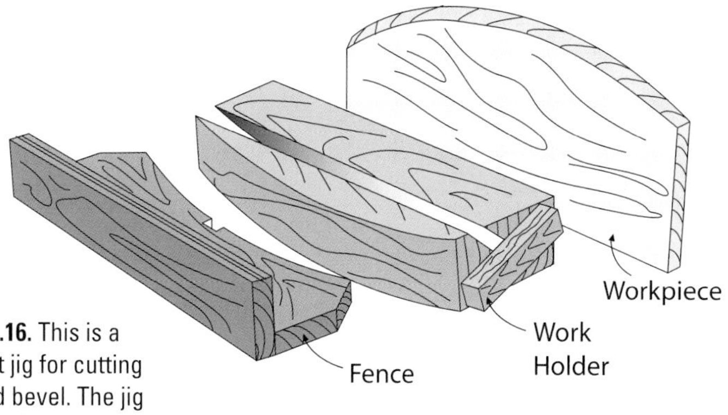

Figure 8.16. This is a two-part jig for cutting a curved bevel. The jig consists of a convex work holder that rides against a matching concave fence.

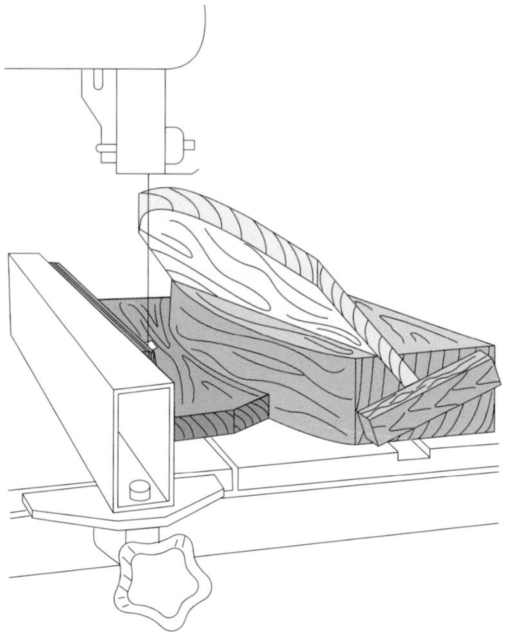

Figure 8.17. The concave fence is secured to the regular saw fence.

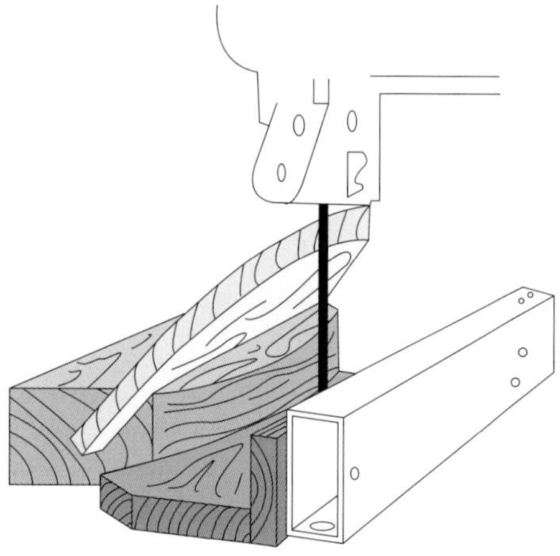

Figure 8.18. The convex work holder is rotated into the blade to saw the beveled curve.

Specialty jigs

Specialty jigs can be used to make curved items that are not circles. A single beveled, curved-edge workpiece can be cut freehand with the saw table tilted. However, if any volume of work is required, it is worthwhile to make the jig shown in **Figure 8.16**. It has two mating parts: a convex work holder and a concave fence. The saw blade passes through a notch in the concave fence. The work holder has an angled groove sawn in it to hold the workpiece, with stop blocks at the ends. The work holder lifts the edge that is to be curved and beveled into the saw blade. The concave fence is secured to the saw's regular rip fence, while the convex work holder is rotated into the saw blade, shown in **Figures 8.17** and **8.18**.

Jig for template sawing

The two most important band saw jigs are the circle cutting jig and the rub block or pattern following jig for template sawing. You've already seen this jig in use in Chapter 7, "Patterns and Templates," page 142. The basic strategy of the rub block is you fasten an accurate template to the top or bottom of the workpiece; then, you guide the template edge against the rub block, which is also called a follower (see **Figure 8.19**) and which ends right at the saw blade. The blade thus traces the shape of the template as it cuts the workpiece, cutting an exact duplicate. While the setup works equally well with the template mounted under the workpiece, as shown here, I prefer to have the template on top of the workpiece because it is easier to see what's going on, as shown in **Figure 8.27** on page 157.

The rub block is simply a flat piece of wood that tapers to a small rounded end with a blade-wide notch in it. It's attached to a mounting block that allows it to be mounted on the rip fence, or it can simply be clamped directly to the band saw table for a template under the workpiece or clamped atop an elevating block when the template is on top. You want to raise the rub block high enough for good contact with the template and no contact with the workpiece. It can be mounted on either side of the blade, but you will have a lot more room for the workpiece if you mount the rub block on the column side. The round end of the rub block has to be just smaller than the tightest curve in the template. If it's too small, steering the workpiece smoothly becomes difficult. If the curve is too flat, the blade won't reach the deepest hollows, and you won't be able to saw out your workpiece accurately. The blade notch allows the template to ride against the rub block without becoming involved with the blade itself (see **Figure 8.20**).

Although it is blindingly simple in concept, the rub block is a very powerful jig because it allows you to saw many duplicate parts accurately and effortlessly.

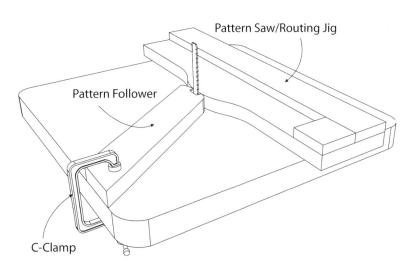

Figure 8.19. When you guide the pattern against the follower, the band saw will reproduce its shape in the workpiece.

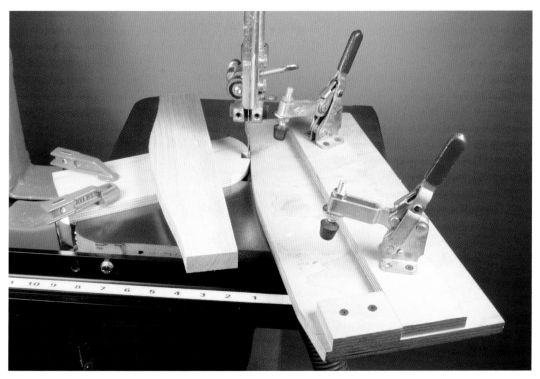

Figure 8.20. This pattern-following jig has a pair of quick-action clamps mounted on it for holding the workpiece in place. This particular example makes the blanks for a chair back.

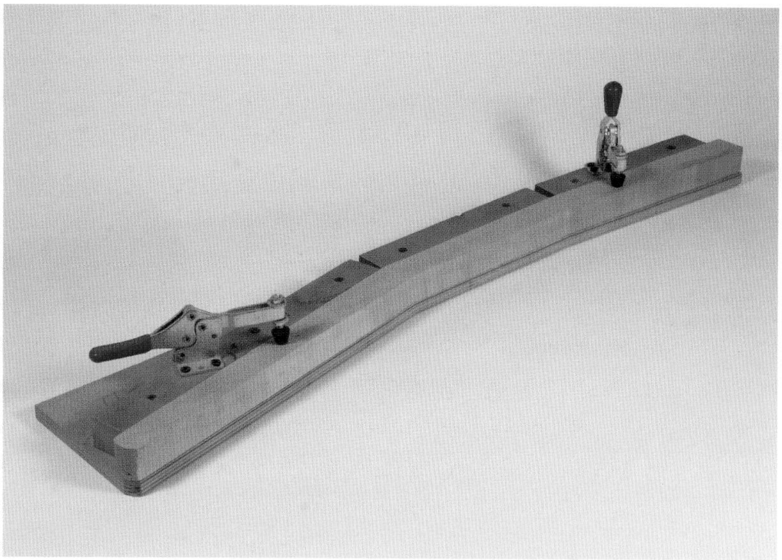

Figure 8.21. For making multiple pieces such as the back leg of a chair, construct a template routing jig and clamp the workpiece to it. In this situation, a flush-trim bit with the bearing on the bottom of the cutter works best.

Figure 8.22. A template jig was used to cut and smooth the four identical brackets on the sides of this Arts and Crafts lamp.

Jigs for template routing

The band saw almost always leaves a pattern of sawing marks on the workpiece. In some situations, this does not matter, but just as often the cut surface is too rough for the desired purpose. It's easy to clean up by planing or jointing when the sawn surface is straight. When the workpiece is curved, cleaning up the band sawn edges can be very tedious and labor intensive. Template routing, shown in **Figures 7.12** and **7.13** in Chapter 7, "Patterns and Templates," on page 143, is a technique for cleaning up the sawn edge with a flush-trimming router bit. In principle, template routing is not different from template sawing. In some cases, the band saw template can be left in place to guide the router bit; in other cases, you'll want to clamp the workpiece and the template to a sled jig, which gives you a safe and secure grip.

For making multiple pieces, such as the back leg of the chair shown in **Figure 7.11** on page 142, create a template routing sled jig and clamp the workpiece to it, as shown in **Figure 8.21**. The clamps are quick-action clamps. In this situation, a flush-trim bit with the bearing on the bottom of the cutter works best. A similar template jig was used to complete the four brackets on the sides of the Arts and Crafts lamp shown in **Figure 8.22**. With this jig, the clamping mechanism is a standard ¼-20 bolt located in an aluminum extrusion, as shown in **Figure 8.23**.

Figure 8.23. This is the jig used for making the four lamp brackets. The clamp is a standard ¼-20 bolt with its head trapped by an aluminum extrusion T-track. The same jig can be used to rough out the part with a rub block on the band saw and to finish the part using a bearing-guided bit on the router table.

Door templates and jigs

Arch-top raised-panel doors, as shown in **Figure 8.24**, are popular projects that require accurate templates for both the top rails and the center panels. Door designs vary from fairly simple to curvy and complicated, as shown in **Figure 8.25**. If you are doing a full kitchen, you will need to elongate the curve to make doors of different sizes, as shown in **Figure 8.26**.

When you want to make perfect mating panel and rail shapes for raised-panel doors and wall panels, you can either take the time to make accurate templates, or you can purchase commercially available sets of templates, as shown in **Figures 8.27** and **8.28**. These templates work with different styles of jigs. Heavy-duty rail and stile jigs, which are used to flush trim the door rails, sandwich the workpiece between a phenolic sled and a plywood template, as shown in **Figure 8.29**. After cutting the curve to shape, the same jig

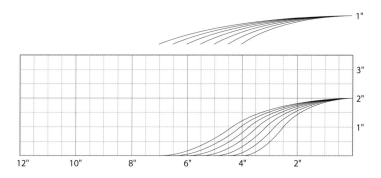

Figure 8.25. Arch-top raised-panel doors range from simple to complex.

Figure 8.26. If you are doing a kitchen, you will need to elongate the pattern curve for different-size doors. Door templates are available in sets of graduated sizes.

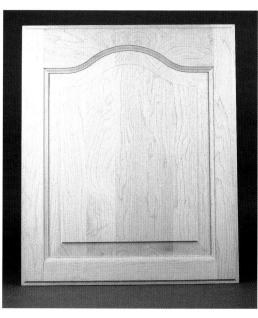

Figure 8.24. Raised-panel doors require accurate templates.

Figure 8.27. This template will accurately cut the curved top for a raised-panel door.

Figure 8.28. This template will cut a curved top rail to match the raised panel.

Figure 8.29. Heavy-duty rail and stile jigs sandwich the workpiece between the phenolic sled and the plywood template. This jig is shown flush trimming the curved door rail.

Figure 8.30. The basic shaper setup uses a sled with the pattern in contact with a rub bearing on top of the panel that is being raised.

can be used to guide a router cutter for the panel groove and the cope-and-stick joint.

Commercial shops often make door parts with shapers instead of routers. Shapers require substantial jigs and fixtures, and extra care when cutting small pieces like the curved door rail. Three-quarter-inch plywood templates are sturdy enough for use with shaper tooling, which can be run with the cutter profile either below the workpiece or above the workpiece. A basic shaper setup uses a sled fixture to hold the workpiece, guided by a top template that is in contact with a rub bearing mounted on top of the raised-panel cutter, as shown in **Figure 8.30**.

Sandwich jigs

Sandwich jigs are complex to make but are worth the trouble when you want to shape a lot of identical parts, as shown in **Figure 8.31**. The jig has the same pattern on top and bottom with the workpiece sandwiched in between. The advantage is that you can flip the jig over when the wood grain changes direction and thus avoid tear-out.

To make a sandwich jig, first make two identical templates. Take a workpiece blank that has been accurately sawn to size, and trace its outline on one of the template blanks. Locate the bolt positions on this pattern, avoiding the area where the workpiece will be. Two or three bolts are usually enough. Clamp the templates together. Drill and counter-bore the bolt holes.

Now, locate stop blocks on one of the two templates for positioning the workpiece. Try to locate the stop blocks so the piece can fit into

the jig in only one way. The stop blocks should be slightly thinner than the workpiece so the workpiece will be held securely once the bolts have been tightened. Check to see whether tightening the bolts distorts the templates, and, if so, add filler pieces. The fillers should be the same thickness as the workpiece. They don't have to fit tightly against the workpiece, but they can if you want to use them as part of the stop block system.

Clamp the workpiece between the templates and rout it to shape. No matter how accurately you make the sandwich jig, there's usually enough play in the bolts to prevent the curves from fairing perfectly smoothly into one another. You can achieve some adjustment by sanding away (or relieving) the pattern where it's not being followed. Finally, however, you may have to hand sand the transitions where the cuts stop and start.

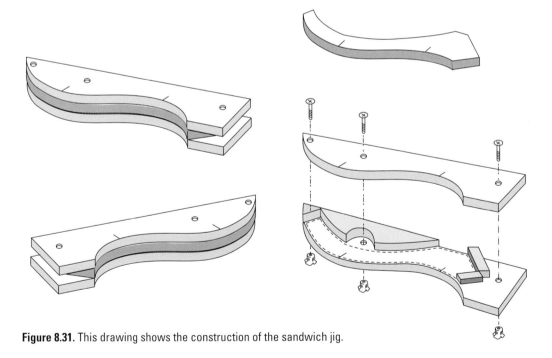

Figure 8.31. This drawing shows the construction of the sandwich jig.

Traditional furniture pieces such as tall case clocks and highboy chests (see **Figure 8.32**) often have a sweeping gooseneck molding atop the bonnet. The traditional way of making this molding is to saw the curve and then carve it with chisels and gouges. I prefer to cut these moldings with a combination of pattern sawing, routing, and sanding.

Figure 8.32. This highboy chest includes an excellent example of gooseneck molding.

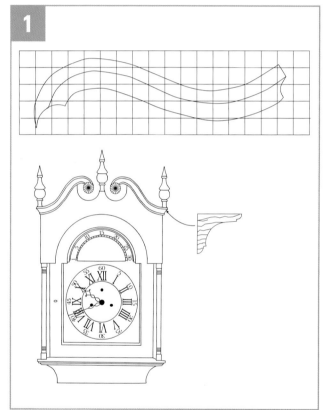

Make an accurate half pattern of the curve, and use it to make a plywood half template.

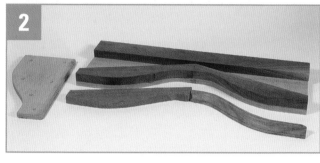

Use the plywood half template to create a full template. A full template is necessary because the two moldings are mirror images of each other and can't be made from a simple half template.

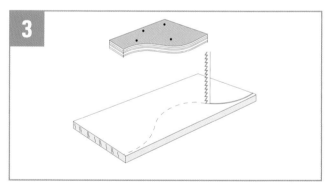

Rough-cut the full plywood template on the band saw.

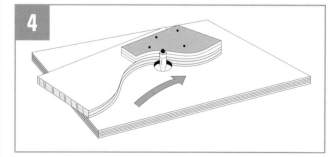

Attach the half template to the full template board and flush trim one side.

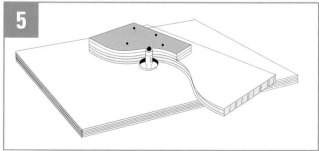

Attach the half template to the other half of the full template board and flush trim the other side.

6

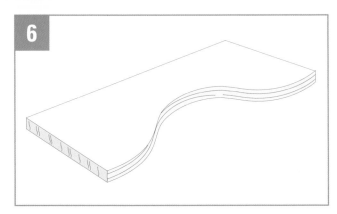

The finished full template will have two identical sides. Attach the two workpieces to the template with screws. Since the molding will be glued to the front of the cabinet, these screw holes will never show. Also, screw a strip of the molding material to the back edge of the full template for shaping into the straight molding you'll need for the cabinet sides.

7

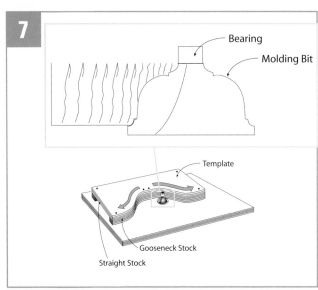

Bearing

Molding Bit

Template

Gooseneck Stock

Straight Stock

Cut the molding to size and shape by template sawing it; then, rout it with a flush-trim cutter to clean up the saw marks. Template rout both the gooseneck and the straight stock to mold the edge. Depending on what you have, you can guide the bit either with a ball bearing or with a rub block follower. Either way, the follower runs along the edge of the template. If you use a rub block, you may need to relieve its underside to provide clearance for the cutter. Start the cuts by pivoting the template against a starting pin. If the pin gets in the way, remove it after the cut is underway. Note that, when routing the molding, part of the cut will be against the grain. You should be taking a small enough bite that you won't lose control. This (along with sharp cutters) will minimize tear-out.

8

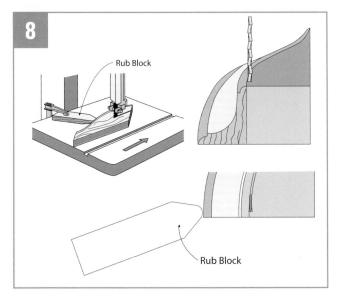

Rub Block

Rub Block

After the shape has been molded on the edge, remove it from the template, and use a rub block on the band saw to cut the opposite curved edge parallel to the original curved edge. Be sure to keep the face of the template (or molding) perpendicular to the rub block.

9

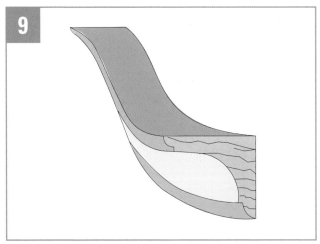

Use a sanding drum in a drill press to sand the gooseneck's front molded edge. Then, use this edge as a guide against the rub block to sand the parallel back edge. After the sawing and sanding, the curved molding will have a curved shape on the bottom and a flat curved shape on the top.

PROJECT: THREE-LEGGED SHAKER TABLE

The popular three-legged Shaker table is typical of furniture with multiple curved parts, such as the leg shown in **Figures 8.33** and **8.34**. First you would use the pattern to lay out and band saw the legs roughly to size. You can use a template with a rub block to do this (see **Figure 8.35**), or you can do it by eye.

The jig shown in **Figure 8.35** is a two-sided jig for use with a rub block on the band saw; then, you can finish the parts with a collar-guided sanding drum on the drill press. It's set up to make the inside curve of one leg and the outside curve of another. Saw and sand both parts; then, reverse their positions in the jig and repeat the operation.

If you would prefer to rout this leg, use a sandwich jig to secure the workpiece between two identical templates, as shown in **Figure 8.36**. You avoid tear-out by flipping the whole assembly over whenever the wood grain changes direction. Marks on the jig locate the change points. Bolts and T-nuts act as clamps. Sandwich jigs are great for shaping a lot of identical parts.

Before turning the jig over, you must start and stop the router cut, and there's always a risk that the router will grab the work. To avoid that risk, equip your router table with a starting pin. The pin acts as a fulcrum that helps you ease the workpiece into the cutter. When you feel the pattern contact the cutter-mounted bearing, pivot it off the starting pin and begin the cut.

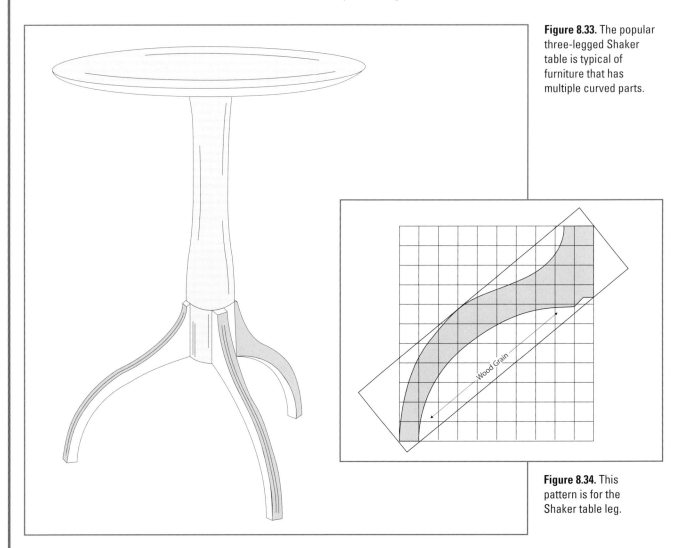

Figure 8.33. The popular three-legged Shaker table is typical of furniture that has multiple curved parts.

Figure 8.34. This pattern is for the Shaker table leg.

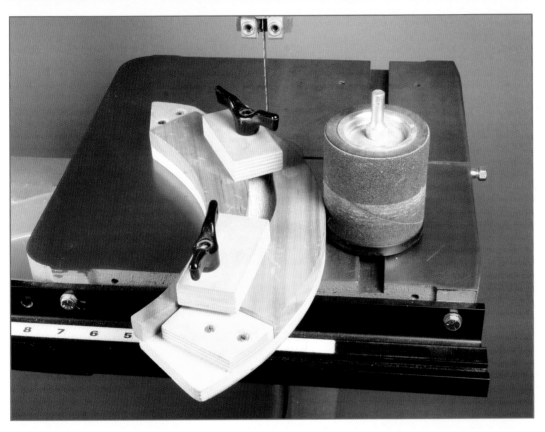

Figure 8.35. The two-sided jig, used with a rub block, helps saw the inside curve of one leg and the outside curve of another. The sanding drum at right has a guide collar on the bottom. When chucked in the drill press, it will follow the same jig to finish the legs.

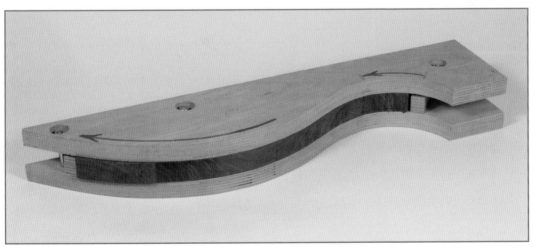

Figure 8.36. A sandwich jig secures the workpiece between two identical templates for routing.

Mortise and Tenon

Because of its strength and resistance to racking and twist, the mortise and tenon joint is ideal for frame construction, such as chairs, tables, cabinets, and frame-and-panel doors. The mortise and tenon is a two-part joint. The mortise, which is an oblong hole, is made first, and then the tenon is made to fit into it, as shown in **Figure 9.2**. The joint can be reinforced with wedges or pins, though the strength of modern glues makes this less important than it once was. Once a well-fit mortise and tenon joint has been glued, the mechanical contact and the large gluing area between the mating long-grain surfaces make it a very strong joint.

The mortise was traditionally made with square corners, but with the advent of powerful plunge routers, it is now easier to make a mortise with round corners. This mortise requires a tenon that is rounded to match the round corner left by the router bit, and making that type of tenon will be discussed at the end of this section.

Figure 9.2. The mortise and tenon is a two-part joint. The mortise, which is an oblong hole, is made first. Then, the tenon is made to fit into it.

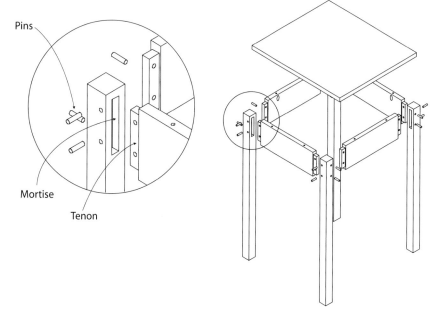

Figure 9.3. There are a large number of variations of the mortise and tenon joint.

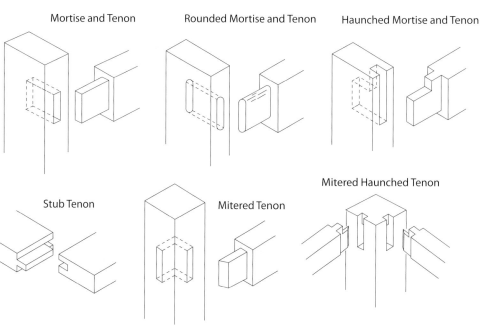

Mortise and Tenon

Rounded Mortise and Tenon

Haunched Mortise and Tenon

Stub Tenon

Mitered Tenon

Mitered Haunched Tenon

Types of Mortise and Tenon

There are many variations of mortise and tenon joints, as shown in **Figure 9.3**. When there is a structural tenon that extends all the way through the mortise piece, the joint is called a through mortise and tenon. In the blind version of the joint, the tenon does not extend through the mortise piece. The haunched mortise and

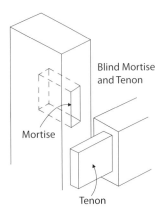

Figure 9.4. The band saw excels at making the tenon portion of the mortise and tenon joint.

tenon, used on corner joints, adds extra surface area for gluing and resists twisting. The haunch is usually made square, but it can be sloped if the appearance of the haunch is undesirable. The stub tenon is a short tenon used in frame-and-panel construction. A mitered mortise and tenon is used for the corners of a chair or a table. The tenons for all of these variations can be made with the band saw (see **Figure 9.4**).

Mortise and Tenon Proportions

Traditionally, mortise and tenon joints are proportioned so that the thickness of the tenon is one-third the thickness of the stock, as shown in **Figure 9.5**. For example, a ¼-inch-thick tenon would be appropriate for ¾-inch wood. The deeper the mortise, the stronger the joint because of the increased contact area between the two pieces. Although the rule of thirds works well in most cases, the tenon can be made thicker, up to half the thickness of the material, though it should not be made any thinner than a third of the piece.

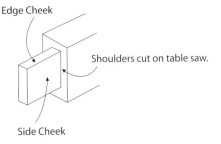

Figure 9.5. Traditionally, mortise and tenon joints are proportioned so that the thickness of the tenon is one-third the thickness of the stock. Using this formula, a ¹/₄-inch-thick tenon would be appropriate for ³/₄-inch stock.

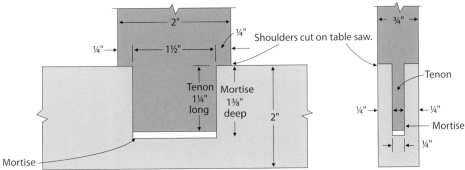

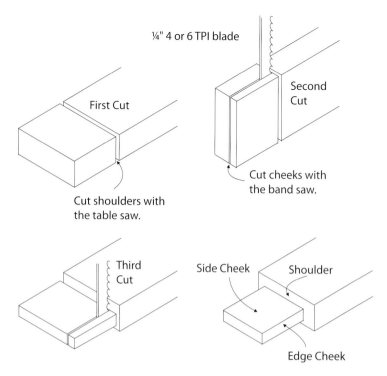

¼" 4 or 6 TPI blade

First Cut

Cut shoulders with the table saw.

Second Cut

Cut cheeks with the band saw.

Third Cut

Side Cheek

Shoulder

Edge Cheek

Figure 9.6. The tenon requires two series of cuts. Crosscut the shoulder first. The setup for cutting the tenon cheeks is the same for making a rip cut.

Figure 9.7. Lay the workpiece on edge to make the side cheek cuts. Position the fence so that the waste is not trapped between the blade and the fence.

Making the mortise and tenon

Mortise and tenon joints are made in the same sequence whether they are cut by hand or machine: The mortise is made first, and then the tenon is cut to fit the mortise. In industry, mortises are made with a specialized machine that is similar to a drill press, except that it usually features a foot or pneumatic feed. I use a plunge router with an up-cut spiral bit to make mortises. The up-cut bit helps evacuate the chips from the mortise.

Sawing the Tenon

After all the mortises have been made, the tenons are cut to fit them. There are a number of ways to do this, but I prefer to use the table saw and the band saw in combination. The tenon requires a crosscut to define its shoulders. This can be done on the band saw, but it is often done on the table saw because this machine leaves a cleaner surface and corner. The cheeks of the tenon also can be cut using either machine, but I prefer to do them on the band saw. Using multiple machines has an advantage in that each setup can be individually fine-tuned. Tenons are cut in three stages, as shown in **Figure 9.6**.

First, a shallow kerf is crosscut all the way around the end of the workpiece to define the tenon shoulder. It is often better to saw the crosscut slightly (⅟₃₂ inch) deeper than the rip cut. This ensures that the corner cut will be complete and provides a space for the excess glue.

Second, after the crosscut has been made, a rip cut with the board on edge defines the tenon side cheek, as shown in **Figure 9.7**. The setup is the usual setup for ripping on the band saw. Third, make a rip cut with the workpiece flat on the saw table to define the tenon edge cheek, as shown in **Figure 9.8**. This is the less critical of the cuts, especially if the tenon is to be made round to fit the round-ended mortise.

Make these band saw cuts with a stop on the rip fence to prevent you from accidentally cutting into the body of the rail. Make the cut for the edge cheek slightly oversize, so you can test fit the joint, as shown in **Figure 9.9**, and remove excess material until it fits. Since glue works best on a smooth surface, saw tenons with a blade of at least 6 TPI. I usually use a ¼-inch x 6 TPI skip tooth blade.

The band saw excels at this type of cutting not only because of its ability to cut into a corner, but also because the workpiece lies flat on the table throughout rather than having an end straight up in the air, as would be the case on the table saw.

To fit round-cornered mortises, the edges of the tenon are chamfered with the band saw. To take off the corner of the tenon, either tilt the table or make a jig for holding the wood at a 45-degree angle, as shown in **Figure 9.10**. Cut opposite corners before resetting for the other two corners, as shown in **Figure 9.11**.

Figure 9.9. Test fit the tenon to the mortise.

Figure 9.10. The V-block jig is a simple fixture that can be used to stabilize round and odd-shaped work on the band saw table.

Figure 9.11. If the mortise was done with a router, the corners will be round. The V-block jig will help you very accurately cut off the tenon corners so the tenons will fit into round-end mortises.

Figure 9.8. Lay the workpiece flat on the table to make the edge cheek cut. A stop block prevents cutting into the workpiece.

Figure 9.12. With a sharp ⅛-inch blade and a shop-made sled jig, you can quickly and accurately cut variably spaced dovetails.

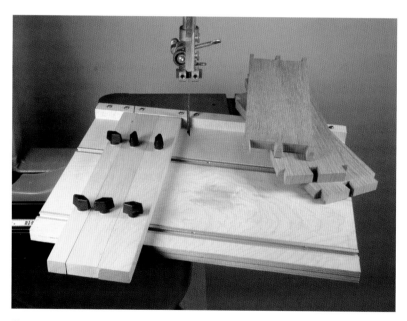

Figure 9.13. This simple, shop-made jig will maintain the dovetail angle and help you accurately space the cuts. The miter bar is attached at a 10-degree angle to the jig platform.

Dovetail joints

The dovetail is the strongest and most attractive joint for boxes, drawers, and carcass joinery. This classic joint is the hallmark of quality craftsmanship, and mastering dovetailing is a big step in learning the craft of woodworking.

The dovetail was traditionally cut by hand, a slow process that requires both skill and patience. Unless you have considerable hand skill, it is not a very practical method, though it must be said that a skilled craftsman can indeed make hand-cut dovetails accurately and efficiently. I have always felt that there was a missing link between the tedium of hand cutting dozens of dovetails and the faster method of producing boring-looking joints with expensive router jigs. Thus, I developed a very simple spacer-block dovetail method that combines hand tool flexibility with power tool speed and accuracy (see **Figure 9.12**).

The band saw method uses a simple shop-made jig to efficiently make dovetails that a master would envy. My dovetail system is fast, accurate, easy to use, costs next to nothing, and allows for design flexibility. I can either make dovetails using the band saw and the table saw in combination, or I can make them on the band saw alone. The key problems of making accurate dovetails are maintaining the correct angle of cut and accurately spacing the cuts. The simple shop-made jig shown in **Figure 9.13** maintains the angle and accurately spaces the saw cuts with spacing blocks. Once the entry cuts have been made, the waste is removed with a ⅛-inch x 14 TPI band saw blade.

With this technique, you can vary both the width and the spacing of the pins and tails for virtually any aesthetic effect. The blocks that set the spacing are self-centering and produce perfectly fitting interchangeable joints, eliminating the need to mark boards so that individual joints will fit, as is necessary with hand dovetailing.

Dovetail Design

The exposed dovetail is both structurally sound and aesthetically pleasing. However, the relationship between design and technique is complex. Just because you have dovetails that are technically sound doesn't mean that your project is well designed. Design without technical skill or consideration is superficial, and technical virtuosity without an eye for design may result in a something that is plain ugly.

The dovetail is a locking joint with two elements, the pin and the tail, as shown in **Figure 9.14**. The pin and tail fit together from only one direction (see **Figure 9.15**), and they hold together without glue. The single dovetail joint can be either a complete pin or a complete tail. The multiple dovetail usually ends with a half pin at each corner (see **Figure 9.16**); the half tail is usually avoided at the ends of the joint because it can break off. The boards with tails on the ends are interchangeable and each side is identical, so they can be turned either way to function as either the inside or the outside of a box. The boards that end with pins are not identical and are not reversible. The outside of the pin board is the side toward which the pins taper.

The dovetail angle provides a mechanical lock. The angle of the pin mates with the angle of the tail, and this contact is the foundation of the joint. If the angle is too slight, the pin can slide between the tails, and the locking mechanism is inadequate. If the angle is too great, the wood at the corner is too fragile and breaks easily under stress. The ideal dovetail angle for hardwoods is approximately 80 degrees, as shown in **Figure 9.17**. It does not matter if this angle is a couple of degrees off either way, but it is important that the pin and tail have the same angle and fit closely without any gaps.

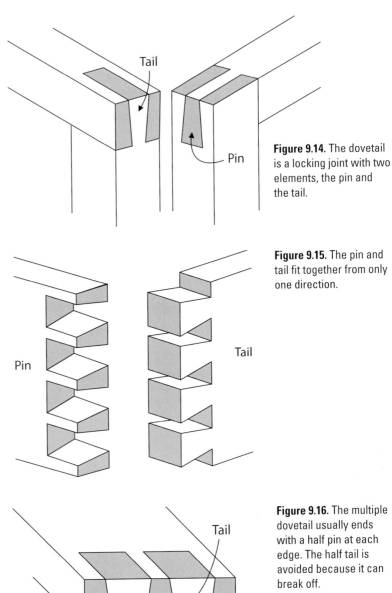

Figure 9.14. The dovetail is a locking joint with two elements, the pin and the tail.

Figure 9.15. The pin and tail fit together from only one direction.

Figure 9.16. The multiple dovetail usually ends with a half pin at each edge. The half tail is avoided because it can break off.

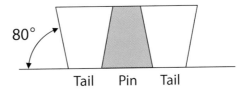

Figure 9.17. The ideal dovetail angle for hardwoods is about 80 degrees.

Anatomy of a Dovetail

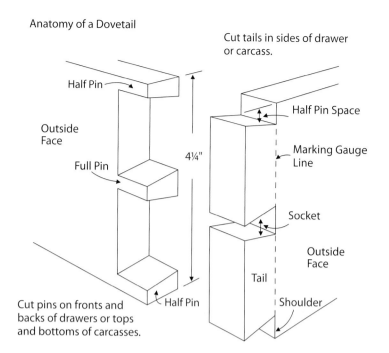

Figure 9.18. Cut the pins on the front and back of the drawer and the tails on the sides of the drawer. This orients the joint for maximum resistance to the stress of pulling the drawer out of the cabinet.

Making the dovetail

Cut the pins on the front and back of the drawer, as shown in **Figure 9.18**. Dovetails are created with a series of straight angled cuts using a taper jig and a series of spacer blocks, which space the cut from the corner of one block to the adjacent block, as shown in **Figure 9.19**. With this block spacing system, the tail size is determined by the block size. One block is equal to the size of the tail plus the size of the pin. When you use tails of different sizes, you affect the design of the joint. Changing the number of blocks and their total width as compared to the workpiece creates different designs. The total width of the blocks and one pin width equals the width of the workpiece, as shown in **Figure 9.20**.

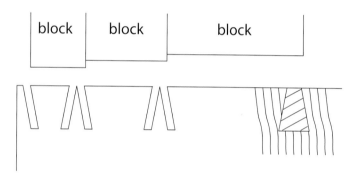

Figure 9.19. Dovetails are created with a series of straight angled cuts with a taper jig, and a series of spacer blocks that space the cut from the corner of one block to the adjacent block. Changing the block size changes the size of the tail.

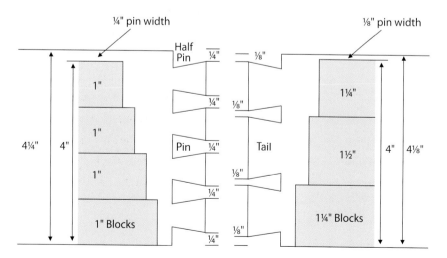

Figure 9.20. The total width of the blocks and one pin width equals the width of the workpiece.

STEP-BY-STEP: MAKING THE DOVETAIL JIG

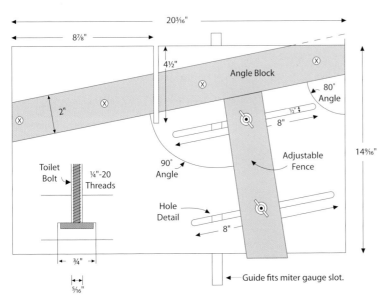

1 The sled jig that is used with the spacer block system should be made of ¾-inch plywood. The fence needs to be adjustable for different widths of stock. You could use aluminum extrusions or use toilet bolts, as shown. Use the ⅛-inch x 14 TPI blade to cut and remove the waste; for maximum accuracy, use closely set phenolic side guides on the band saw.

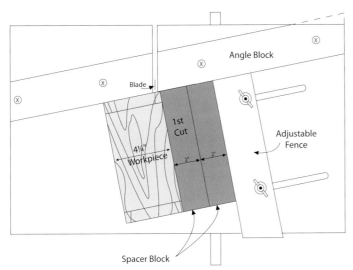

2 The tails workpiece is sawn first. Make the first cut with all of the blocks in place. Cut all four corners of the workpiece.

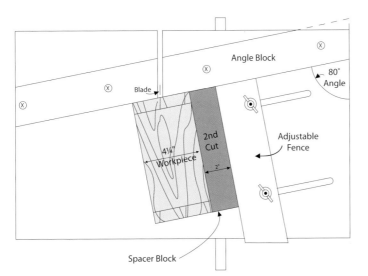

3 For the second series of tail cuts, remove one block to space the kerf. Machine the spacer blocks very accurately.

4 To saw the mating pins workpiece, tilt the saw table to the dovetail angle, and space the cuts by using the spacer blocks with the band saw fence; the sled jig is not used to saw the pins. These steps will become clearer in the photos with the next section.

STEP-BY-STEP: SAWING THE TAILS

1 Prepare all of the workpieces by gauging a sharp line around the wood that is the same distance from the end of the board as the thickness of the workpiece. Use a cutting gauge or a sharp knife with an accurate square.

2 The pin and half pin size is determined by the difference between the workpiece and the measuring blocks. Place the blocks on edge next to the tails workpiece, and mark the starting line with a pencil.

3 The first cut on the tails workpiece is made with the blocks (dark wood) in place. Place the blocks on the jig, and move the adjustable fence to align the saw blade with the pencil mark. Make a cut down to the knife line, and then set a stop block to limit the forward movement of the jig.

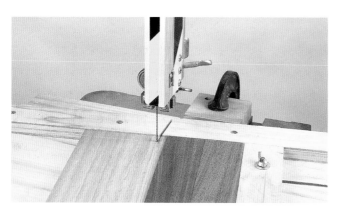

4 With the two spacing blocks against the fence, cut all four corners.

5 Remove one spacer block and repeat the series of four cuts, rotating and turning the workpiece end for end.

Remove the material in the pin area by nibbling with the ⅛-inch blade. An eighth inch of material is first nibbled to make space for the blade. Next, make a cut ⅛ inch away from the first cut, and then slide the board laterally and make a series of cuts to remove the waste material.

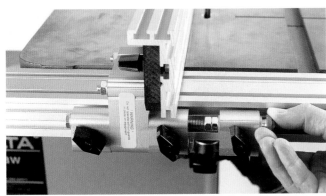

6 Because you want to cut the gauge line in half, you have to accurately adjust the fence. Some saw fences are fitted with an optional microadjuster, which is ideal for this kind of task.

7 Test the fence position on scrap. Then, slide the tails board into the blade to remove the half-pin waste from the corner.

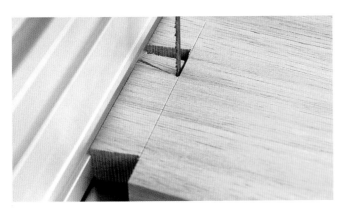

8 To remove the pin waste from between the tails, slide the blade into the wide kerf and saw, as shown. Cut into the corner from one side. If there is material in the corner that prevents the blade from touching the line, don't worry about it because the blade will flex back to the line. Cut into one corner, remove the wedge of waste, and then flip the board to cut into the opposite corner.

STEP-BY-STEP: SAWING THE PINS

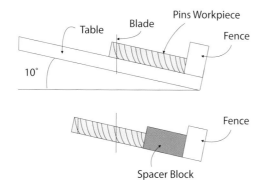

1 With the tails complete, make the pins by two series of cuts with the table tilted at 10 degrees. The tail jig is removed, and the rip fence guides the work. The first series of cuts is made with the table tilted 10 degrees in one direction, and then the second series is made with the table tilted in the opposite direction.

2 The blocks will accurately space the cuts, but locating the cut in the correct position is important. Use the tails workpiece to line up the fence with the blade. Adjust the fence using the tails workpiece so the blade would cut into its corner. The side of the blade tooth should line up with the corner of the tail. Remember that you are cutting the waste, so you want to remove the material opposite the tail.

3 When you cut the tails, the blocks were located between the workpiece and the fence. When cutting the pins, the workpiece initially rests against the fence, and you add blocks rather than removing them.

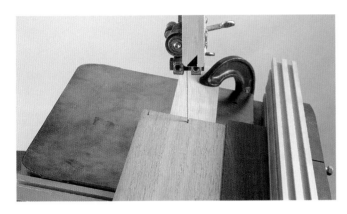

4 Make the first cuts in opposite corners of the workpiece. For the second series, add a spacing block. Rather than making four cuts as you did on the tails workpiece, you make only two cuts on the pins workpiece with each setup—one cut on each side. Make the first pair of pin cuts, and then add a block to make another pair of cuts.

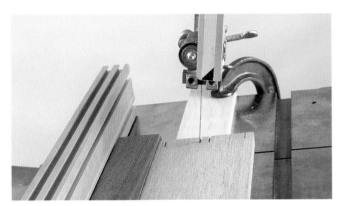

5 After you complete the first series of pin cuts, tilt the table 10 degrees in the opposite direction and repeat the process. Then, return the table to the level position, and nibble the material between the pins in the same fashion as you did the tails.

6 Here are the sequential steps in making the pins.

7 The completed dovetail.

PROJECT: BAND SAW DOVETAILED STEP STOOL

The Shaker-style dovetailed step stool in **Figure 9.21** was made using the spacer block technique on the band saw. **Figure 9.22** is the plan for the step stool. The stool is a good exercise for mastering this technique.

Step 1: Begin by choosing the wood—the stool shown is made of walnut—and glue up the two boards that make each of the side panels. Cut all the pieces a couple of inches longer than the finished size, and, during the glue-up, check the location of the top of the shorter piece. You want to be sure there is more than enough wood at both ends of the longer piece so that you can crosscut the glued-together pieces to length without having to recut the L shape that forms the step itself.

Step 2: After sawing the side pieces to length, use a circle cutting jig on the band saw to make the semicircular cutouts.

Step 3: Make the through dovetail joints that connect the two steps to the sides using the spacer block technique.

Step 4: Blind-mortise the cross rails under the steps into the sides, using a couple of biscuits in each end or using pocket-hole screws from their bottom edges. If you glue the rails to the underside of the steps, you'll be making the step stool strong enough for elephants.

Figure 9.21. The Shaker-style dovetailed step stool was made using the spacer block technique on the band saw.

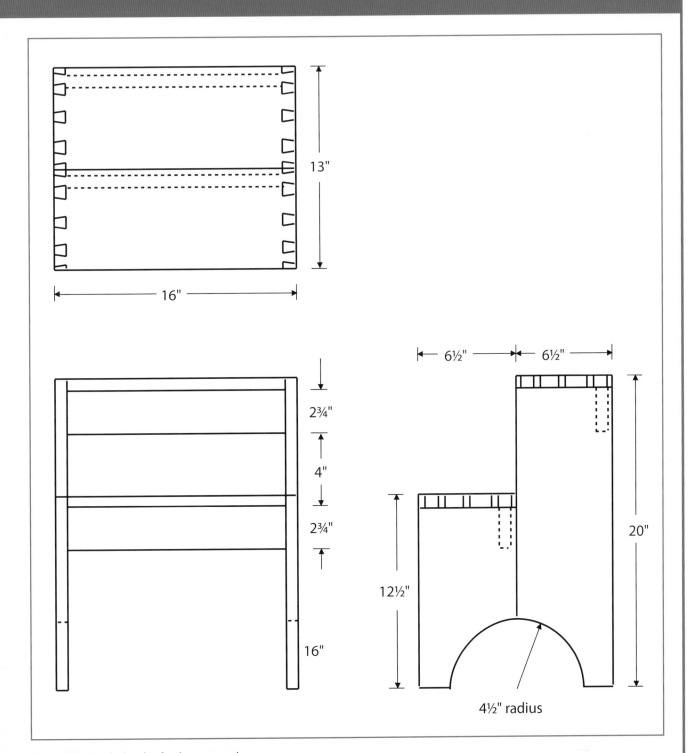

Figure 9.22. Here is the plan for the step stool.

Glossary

Alternate Set Teeth. Each tooth is set, or bent, alternately left or right. Alternate set blades are generally used in woodworking because they cut a slot or kerf wider than their own bodies and thus do not bind in the workpiece.

Band Saw Box. A free-form container band sawn from small logs and thick slabs of wood, often containing a drawer, is called a band saw box.

Barrel Cut. The curve cut into a piece of wood when a blade deflects due to under-tensioning.

Beam Strength. Beam strength is the ability of the blade to resist deflection. It results from a combination of band hardness, thickness, and width. A wide blade, properly tensioned, has greater beam strength than a narrow one and usually produces straighter cuts.

Belly, Bellying. An under-tensioned blade can create a curve or "belly" in the thickness of the wood, a condition called "bellying."

Bench-Top Band Saw. A small two or three wheel band saw that can be mounted on a table or workbench is called a bench-top band saw.

Bevel. A bevel is any angle other than 90 degrees (square) between the edge and face of a piece of wood.

Bimetal Blade. Bimetal blades are specifically designed for durability with a hard tooth face material laminated to a back of softer metal.

Blade Back. The blade body, not including the tooth portion, is the blade back.

Blade Body Width. The width of the blade, minus the width of the tooth gullet, is called the body width.

Blade Cutting Edge. The toothed edge of the blade from the points of the teeth to the base of the gullets is its cutting edge. The rest of the blade is considered the blade back.

Blade Lead. Band saw blades tend to steer themselves to one side or the other, or lead, while cutting. Lead is correctible by adjusting the band saw rip fence to match the lead angle.

Blade Length. The length of a band saw blade is the length it would be if the weld were broken and the metal straightened out.

Blade Pitch. The distance from one tooth tip to the next tooth tip is its pitch. Variable-tooth blades are specified by two numbers because their tooth pitch and the gullet depth vary.

Blade Speed. Velocity in surface feet per minute (SFM) of a band saw blade is its speed.

Blade Thickness. See "Gauge."

Blade Width. The width of a saw blade is measured from the tip of the tooth to the back of the blade.

Bookmatching. Joining two identical resawn boards so that they mirror one another is called bookmatching.

Circle Cutting Jig. A sled jig that has a center point for mounting the workpiece can saw circular disks of wood.

Column. The vertical backbone of the band saw is called its column.

Crosscut, Crosscutting. Sawing wood across the grain direction, which in most cases means sawing across the width of a board, is called crosscutting.

Crown. The top of the ridge on band saw wheels, which aids in tracking thinner blades, is called its crown.

Cut-and-Glue Technique. To saw a cutout shape that is entirely enclosed, divide the workpiece into two or more parts, saw the cutout, and then glue the parts back together.

Cut by Eye Technique. By sighting the saw blade against the layout line and steering the wood accordingly, the operator can saw to a line without the aid of jigs and fences.

Drift Angle. The drift angle is the amount that a band saw blade tends to lead the cut to one side or the other, gauged from the edge of the saw table.

Feed Speed. The speed at which the material is fed through the blade is the feed speed. "Feed speed" is a relative term used to distinguish between a rapid feed and a slow feed, and normally is not calibrated in any units.

Figure, of Wood. Visible whorls and lines of color in the surface of smooth wood constitute its figure.

Fixture. A fixture is a device, often shop-made, that holds the workpiece in position so it can be cut and shaped by machine. Also see "Jig."

Flat Sawn. Flat sawing is a method of sawing a softwood log into edge-to-edge slices, with the resulting figure characterized by Vs and whorls. Also called "sawn through and through" and "plain sawn."

Flex Back Blade. Carbon steel blades that have hardened teeth and back are called flex back blades.

Floor Model Band Saw. Large band saws are installed directly on the shop floor without a stand or table. Floor model band saws typically have wheels that are 20 inches in diameter or larger.

Flutter. Rhythmic vibration by a band saw blade can cause crisscrossing diagonal saw marks on the cut surface. Flutter indicates that the blade is under-tensioned.

Follower. A jig built around a pointed or rounded stick that bears against a template and can reproduce the template's shape in the workpiece is called a follower. See "Rub Block."

Frame. The steel and cast-iron apparatus that holds the band saw wheels, table, and guides in a fixed relationship to one another is called the frame or the skeleton of the machine.

Gauge. The blade's thickness is its gauge.

Grain, of Wood. Wood is made of cellulose fibers, bound by a natural glue called lignin. The grain of wood tends to run from one end of a board to the other, and woodworkers need to be aware of whether they are working with the grain or across or against the grain.

Guide Bearing. A guide bearing is a circular ball-bearing device that keeps the band saw blade cutting straight without side-to-side deflection or twist.

Guide Block. Rectangular blocks of metal, plastic, or composite material such as phenolic, mounted close to the saw blade, can help keep the band saw cutting straight without side-to-side deflection or twist.

Guide Post. The guide post is a metal rod attached to the band saw frame that permits the upper blade guides to move up and down to accommodate the thickness of the workpiece.

Gullet. The curved area at the base of the tooth, which is designed to carry the chip from the kerf, is its gullet.

Gullet Depth. The distance from the tooth tip to the bottom of the gullet is its depth.

Hook Tooth. The cutting tooth may project at a right angle from the blade body, or it may point downward in the direction of cut, which is called "hook" or "positive rake." Hook teeth cut aggressively and have rounded gullets to help clear the chips.

Inside Cuts. Enclosed openings in a design that cannot be sawn from the edge of the workpiece are called inside cuts.

Intarsia. Intarsia designs are made by assembling thin pieces of wood of various species. Intarsia pieces typically range from $1/8$ inch to $1/2$ inch thick, and intarsia pictures typically have a three-dimensional surface.

Jig. A device that guides a cutting tool along or through the workpiece on a prescribed path is called a jig. Also see "Fixture."

Joinery. Strictly, "joinery" refers to wooden frame-and-panel constructions that are attached to a building, such as paneled walls and cabinets, as well as to the act of making such constructions. In contemporary usage, it refers to the act of making joints to connect pieces of wood.

Joint. A joint is the mechanical interlock between two pieces of wood, most commonly the mortise and tenon joint for table bases and paneled frames and the dovetail joint for cabinet boxes and drawers.

Jointing (v), jointer. Jointing is the act of preparing a straight, flat, and square edge or face on the workpiece. The jointer is a machine designed to cut a straight, flat, and square edge or surface on the workpiece.

Kerf. The total thickness of the blade at tooth tips, measured from a right-set tooth to a left-set tooth, is the width of the slot, or kerf, it will cut in the wood.

Lead. Lead is the tendency of a band saw blade to steer itself one way or the other away from a line parallel to the edge of the saw table.

Marquetry. Marquetry is the art of cutting variously colored wood veneers into pieces that can be assembled together to make pictures and designs. Wood veneers typically range from $1/28$ inch thick to $1/40$ inch thick, and marquetry pictures typically have a flat and smooth surface.

Miter Gauge. A semicircular gauge mounted on a steel bar can be adjusted to hold an angle with respect to the band saw's normal cut. The miter gauge is an aid to making crosscuts that are square to the edge of the wood as well as making cuts at various angles.

Modified Hook Tooth. Blades with modified hook teeth are most often used to cut wood but are sometimes used to cut aluminum. The difference between this blade and the regular hook tooth is in the gullet shape. The gullet of the modified hook tooth acts like a chip breaker to help prevent clogging.

Nibbling. Repeatedly cutting up to the layout line in order to remove waste from a band-sawn pattern is called nibbling.

Pattern. The pattern is a drawing that accurately describes the design one intends to saw from the wood.

Phase. Orientation of alternating current supply is called a phase. Household electrical current is single phase, whereas industrial machinery—including large band saws—runs on three phase and cannot be operated on household circuits without adding an electrical phase converter.

Phenolic Replacement Blocks. These are blade guides made from graphite impregnated phenolic laminate, which coats the blade with dry lubricants when contact occurs.

Plain Sawn. A hardwood log sawn through and through into edge-to-edge slices, with the resulting figure characterized by Vs and whorls, is said to be plain sawn. See "Flat Sawn."

Point Fence. A piece of wood with one rounded edge, mounted on end alongside the band saw blade and used to guide a deep cut, as when resawing, is called a point fence.

Positive Rake. A positive rake tooth leans forward in the direction of the cutting action, and teeth with positive rake are also called hook teeth. The higher the positive rake angle, the more aggressive the blade.

Quarter Sawn. When a quartered log is sliced into boards, the resulting wood figure is characterized by straight, closely spaced lines and is referred to as "quarter sawn." Quarter-sawn wood is notably stable.

Quick-Release Tension Lever. This convenient feature allows quicker blade changes and also provides the option of releasing the tension on the blade when the saw isn't in use, thus lengthening blade life.

Rack-and-Pinion Guidepost. This guidepost utilizes a circular gear and a flat bar to move up and down.

Rake Angle. The angle of the tooth face measured from a line perpendicular to the direction the blade is moving is the rake angle. Most band saw blades have a rake angle of zero or a small positive rake angle.

Raker. Some blades have straight unbent teeth in between alternately set teeth to help rake the chips out of the cut.

Raker Set. A band saw blade on which each triplet of teeth has one tooth tilted left, the next tooth to the right, and the third straight, is said to have "raker set."

Relief Cut. A relief cut is a preliminary band saw cut from the edge of the workpiece to the pattern line meant to release a piece of the waste when the pattern itself is being sawn.

Resaw, Resawing. Resawing is cutting a board from edge to edge through its width in order to produce two thinner boards. A resaw is a band saw specially equipped for resawing; the word "resaw" is also used as a verb and as an adjective.

Rift Sawn. Rift sawing is a method of sawing a log that produces boards whose grain is halfway between plain sawing and quarter sawing. When a complete log is plain sawn or sawn through and through, some of the wood will be rift sawn, and one or two boards will be quarter sawn.

Rip Fence. A straight, movable device mounted on the band saw table parallel to the saw blade as an aid to sawing the workpiece lengthwise is called a rip fence.

Rip, Ripping. A rip cut divides a piece of wood into two parts lengthwise, that is, with the wood grain.

Riser Block. A riser block is a cast-iron section that can be bolted between the two parts of the band saw column in order to increase the machine's depth of cut.

Rub Block. A rub block is a jig that rubs against a template in order to reproduce the template's shape in the workpiece. See "Follower."

Sandwich Jig. A sandwich jig is a fixture that traps the workpiece between two plates that have a template shaped on their edges in order to hold the workpiece safely while guiding it past a rotating cutter.

Scroll Saw. A small bench-mounted or stand-mounted woodworking machine that can cut intricate shapes by using a short, straight blade that moves rapidly up and down is called a scroll saw. Though an alternative to the band saw for small work, the scroll saw cannot handle thick wood, nor is it especially good at long, straight cuts.

Set. The band saw teeth are alternately bent, or set, to the right or the left to allow clearance for the blade back in the cut. Set is measured at the widest point of the blade; the more set, the wider the kerf.

SFM. The speed of blade travel is measured in surface feet per minute (SFM). The blade speed is typically 2,800 to 3,000 SFM on consumer-grade saws and twice that on large industrial saws.

Side Guides. The band saw's side guides are blocks or bearings that keep the blade moving straight without side-to-side deflection or twist.

Single-Point Fence. A pointed stick or a bolt head mounted on the regular saw fence alongside the band saw blade can help the operator steer the workpiece along a curved line. The single-point fence can also be used for resawing.

Skip Tooth. Some blades have widely spaced teeth with a large gullet capacity. This skip tooth design prevents clogging when cutting soft, sticky materials such as softwood, aluminum, and magnesium. Skip tooth blades have a zero-degree rake angle.

Sled Jig. A flat fixture with a clamping apparatus that holds the workpiece while guiding it past a rotating cutter is called a sled jig.

Spacer Block. An accurately sized wooden block used to space the edge of the workpiece a known and fixed distance from the band saw blade is called a spacer block. They commonly are used to make dovetail joints.

Stand-Mounted Band Saw. Medium-size band saws typically are mounted on a metal stand. The stand usually contains the saw's motor.

Table. The horizontal table, typically a flat plate made of cast iron, supports the workpiece as it approaches the band saw blade.

Table Insert. The band saw table has a circular opening for the blade, and the table insert fills the blade opening.

Table Rail. The rail is a metal bar bolted to the front edge of the band saw table, providing a secure point of attachment for the rip fence and other jigs.

Taper Jig. A sled jig that holds the workpiece in position and guides it against the band saw fence for cutting a taper on one or more edges is called a taper jig.

Taper. A workpiece that is wider at one end than at the other is said to "taper." The workpiece may be tapered on one, two, three, or all four sides.

Template. A plate of wood, plastic, or metal that reproduces the shape specified by a pattern, and which may be used to transfer that shape to the workpiece, is called a template.

Template Routing. This method involves guiding a router cutter along the edge of a template in order to reproduce the template's shape in the workpiece.

Template Sawing. This method entails guiding the workpiece past the band saw blade using the edge of a template in order to reproduce the template's shape in the workpiece.

Tension Gauge. The tension gauge is a scale on the band saw tensioning apparatus that indicates when a particular blade is tight enough on the machine's wheels.

Tension, Tensioning. Tension is a force that tends to pull an object apart. The band saw includes a spring-loaded apparatus for changing the distance between the saw's wheels in order to put tension on the blade and help keep it running straight.

Throat Depth. The vertical distance between the band saw table and the uppermost setting of the blade's top guides is the throat depth, which equals the maximum thickness that can be sawn.

Throat Width. The horizontal distance between the band saw blade and the machine frame or column is the throat width, which determines how far the band saw can reach into a sheet of plywood.

Thrust Bearing. A circular bearing mounted behind the band saw blade to stop the blade from moving backward under the pressure of sawing is a thrust bearing.

Tire. Band saw wheels have a rubber tire to cushion the moving blade.

Tooth, Teeth. The points on the band saw blade that do the actual cutting are called its teeth. The teeth on some blades are hardened.

Tooth Back. The surface of the tooth opposite the cutting edge, or tooth face, is the tooth back.

Tooth Back Clearance Angle. The angle between the back of the sharpened tooth and a line connecting all the tooth points is called its back clearance angle.

Tooth Face. The cutting surface of the tooth is the tooth face.

Tooth Point. The tooth's cutting or scraping edge is its point; it does most of the work and suffers the most wear while sawing.

Tooth Spacing. This relative term describes how far apart the teeth are. "Fine" refers to a blade with many teeth per inch. "Coarse" refers to a blade with few teeth per inch.

TPI. Blades are measured by their length, thickness or gauge, and their number of teeth per inch (TPI).

Track (v), tracking. While being propelled by the band saw wheels, the blade will move across the rim of the wheel until it finds an equilibrium position. By minutely tilting the top wheel's axle, the operator can control where that position is, a process called tracking.

Trunnion. A semicircular metal plate that fits a matching metal cradle is a trunnion. Mounting the band saw table on a pair of trunnions allows it to be tilted.

Turning Holes. Holes drilled along or adjacent to a pattern provide space for sharply changing the direction of the band saw cut.

Variable Pitch. Some blades, usually designed for cutting metal, have more than one tooth pitch and gullet depth. Their tooth pitch and gullet depth vary rhythmically along the length of the blade.

Wavy Set. Wavy set blades have groups of teeth set to the left and to the right alternating throughout the band length. A wavy set helps avoid stripping teeth off the blade body when sawing thin sections such as tubing, pipe, and sheet metal.

Wheel. The band saw has two or three metal wheels, around which the saw blade orbits. Band saws are often described by their wheel diameter.

Wheel Crown. Small band saws have a crown, or raised center, on the rim of their wheels. The crown helps the moving blade find its equilibrium position.

Wheel Tilt. A small tilt in the plane of the band saw wheel helps track the blade. The tilt adjustment is governed by a knob with a locking nut, mounted on the back of the machine's top wheel.

Zero Rake Angle. The face of a tooth with zero rake angle falls on an imaginary line perpendicular to the direction the blade is moving.

Resources

Bridgewood
801 N. Duke St.
York, PA 17404
(800) 235-2100
www.wilkemachinery.com
Band saws, blades, band saw
accessories

Carter Products Company, Inc.
2871 Northridge Dr. NW
Grand Rapids, MI 49544
(616) 647-3380
(888) 622-7837
www.carterproducts.com
Blade guides, electronic
tension gauge, band
saw accessories

Cattail Foundry
167 West Cattail Road
Gordonville, PA 17529
Castings

CMT Tools
P.O. Box 2063
Greenville, SC 29602
www.cmt-tools.com
Door templates, router bits

Daily Saw
4481 Firestone Blvd.
South Gate, CA 90280
(323) 564-1791
www.dailysawservice.com
Lenox blade resharpening

Delta International Machinery
4825 Highway 45 North
P.O. Box 2468
Jackson, TN 38302
(800) 223-7278
www.deltawoodworking.com
Band saws

Eagle Tools
3027 Treadwell Street
Los Angeles, CA 90062
(323) 999-2909
www.eagle-tools.com
Band saws, Lenox blades,
Lenox blade resharpening

Felder USA East
2 Lukens Drive
Suite 300
New Castle, DE 19720
(866) 792-5288
Band saws

Garrett Wade Co.
5389 E. Provident Dr.
Cincinnati, OH 45246
(800) 221-2942
www.garrettwade.com
Band saw accessories

Grizzly Industrial, Inc.
1821 Valencia St.
Bellingham, WA 98229
(800) 523-4777
www.grizzly.com
Band saws, blades, band saw
accessories

Highland Hardware
1045 North Highland Avenue, NE
Atlanta, GA 30306
(800) 241-6748
www.highlandwoodworking.com
Band saws, blades, band
saw accessories

Jasper Parts
(508) 653-4480
Industrial blade guides

Jet/Powermatic
WMH Tool Group
(800) 274-6848
www.wmhtoolgroup.com
Band saws, blades, band
saw accessories

Kreg Tool
201 Campus Drive
Huxley, IA 50124
(800) 447-8638
www.kregtool.com
Band saws accessories

Laguna Tools
17101 Murphy Avenue
Irvine, CA 92614
(800) 332-4094
www.lagunatools.com
Band saws, blades, band
saw accessories

Lee Valley Tools
P.O. Box 1780
Ogdensburg, NY 13669
(800) 267-8735 (US only)
www.leevalley.com
Blades, guides, books

Lenox
301 Chestnut Street
East Longmeadow, MA 01028
(800) 628-3030
www.lenoxsaw.com
Tension gauge, blades
(wholesale only)

L.S. Starrett Co.
121 Crescent Street
Athol, MA 01331
(978) 249-3551
www.starrett.com
Tension gauge, blades
(wholesale only)

Olson Saw Company
16 Stony Hill Road
Bethel, CT 06801
(203) 792-8622
www.olsonsaw.com
Band saw blades, band
saw accessories such
as Cool Blocks

Oneida Air Systems
1001 West Fayette Street
Syracuse, NY 13204
(800) 732-4065
www.oneida-air.com
Dust collection

**Rockler Woodworking and
Hardware**
4365 Willow Drive
Medina, MN 55340
(800) 279-4441
www.rockler.com
Band saws, blades, band
saw accessories

Suffolk Machinery Corp.
12 Waverly Avenue
Patchogue, NY 11772
(800) 234-7297
www.suffolkmachine.com

Tannewitz, Inc.
0-794 Chicago Drive
Jenison, MI 49428
(800) 458-0590
www.tannewitz.com
Band saws

Tod Engine Works
2261 Hubbard Road
Youngstown, OH 44505
(330) 272-4089
www.todengine.org
Castings

Woodcraft Supply
Woodcraft
P.O. Box 1686
Parkersburg, WV 26102
(800) 225-1153
www.woodcraft.com
Band saws, blades, band
saw accessories

Woodhaven
501 West First Avenue
Durant, IA 52747
(800) 344-6657
www.woodhaven.com
Door templates

Woodworker's Supply
5604 Alameda Pl. NE
Albuquerque, NM 87113
(800) 645-9292
www.woodworker.com
Band saws, blades, band
saw accessories

Index

Index (continued)

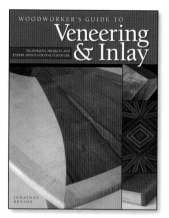
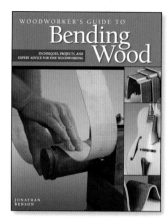
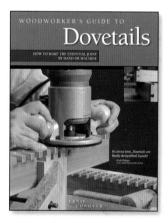
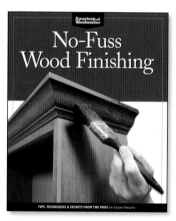
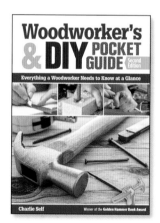